Mediating Nature

Mediating Nature considers how technology acts as a mediating device in the construction and circulation of images that inform how we see and know nature. Scholarship in environmental communication has focused almost exclusively on verbal rather than visual rhetoric, and this book engages ecocritical and ecocompositional inquiry to shift focus onto the making of images.

Contributors to this dynamic collection focus their efforts on the intersections of digital media and environmental/ecological thinking. Part of the book's larger argument is that analysis of mediations of nature must develop more critical tools of analysis toward the very mediating technologies that produce such media. That is, to truly understand mediations of nature, one needs to understand the creation and production of those mediations, right down to the algorithms, circuit boards, and power sources that drive mediating technologies.

Ultimately, *Mediating Nature* contends that ecological literacy and environmental politics are inseparable from digital literacies and visual rhetorics. The book will be of interest to scholars and students working in the fields of Ecocriticism, Ecocomposition, Media Ecology, Visual Rhetoric, and Digital Literacy Studies.

Sidney I. Dobrin is Professor and Chair in the Department of English at the University of Florida, USA. He is the founding director/editor of TRACE Innovation Initiative.

Sean Morey is Associate Professor in the Department of English at the University of Tennessee, Knoxville, USA.

Routledge Environmental Literature, Culture and Media

Series editor: Thomas Bristow

The urgency of the next great extinction impels us to evaluate environmental crises as sociogenic. Critiques of culture have a lot to contribute to the endeavour to remedy crises of culture, drawing from scientific knowledge but adding to it arguments about agency, community, language, technology and artistic expression. This series aims to bring to consciousness potentialities that have emerged within a distinct historical situation and to underscore our actions as emergent within a complex dialectic among the living world.

It is our understanding that studies in literature, culture and media can add depth and sensitivity to the way we frame crises; clarifying how culture is pervasive and integral to human and non-human lives as it is the medium of lived experience. We seek exciting studies of more-than-human entanglements and impersonal ontological infrastructures, slow and public media, and the structuring of interpretation. We seek interdisciplinary frameworks for considering solutions to crises, addressing ambiguous and protracted states such as solastalgia, anthropocene anxiety, and climate grief and denialism. We seek scholars who are thinking through decolonization and epistemic justice for our environmental futures. We seek sensitivity to iterability, exchange and interpretation as wrought, performative acts.

Routledge Environmental Literature, Culture and Media provides accessible material to broad audiences, including academic monographs and anthologies, fictocriticism and studies of creative practices. We invite you to contribute to innovative scholarship and interdisciplinary inquiries into the interactive production of meaning sensitive to the affective circuits we move through as experiencing beings.

Mediating Nature
The Role of Technology in Ecological Literacy
Edited by Sidney I. Dobrin and Sean Morey

Mediating Nature
The Role of Technology in Ecological
Literacy

Edited by
Sidney I. Dobrin and Sean Morey

Routledge
Taylor & Francis Group

LONDON AND NEW YORK

First published 2020
by Routledge
2 Park Square, Milton Park, Abingdon, Oxon OX14 4RN

and by Routledge
605 Third Avenue, New York, NY 10017

First issued in paperback 2021

Routledge is an imprint of the Taylor & Francis Group, an informa business

British Library Cataloguing-in-Publication Data
A catalogue record for this book is available from the British Library

Library of Congress Cataloging-in-Publication Data
A catalog record has been requested for this book

Typeset in Goudy
by Taylor & Francis Books

ISBN 13: 978-1-03-223978-1 (pbk)
ISBN 13: 978-0-367-02518-2 (hbk)

DOI: 10.4324/9780429399121

For Judd and Penni Wise

Contents

Figures

Contributors

Melissa Bianchi is an Assistant Professor of Writing at Nova Southeastern University (NSU), USA. Her scholarship focuses on the intersections between rhetoric and composition, game studies, and ecocriticism. She has presented her scholarship on these topics at national and international conferences, and her research is published in referred journals including *Green Letters* (2017), *Ecozon@* (2017), and others. Her latest works will appear in the edited collections *Madness in the Woods* (Lexington Books) and *EcoComix* (McFarland). Melissa also teaches undergraduate and graduate courses at NSU that focus on writing and digital media.

Dan Brayton holds the Julian W. Abernethy Chair of Literature at Middlebury College, USA, where he is Professor of English and American Literatures, and Director of the Environmental Studies Program. His book, *Shakespeare's Ocean: An Ecocritical Exploration* (University of Virginia Press) won the Northeast Modern Language Association Book Prize. He publishes on early modern natural history, blue cultural studies, Shakespeare, and traditional boat building in such journals and magazines as *ELH*, *Forum for Modern Language Studies*, and *WoodenBoat*. In addition to teaching at Middlebury, he has taught for the Sea Education Association, the Williams-Mystic Program in Maritime Studies, and Semester-at-Sea.

Shannon Butts is a doctoral candidate at the University of Florida, USA, working with digital rhetoric, writing, and locative media. Her research and teaching examine how emerging technologies, such as augmented reality and 3D printing, create new literacy practices and opportunities for civic engagement.

Jason Crider is a PhD candidate and Graduate Research Fellow in the Department of English at the University of Florida, USA, where he researches and teaches on the rhetorics of ecomedia and biotechnologies. His work appears, or will soon appear, in *Computers and Composition*, *ISLE*, *Kairos*, *Technoculture*, and *Textshop Experiments*. He is currently preparing to build his first artificial pancreas.

Sidney I. Dobrin is Professor and Chair in the Department of English at the University of Florida, USA. He is also the Director of the Trace Innovation Initiative housed in that department. He is the author of numerous books and articles about things.

Joe Marshall Hardin is former dean of the College of Languages and Communication at University of Arkansas, Fort Smith, and was Writing Program Administrator at Western Kentucky University and Northwestern State University, USA. Hardin is a former member of the Executive Board of the Council of Writing Program Administrators (2006–2009) and member of the Conference on College Composition and Communication (CCCC) Committee on Teacher Preparation (2005–2008). His books include *Opening Spaces: Critical Pedagogy and Resistance Theory in Composition* (State University of New York Press) and *Choices: Situations for College Writing* (Fountainhead Press). Hardin has published in the areas of writing program administration, composition theory, sound production and composition, and food studies. He is also a songwriter and musician.

Steve Holmes is an Associate Professor of Technical Communication and Rhetoric at Texas Tech University, USA. He has published two books on digital rhetoric, ethics, and embodiment (*The Rhetoric of Videogames as Embodied Practice: Procedural Habits* (Routledge) and *Rhetoric, Technology, and the Virtues*, with Jared S. Colton (Utah State University Press)), as well as several articles and chapters in edited collections.

Madison Jones is a doctoral candidate in the Department of English at the University of Florida, USA, specializing in Rhetoric and Writing Studies with a secondary focus on Technical and Professional Communication. His dissertation project, 'Writing, place, network', uses an ecological methodology to understand the place-based affordances of digital writing technologies, and was awarded the Fall 2019 Graduate School Doctoral Dissertation Award. He teaches courses in digital rhetoric, writing/argumentation, and technical/professional communication. His articles have appeared in *Enculturation*, *Rhetoric Review*, *Computers and Composition Online*, *Kairos*, and *Interdisciplinary Studies in Literature and Environment*.

Lisa King is Associate Professor of Rhetoric, Writing, and Linguistics in the Department of English at the University of Tennessee, Knoxville, USA. Her research and teaching interests are interdisciplinary, and include cultural rhetorics with an emphasis in contemporary Native American and Indigenous rhetorics. Her focus rests on the rhetorics of cross-cultural sites such as Indigenous museums and cultural centers, and theorizing cross-cultural pedagogy through the teaching of Indigenous texts in rhetoric and composition classrooms. She is co-editor of *Survivance, Sovereignty, and Story: Teaching American Indian Rhetorics* (Utah State University Press), and author of *Legible Sovereignties: Rhetoric, Representations, and Native American Museums* (Oregon State University Press).

Anastasia Kozak holds an MFA in Creative Writing and a PhD in English from the University of Florida, USA. Her research and writing focus on the role of technology in language translation, textual analysis, and visual communication.

Sean Morey is an Associate Professor of English at the University of Tennessee, Knoxville, USA, where he teaches writing and digital media in the Department of English. His research focuses on developing theories of environmental studies at the intersections of rhetoric, digital media, and technology, primarily through the lens of electracy. He is the author of *Network of Bones: Conjuring Key West and the Florida Keys* (Texas A&M University Press); *Rhetorical Delivery and Digital Technologies* (Routledge); *The New Media Writer* (Fountainhead Press); and *The Digital Writer* (Fountainhead Press). He co-edited the collection *Ecosee: Image, Rhetoric, Nature* (SUNY Press) with Sidney I. Dobrin, and *Augmented Reality: Innovative Perspectives across Art, Industry, and Academia* (Parlor Press) with John Tinnell.

Glen Southergill is an Associate Professor of Writing at Montana Technological University, USA, where he also teaches interactive media and professional communications courses. His research centers on the emerging extensions and complications of dramatism in public, spatial, and digital rhetorics. He serves on the editorial collective of the *Journal for Undergraduate Multimedia Projects* (*Jump*+) and has published works in *Textshop Experiments*.

1 Mediating interfaces

Getting in between

Sidney I. Dobrin and Sean Morey

In 2009, editors Sid Dobrin and Sean Morey published the collection *Ecosee: Image, Rhetoric, Nature* in which contributors addressed how images have shaped popular notions of environmentalism, the environment, and more-than-human nature. *Ecosee* took up the position that despite the rhetorical power of images connected with environmental movements over the past forty years, scholarship in environmental communication has focused almost exclusively on verbal rather than visual rhetoric, as exemplified by M. Jimmie Killingsworth and Jacqueline S. Palmer's landmark book *Ecospeak: Rhetoric and Environmental Politics in America*. Contributors to *Ecosee* offered a deeper and fuller understanding of the communicative strategies and power of environmental politics by looking closely at the visual rhetorics involved in photographs, augmented reality applications, television and filmic images, video games, comics, and other forms of image-based media. While the editors maintain that verbal/textual rhetorics still capture the most attention in environmental and ecological studies—particularly within ecocriticism—rapid advances in digital technologies and the ever-growing role of image-based information and data visualization in public communication demand critical consideration of what it means to image nature.

Mediating Nature: The Role of Technology in Ecological Literacy asks the next question in research pertaining to the visual rhetoric of environmental politics and ecological thinking, questioning the very technologies that mediate the construction and circulation of images that inform how we see and know nature. *Mediating Nature* engages ecocritical and ecocompositional inquiry about the making of image as meaning making. Contributors to this dynamic collection focus their efforts on the intersections of digital media and environmental/ecological thinking, bringing Environmental Humanities into conversation with Digital Humanities, expanding the very notion of what the image of nature might be.

Mediating Nature addresses questions about the technologies used to construct representations of nature, including visual and other sensory representations. Part of the argument that emerges throughout the collection is that the study of media and nature requires the development of critical tools and methodologies for considering the very mediating technologies that produce and circulate representations of nature. That is, to understand mediations of nature, one needs to understand the creation and production of those mediations, right down to the algorithms, circuit boards, and power sources that drive mediating technologies. The need for such understanding is driven not merely by the desire to see the whole picture of mediated nature, as such, but by the fact that such mediations are always already political. As Angela Haas (2008) explains, "just as the rhetoric we compose can never be objective, neither can the technologies we design" (288).

Mediating Nature begins to galvanize and encourage conversations about how such critical tools might unfold beyond the few conversations that have begun to appear in ecocritical and ecocompositional work. For instance, in his article "The Ecocinema Experience," Scott McDonald (2012) has demonstrated how technologies of film rely upon the bones and tissues of animals, as celluloid film strip is made with collagen, a compound separated from dead animals by boiling these dismembered parts. Similarly, of digital camera technology, Steve Holmes (2017) has argued that the cameras in smartphones that are used to create images of nature need to be disassembled and examined for how their components capture light, process color, and create digital photos in order to understand how the camera mediates the "real" of nature (168–174). Through his analysis of the ways that the San Antonio Zoo mediates encounters with animals through augmented reality exhibits, he argues that this "means that technological black boxes have to be pried apart by cultural studies theorists and exhumed to locate the ways in which mobile media technologies radically restructure experience at multiple affective levels" (174). Thus, questions about mediation target a gamut of kinds of mediating technologies, and though the majority of the discussions in *Mediating Nature* take up digital imaging technologies, the collection intends to open discussion of mediation by ways of other technologies and materialities as well. That is, the inquiries and methods forwarded in *Mediating Nature* are intended to generate further questions about old media, as well as new and emerging media, and how those technologies engage sensory perception in addition to the visual.

In addition to the inner workings of mediating technologies, *Mediating Nature* also addresses the outputs of mediating technologies beyond visual representations. Mediating technologies themselves require humans to make changes to their environments in order to accommodate their technological requirements. For instance, the chemicals used to make and process film are toxic and often end up contaminating the environment. Similarly, the minerals required for the construction of digital devices must be extracted from environments, and as many new media ecologists have identified, those same minerals are dumped as e-waste in mass back into other environments—most often in developing countries—resulting in pollution and causing human health issues. But such concerns extend beyond the immediate, evident material consequences. For example, digital computer code and algorithms create real material effects throughout multiple environments. They require us to alter our buildings, our streets, and the planet in general to accommodate their needs (or our desires that their needs support). As Kevin Slavin (2011) has discussed, companies are gutting hotels and filling the floors with servers in order to be closer to Internet distribution centers. Such proximity allows algorithms (particularly Wall Street trading algorithms) to enact their transactions milliseconds faster. Toward such speed (what Paul Virilio identifies as the dromosphere), we authorize companies to terraform the planet, cutting through the earth to lay cables that more directly traverse the land from city to city, such as the infrastructure being laid by Spread Networks from New York to Chicago. Similarly, as Nicole Starosielski (2015) makes visible in her magnificent book *The Undersea Network*, the often-veiled global dependence on undersea cable systems reveals the environmental, historical, and cultural impact of that system on media and data circulation. Thus, *Mediating Nature* considers not only the capture and production of images, but the mediation that occurs in circulating those images as well.

Ultimately, *Mediating Nature* contends that ecological literacy and environmental politics are inseparable from digital literacies and visual rhetorics. Such a claim also demands consideration beyond the ecocritical and ecocompositional to a broader understanding of such mediations within Environmental Humanities and Digital Humanities, as well. Contributors to this collection push the borders of such thinking in order to forward theoretical considerations and implications of such relationships.

Ecological literacy

To claim that ecological literacy and environmental politics are inseparable from digital literacies and visual rhetorics requires consideration of the very ideas of environmental or ecological literacies, and in turn, digital literacy. We acknowledge the distinction between ecological and environmental literacies in the same way in which ecocriticism has come to identify differences between environmental and ecological, and we do not wish to conflate the two terms as interchangeable, as often happens. Rather, the focus here falls not on the distinctions between environmental and ecological literacies, but on the very idea of literacy as a component of ecocriticism and ecocomposition, on the very idea that we might identify something as an ecological or environmental literacy—or even a digital literacy. That is, the address of mediation in the imaging of nature/environment requires consideration of the very idea of literacy, as well, as the act of mediation is irrevocably bound to literacy. Similarly, histories of literacy often bind literacy with technological development. Reading and writing—a reductive definition of mass literacy—after all, are bound to technologies of writing and circulation (see, for example, Christina Haas, 1996).

Historically, literacy's value, in part, grows from its opposition to illiteracy, a concept rhetorically imbued with value. The illiterate lacks. *Illiterate* suggests more than not having the ability to read and write, more than being uneducated; it conveys, as all language does, an ideology of value and individual worth. Describing an individual as being "illiterate" is not merely an identification of lacking a particular skill set—reading and writing, for example—it is a statement of imposed difference. The lack of literacy is conveyed as derogatory, and the label used historically to mark particular populations as Other. As David Barton (1994) has explained, in various moments in history, illiteracy has been characterized as a disease, as a contributor to criminal activity, as an economic burden, and as a factor in unemployment, among other negative attributes. Literacy was employed as a measure of civilization. Those who are literate are understood to be civilized; those not literate deemed uncivilized. Often, such demarcations stood as foundational to colonial enterprise and were employed to silence Indigenous literacies. Sylvia Scribner explains it this way: "Historically, literacy has been a potent tool in maintaining the hegemony of elites and dominant classes in certain societies" (1984: 11). As Annette Vee (2017) explains in *Coding Literacy: How Computer Programming is Changing Writing*, literacy might be better understood in terms of access rather than as a synonym for education (47). Some are granted access, others are not. Vee goes on to show how educational systems are frequently designed to provide that access, but in ways that maintain hegemonic power structures by way of determining what constitutes literacy/education. That is, what education systems promote as knowledge, as literacy, is always already the reinforcement of a particular ideological worldview.

Clearly, this is a reductive overview of the politics of literacy, and this collection focuses on technological mediation, not histories of literacy. However, it is critical that we always be alert to the politics and power invoked in notions of environmental or ecological literacy. Such politics and power may be considered from ideological standpoints, but as this collection shows, the materiality of mediating devices plays a significant role in such literacies. Consider, for example, the ramifications of mediating devices such as medical X-ray machines on bodies. When a patient requires an X-ray, few patients ever ask what kind of X-ray machine the doctor will use to make the images that will inform diagnosis. Few of us are even likely to be aware that there are different kinds of medical imaging devices that can be used to produce X-ray images. Likewise, as one radiologist has explained,[1] there are many companies that make X-ray machines, and each type of machine can provide a different type of image. The same radiologist explains that, like any other manufactured object, there are good X-ray machines and bad X-ray machines. The images one machine makes may be very different from the image of the same object that another machine makes, just as a professional photographer will explain that the image made with one company's lenses are inherently different from images made with another company's lenses because the designed grind of the glass is unique to each company's lenses. The differences in image can direct significantly different diagnosis and intervention. Thus, the variance in imaging contributes to a difference in what is known—literacy—about the object. In this way, then, we see the effect the mediating device plays as never apolitical or innocent. The same should be considered about all mediating devices and the role they play in constructing the ideological positions of literacies. Consider, too, the ways in which variations in ultrasound machines contribute to literacies about women's bodies and reproduction as a medical process. Or, the ways in which technologies like ultrasound "translate" audio data into visual data to contribute to how we "see" women's bodies without consideration of the algorithms or circuitry required for such translations. Alternatively, consider how deep space telemetry is translated from radio and other forms of data into visual images that viewers tend to accept as accurate representations of nature, without questioning the politics of the devices themselves or the ideologies supported or refuted through their use. Thus, any invocation of ecological or environmental literacy requires a deeper consideration of the roles mediating technologies play in determining the substance and politics of that claim of literacy. Neither literacy nor technology is ever free of ideological agenda.

Mediation

More often than not—and certainly not unproblematically—mediation in media studies is tied primarily to theories of communication. Prior to the advent of digital media, such theories reduced communicative interaction to distinctions between human-to-human communication and mediated communication, and presumed active engagement with media. Questions of mediation focused primarily on the effects media *imposed on* communicative situations and, in fact, early theories of mediation did not address media in the act of mediation. However, as Leah A. Lievrouw explains,

> In the 1980s and 1990s, the introduction of digital media and information technologies confounded established distinctions between interpersonal and mass communication, and generated another wave of theorizing that brought conversation, symbolic interaction, social constructionism and small group process into accounts of computer-mediated communication, virtuality, online community, and other novel forms of mediated communication.
>
> (2009: 304)

The generation of media scholars that followed these shifts, scholars who emerged native to the digital age, began to examine the complexities of digital mediation in ways that account for the dynamic connections between the digital, the material, and the social that had not previously been accounted for. Thus, communications theorists now identify mediation as the prevailing characteristic of communication, particularly as the use of digital tools evolved from limited, professional settings to ubiquitous personal or domestic uses. That is to say, as Sonia Livingstone explains it, whereas media and communication studies would analyze the relation between media and politics, say, while in other disciplines they analyze the relation between politics and the environment, or society and the family. But in a heavily mediated world, one cannot analyze the relation between politics and the environment, or society and the family without also recognizing the importance of the media—all these spheres and their intersections have become mediated.

(2009: 2)

Mediation emerged in the late 1970s and early 1980s as way of addressing connections between media and interpersonal communications within social and cultural contexts (Lievrouw, 2009: 309). The editors of the landmark collection *Inter/Media* argued for mediation as a key term for emerging communications theories (Gumpert and Cathcart, 1982: 135) and later James A. Anderson and Timothy P. Meyer (1988) would contend that such frameworks focus on emerging media forms. Many of these newer theories of communication, mediation, and emerging technologies focused on the effects the varying technologies had on communicative situations, often focusing on the "impacts" of "new technologies on users' attitudes, values, behaviors, and perceptions" (Lievrouw, 2009, 309). Similarly, those researchers concerned with media policies began to consider the role of new media in traditional regulatory structures in industry, including things like privacy, decency, and service obligations. Others began to question the role of mediation in technological determinism. Such inquiries also encouraged more interdisciplinary perspectives regarding mediation and communication; theories developed in science and technological studies, for example, necessarily were brought into conversation with communications theories. Such cross-pollinations invigorated new perspectives. For example, science and technology studies provided mediation theories the idea of mutual-shaping, the argument that "society and technology are co-determining and articulated in the on-going engagement between people's everyday practices and the constraints and affordances of material infrastructure" (Lievrouw, 2009, 310). Similarly, such interdisciplinary influences allowed communications theorists to begin to consider localized and individual subject-focused ideas about meaning and interaction and, later, to be able to make distinctions in mediation between presence and telepresence and the role of interactivity in meaning making. Much of this work focused on the role specific media forms play in communication and information circulation.

Most recently, considerations of mediation have turned from the media to the very act of mediation, influenced by a larger cultural turn and research from the humanities. As Lievrouw explains, "key approaches and concepts from critical and cultural studies have been imported into the new media context, particularly a 'cultural transmission' view of media as powerful instruments in the reproduction and transmission of dominant ideologies, interests, and power structures" (2009: 312). Lievrouw shows how such a turn has accounted for mediation and representations of ideas like "gender, sexuality, ethnicity, and class and the influence of these representations on people's senses of self or identity (especially among children and youth)" (312). Noticeably absent from Lievrouw's summary—and, in turn from the overall larger conversation about mediation—is the mediation and representation of nature, environment, and other non-human entities and subjects. Consider, too, the opening lines of Lievrouw and Livingstone's *Major Works in New Media*:

> No part of the world, no human activity, is untouched by the new media. Societies worldwide are being reshaped, for better or for worse, by changes in the global media and information environment. So too are the everyday lives of their citizens. National and subnational forms of social, political and economic inclusion and exclusion are reconfigured by the increasing reliance on information and communication technologies in mediating almost every dimension of social life.
>
> (2009: 1)

Mediating Nature takes up this conversation at this specific moment in communication and media theory's address of mediation, not only bringing the ecocritical and ecocompositional perspective to mediation studies, but rethinking the very idea of such intersections as having been pre-established by the cultural turn in communications and mediation studies.

Like many working in media studies or communications studies, this collection does not situate new media as simply an extension of mass communications media forms. Doing so would limit the understanding of new media technologies as little more than new iterations of the same communicative interactions. Instead, the writers in this collection attend to new media and emerging media technologies as providing new methods for communicative interaction that require new theories, including new theories of mediation. To cast new media simply as new approaches to entrenched methods of personal and mass communication is to reduce our understanding of the very idea of mediation as merely the act of communicating via media. Mediation must now be considered in light of more than just production/consumption communication models. We must now account for ideas and functions like circulatory velocity, "always-on" technology, mobility, ubiquitous computing, the internet of things, global social networks, optimization, targeted marketing, and so on. Perhaps, as Roger Silverstone (2006) has contended, the most relevant of all such influences in mediation is the emerging role of domestication, the appropriation of new media technologies into our individual, daily lives. Central to Silverstone's idea of media domestication is the understanding that new media are always already both material and symbolic. For Silverstone, mediation is a dialectic circulation of meaning.

In her Presidential Address to the International Communication Association entitled, "On the Mediation of Everything," Sonia Livingstone (2009) asks what it might mean that we now claim that "information and communication technologies now mediate every dimension of society" (2). Such claims echo Kenneth Burke's notion of "Terministic Screens," the systems that influence—if not control—the ways in which individual subjects perceive the world and the ways such perceptions then dictate actions in the world. Burke explains that "the nature of our terms affect the nature of our observations, in the sense that the terms direct the attention to one field rather than another" (1966: 46). Thus, how we talk about mediation is as relevant as the mediation itself, or how we identify what it is to mediate. The contributors to *Mediating Nature*, of course, add nature and environment to this question of the terministic in mediation. For Livingstone, asking such questions, on the one hand, is asking about changes in the discipline of communication studies, but it is also, on the other, asking as to the implications of mediation for the ways in which we come to know and interact with the world and the grand claims that "everything is mediated." What Livingstone's analysis makes evident is that whether or not communication is changing in a mediated world, clearly the technologies through which communication occurs are, and that those changes require new theories and new ways of thinking about mediation and communication. Similarly, her analysis looks to definitions of mediation across multiple languages and a prevailing understanding that in English the concept is most frequently understood to mean something akin to "getting in between," often linked with ideas of negotiation or resolving disputes to carry a positive sense of resolution. However, Livingstone acknowledges that in academic inquiry, the positive attribution is often set aside in questioning media mediation in order to ask questions about control over media, ideology, capital, and so on.

The very notion of "getting in between" echoes the Hegelian claim that there is no pure experience prior to mediation. If this claim is accurate, Livingstone posits, then there is need for understanding how media mediate (2009: 4). Livingstone and many other communications and media theorists invest in this claim; yet, in their interrogations into mediation, few extend their inquiries of mediation beyond the social into the environmental, ecological, or natural. This collection takes up that specific task: developing theoretical approaches to understanding how media mediates ecology, environment, and nature. The collection looks at what comes between environment/nature and the individual and collective experiences of knowing those environments and natures.

Often, this notion of "in between" is also understood to suggest interface. Similarly to Burke's terministic screens which point to the mediative qualities of language systems, "interface" is understood to suggest the device or process in between the subject and the experience. Interface is not only the facilitator of interaction, but is the determiner of interaction. The interface dictates how interaction can occur. Famously, Alexander Galloway argues in *The Interface Effect* that the "interface is not a thing, it is always an effect" (2012: 33); however, the digital turn brings to light that, in fact, interfaces are always already also things, they are material, whether digital, mechanical, or even biological and physiological. The interface is understood as the thing *and* the process through which independent systems interact and communicate with each other. Imbricated in interface and mediation, then, is also an understanding of separation and distinction. Interface reinforces boundary at the same moment as facilitating interaction. For mediation, particularly mediation by way of new media, these boundaries fortify separation between viewing subject and object viewed. In the case of mediated environmental or ecological understanding and experience, what comes in between reinscribes separation between the human subject and the natural world. The contributors to this collection turn a critical gaze upon the moments of and interfaces of what comes in between.

Beyond officially-created/endorsed mediations of nature, mediating nature is now crowdsourced, being produced by millions of hikers, bikers, anglers, hunters, mountaineers, park-goers, RVers, ATVers, and general outdoor enthusiasts. With easy access to mediating equipment such as action cams, smartphones, GPS-enabled tracking software, motion-sensor cameras, con-sumer drones, and other technologies, everyday experiences of nature are becoming mediated and shared every second. Of course, while many of these encounters are mundane, the more exotic encounters become super-mediated, virally-shared to the point that, as Sid Dobrin might describe, they saturate multiple networks, each re-mediating the encounter a bit differently. Such encounters, like dramatic shark attacks on humans or fauna, fuel stereotypes about these species, playing into fears that scientists have tried to debunk for decades, fears that can negatively affect such species. While this collection does not take up "self-produced" media explicitly, any consideration of mediation and media must now begin to account for the implications of how mass-acces-sed media creates (or makes evident) distinctions between official and unofficial language in representation, as well as how collective and cultural memories are constructed through the tropes and archetypes of self-produced media. This, we believe, warrants significant consideration beyond this collection.

Collected voices

In order to open the gates of inquiry regarding mediation, new media, media ecology, ecocriticism, ecocomposition, and digital studies and representa-tions of nature and environment, the contributors to *Mediating Nature* take up a diverse range of communicative technologies. You will notice that a majority of the contributions focus on visual representation; this is the case primarily because, as we noted at the outset of this introduction, *Mediating Nature* follows in agenda the work the Editors initiated in *Ecosee*. However, mediation requires consideration beyond just the visual; it requires more dynamic engagement with sensory representations—see, for instance, Joe Marshall Hardin's discussion of audio representations of nature in Chapter 5 of this collection. Thus, the contributors to this collection each offer glimpses into the growing and necessary conversation about mediation, emerging technologies, and ecological literacies.

In "Ecoplay: The rhetorics of games about nature" (Chapter 2), Melissa Bianchi considers the role video games play in constructing nuanced understandings of ecological and environmental issues. Bianchi looks to both small, independently-developed games and widely-distributed, mass-produced games in order to show how the very notion of computer games supports, critiques, and reflects upon how humans conceive of "nature." She situates her eye-opening analysis in an emerging body of critical work about computer games and representations of nature in order to further developing methods for studying games as ecomedia. Bianchi proposes an alternative framework for analyzing the representations of nature, environment, and ecology in computer games that she identifies as "ecoplay," a method that connects elements of play theory to scholarship about environmental rhetorics. Bianchi shows how by connecting play to other rhetorical forms we can "contextualize gameplay ecologically within networks of environmental rhetoric appearing across different modes and media."

Also concerned with video games, Steve Holmes' "Visualizing ecocritical euphoria in Red Dead Redemption 2" (Chapter 3) considers an on-going debate about the role of realistic visual representations of nature in ecocritical approaches to video games. By way of seeing the video game Red Dead Redemption 2 as a kind of "living game," Holmes takes up the degree to which visual realism in video games might be approached ecocritically. He contends that much of how ecocriticism has approached video games privileges what he identifies as a form of "metaphorical proceduralism." Holmes contends that what is needed are "better figurations of how nature's agency is figured as an active presence" in computer games. He posits that ecocritics "can benefit not only from metaphorical forms of proceduralism, but also by better understanding literal forms of the ways in which visual rendering technologies themselves figure and unfigure nature/culture divides."

Shannon Butts' insightful "Stereoscopic rhetorics: Model environments, 3D technologies, and decolonizing data collection" (Chapter 4) examines the role of 3D modeling in preservation efforts of cultural and natural locations. Butts makes us aware of how 3D modeling works as a mediation process that incorporates many traditional aspects of 2D and screen-based visual mediation, but also relies on dynamic dimensionality to provide visual information not found in traditional images. However, rather than applauding the value of modeling efforts, Butts shows us that as "3D technologies measure and remediate select sites, they create models dislocated from the complex ecology of the surrounding environment." She explains that 3D models inscribe a way of seeing cultural heritage that isolates the physical structures of a location. As such, in digitally preserving historical structures, we often lose local context or marginalize the voices of Indigenous communities.

While Butts' work expands our understanding of visual mediation, Joe Hardin's "If a tree falls: Mediations into and of natural sound" (Chapter 5) moves our consideration of mediating technologies beyond the visual to the auditory. Moving from the familiar question as to whether or not a tree falling in the woods makes a sound, Hardin shows that "the world is full of sound waves, both observed and unobserved." He considers the role of "soundscaping" as a kind of audio technology mediation, and proposes that "attention to the sounds of the world can be a powerful means to stimulate a shift in how humans live as a part of the natural world instead of apart from it." He contends that acoustic ecology, bioacoustics, and ecoacoustic theories, as well as art and music grounded in the non-objectification of nature, can "contribute to our understanding of the problems in our world and how we might best manage them."

Like Butts' expanded view of visual representations, Madison Jones also pushes us toward more complex understandings of the visual. In "(Re)placing the rhetoric of scale: Ecoliteracy, networked writing, and MEmorial mapping" (Chapter 6), Jones examines the role of scale in environmental communication, "specifically in the use of visualization technologies to promote ecoliteracy and communicate massive environmental issues (such as sea-level rise or climate change) to public audiences." Jones shows us how scalar technologies produce discrete challenges for environmental communication. Jones argues that by "presenting geological perspectives of deep time, digital technologies undermine human(ist) conceptions of place and environment." Jones understands Gregory L. Ulmer's concept of MEmorials as providing ways to "engage places of change and catastrophe as networked, ecological, and emergent." Rather than relying on Cartesian topologies, Jones proposes practices that stand to engage place as a trans-scalar network.

In his manifesto-inspired essay, "Imagining the Eastern Garbage Patch: Ocean plastics as a problem of representation and scale," Dan Brayton (Chapter 7) also attends to scale, providing a first-hand account of his encounters with plastic and how we mediate such pollution that operates on oceanic scales. By recounting a sea voyage in July of 2007 through the North Pacific Subtropical Gyre, home to the notorious concentration of ocean plastics known as the Great Garbage Patch (or the Eastern Garbage Patch), he discusses how scientists and journalists mediate this phenomenon, and makes a case for the humanities in the study of ocean plastics by approaching the topic through the lens of narrative criticism. Ultimately, Brayton concludes that "it may well be the arts and the humanities, not the natural sciences, that have the most to say about the significance of ocean plastics, for to make the vastness and complexity of the phenomenon meaningful on a human scale they must enter our cultural narratives."

Returning back to terra firma, Lisa King (Chapter 8) shares her own experience of visiting the Wampanoag Homesite as a way to think through the process by which interaction with Indigenous technologies mediates a specific kind of relationship to and vision of the land. In her essay "Meaning in the growing, the harvest, the weaving, the making: Indigenous technologies at Plimoth Plantation's Wampanoag Homesite," King focuses less on museum technologies that are typically used as an interface between museum-goers and exhibits, and instead on how the experience at the Wampanoag Homesite is largely devoid of these kinds of technologies, relying upon "human demonstration and interaction to teach." Doing so focuses on mediating technologies that are not relegated to the past, but still with us in the present, so that "the Wampanoag Homesite interprets traditional Indigenous (Wampanoag) knowledges, lifeways, and technologies as on-going, living, and still deeply connected to a vision of and relationship with the land that is unique to Wampanoag peoples."

Anastasia Kozak engages with the ways photography mediates how we see nature, examining in what ways the production and circulation of digital landscape photography signals a different way of mediating the natural world. In her essay "Translating nature: Capture and exposure in contemporary digital landscape photography" (Chapter 9), Kozak examines not a particular technology of photography, but "certain practices of seeing and capturing nature that, in spite of Adobe Lightroom and Photoshop 'magic,' have not only withstood the test of time but became even more entrenched in an age that ... erases the chronodiversity of past-present-future and makes everything instantly updatable and shareable, the so-called age of the instant." By analyzing the concept of exposure and what this term's various meanings can tell us about photographic mediation, Kozak discusses how photographic technologies affect landscape photography, and argues that exposure "is as applicable to analog as to the digital photographic practices, a constant that provides continuity in the field in spite of the ever-present advancements of technology."

While Kozak discusses the technologies of cameras, in Chapter 10 Glen Southergill discusses how computer programming and algorithmic logic influence how we experience nature through web-based platforms. In his essay "(Re)coding environmental activism: An examination of *Hike Montana*," Southergill provides a case study of *Hike Montana*, a smartphone app that guides users through the natural beauty and natural heritage of Montana. Through his synthesis of Wendy Hui Kyong Chun's theorization of code, Kenneth Burke's treatment of induced action, and the World Wide Web Consortium's crowdsourced approach to generating standards, Southergill argues that the programmers who design such apps influence how nature becomes mediated through their coding. By looking closely at the JavaScript programming of *Hike Montana*, Southergill shows "how the work of environmental writing extends into domains of pixel and tracker, as well as derives significant meaning from the discipline-specific languages and discourse communities of programmers."

Complicating the inside/outside dimensions of mediating nature, Jason Crider (Chapter 11) returns to the human body as the site of all human-based mediation. In his contribution "I see the body electrate," Crider situates the always interrelated systems of the human body with an exterior environment within his personal account of contending with Type I diabetes. By noting the ways that his own body has become cybernetic as he connects with a variety of technologies that keep him alive, he learns how his own body is itself mediated and how "the functionings of these bodies might open up new rhetorical affordances and offer an escape from systemic, problematic logics in order to open new inventive possibilities via digital technologies." Ultimately, Crider finds that "There is no longer a binary between body and nature, body and technology, body and other, but rather interconnected systems of production and desire."

While each contributor's intervention in conversations regarding mediation and nature/environment varies, the exigencies for analyzing and theorizing the role of new media technologies in the construction and circulation of images that inform how we see and know the world remain consistent. This collection begins to establish theoretical frameworks for engaging the relationship between new media artifacts, mediating technologies, and nature/environments. However, this collection is by no means comprehensive or complete; it is merely an opening. Clearly, further work bringing Game Studies and ecocriticism together will need to unfold in examining the materialities of games as mediators. Likewise, Comics Studies is ripe for consideration of comic media as mediating technology, particularly as digital comic forms emerge.

Technologies of mediation have always influenced the ways that humans interact with and view nature, whether through the development of oral speech and the ability to label nature, or the development of writing, which allowed humans to more systematically define, categorize, and control nature and natural environments. As ecocinema scholars such as Sean Cubitt and Steven Rust have discussed, film and other visual media have continued to shape the ways that we relate to nature. *Mediating Nature* enters into this history of inquiry in order to establish the need to look at emerging digital technologies and how they further augment the ways that we see nature. *Mediating Nature* facilitates a dynamic discussion in order to institute this theoretical space as a critical aspect in emerging scholarship in media ecology, ecocriticism, ecocomposition, and digital studies.

Note

1 Trish Moser (physician) in discussion with the author, April 24, 2016.

References

Anderson, James A. and Timothy P. Meyer. *Mediated Communication: A Social Action Perspective*. London: Sage. 1988.

Barton, David. *Literacy: An Introduction to the Ecology of Written Language*. Oxford: Blackwell, 1994.

Bolter, Jay David and Richard Grusin. *Remediation: Understanding New Media*. Cambridge, MA: MIT Press, 2000.

Burke, Kenneth. "Terministic Screens." *Language as Symbolic Action: Essays on Life, Literature, and Method.* Oakland, CA: University of California Press, 1966. 44–62.

Dobrin, Sidney I. and Sean Morey, eds. *Ecosee: Image, Rhetoric, Nature.* Albany, NY: State University of New York Press, 2009.

Galloway, Alexander R. *The Interface Effect.* New York: Polity Books, 2012.

Gumpert, Gary and Robert S. Cathcart. *Inter/Media: Interpersonal Communication in a Media World.* Oxford: Oxford University Press, 1982.

Haas, Angela. "Wampum as Hypertext: An American Indian Intellectual Tradition of Multimedia Theory and Practice." *Studies in American Indian Literatures* 19. 4(2008): 77–100.

Haas, Christina. *Writing Technology: Studies on the Materiality of Literacy.* Mahwah, NJ: Lawrence Erlbaum, 1996.

Holmes, Steve. "SAZoo-AR, Ethea, and Computer Vision." *Augmented Reality: Innovative Perspectives across Art, Industry, and Academia.* Eds. Sean Morey and John Tinnell. Anderson, SC: Parlor Press, 2017. 155–175.

Killingsworth, M. Jimmie and Jacqueline S. Palmer. *Ecospeak: Rhetoric and Environmental Politics in America.* Carbondale, IL: Southern Illinois University Press, 1992.

Lievrouw, Leah A. "New Media, Mediation, and Communication Study." *Information, Communication, & Society* 12. 3(2009): 303–325.

Lievrouw, Leah A. and Sonia Livingstone. "Introduction." *Major Works in New Media.* Eds. Leah A. Lievrouw and Sonia Livingstone. London: Sage, 2009. xxi–xl.

Livingstone, Sonia. "On the Mediation of Everything." Presidential Address 2008. *Journal of Communication* 59. 1(2009): 1–18.

McDonald, Scott. "The Ecocinema Experience." *Ecocinema Theory and Practice.* Eds. Stephen Rust, Salma Monani and Sean Cubitt. London: Routledge, 2012.

Scribner, Sylvia. "Literacy in Three Metaphors." *American Journal of Education* 93. 1(1984): 6–21.

Silverstone, Roger. "Domesticating Domestication: Reflections on the Life of a Concept." *The Domestication of Media and Technology.* Eds. Thomas Berker et al. Maidenhead: Open University Press, 2006. 229–248.

Slavin, Kevin. "How Algorithms Shape Our World." TED: Ideas worth Spreading. July 2011. Accessed April 20, 2012. https://www.ted.com/talks/kevin_slavin_how_a lgorithms_shape_our_world

Starosielski, Nicole. *The Undersea Network.* Durham, NC: Duke University Press, 2015.

Vee, Annette. *Coding Literacy: How Computer Programming is Changing Writing.* Cambridge, MA: MIT Press, 2017.

2 Ecoplay

The rhetorics of games about nature

Melissa Bianchi

From small, independently developed projects to massively popular titles, digital games continue to nuance our understandings of environmental issues. In our contemporary moment, a wide range of computer games support, critique, and reflect upon how humans conceive of "nature." These claims are supported by innovative, though mostly isolated, scholarly essays. For example, Benjamin Abraham and Darshana Jayemanne's 2017 analysis of the relationship between climate fiction and digital games, Colin Milburn's 2014 codification of "green games," Alenda Chang's 2011 argument that games are environmental texts, and Matt Barton's 2008 examination of weather simulations demonstrate the value of identifying and assessing how digital games communicate ideas about nature. Similarly, Melissa Bianchi's and Kyle Bohunicky's articles in the 2014 special issue of *Green Letters* also contribute to this expanding field of scholarship by explaining how specific games operate as critical lenses for environmental perspectives. These works and others illustrate the importance of studying digital games as environmental and ecological media, or ecomedia.

In a groundbreaking special issue of *Ecozon@: European Journal of Literature, Culture and Environment*, several scholars propose frameworks for analyzing games as ecomedia. The issue, called *Green Computer and Video Games* (2017), illustrates the significance of digital games to studies of environmental thinking by examining the complex and varied ways that games raise environmental awareness, encourage thoughtful actions, challenge unsustainable practices, and more. The editors of the issue, Alenda Chang and John Parham, firmly situate the project at the intersection of ecomedia studies and games studies, characterizing its contents as an extended conversation about games' ecological impacts and the strategies we can use to "green" game studies. The essays contained in *Green Computer and Video Games* highlight the many and varied methods used to study how digital games engage in environmental thinking. In the issue's introduction, Chang and Parham provide an overview of these methods, including "'contradictory' ecocritical readings and playthroughs of games produced within mainstream, industrial (mass) culture"; "analyses of environmentally educational serious games"; studies of fan culture, player creations, and player communities; "'tactical' and/or counterculture gaming"; and the design and development of "dissonant" games that challenge ideas presented in mainstream media (2017: 7). This list offers a necessary foundation for the burgeoning field of green game studies while also providing valuable direction for cultivating further research at the intersection of ecomedia studies and game studies.

To continue establishing methods for studying games as ecomedia, this chapter elaborates on an alternative framework for analyzing how games make arguments about nature, the environment, and ecologies. This perspective, called "ecoplay," was briefly described in the introduction to the second issue of *Trace: A Journal of Writing, Media, and Ecology* (2018). At its core, ecoplay links elements of play theory to scholarship on environmental rhetorics. By connecting play to other rhetorical forms, we can contextualize gameplay ecologically within networks of environmental rhetoric appearing across different modes and media. Locating digital games and play within broader discursive and rhetorical ecologies through ecoplay can further illuminate how digital games cultivate environmental awareness; continue to establish the importance of green game studies to ecocriticism and game studies; and change how we play, analyze, and design games about nature.

Environmental rhetorics in games: ecospeak, ecosee, ecoplay

Ecoplay is inspired by two concepts, "ecospeak" and "ecosee," each of which vitally informs the context and scope of the proposed portmanteau. The former, "ecospeak," comes from M. Jimmie Killingsworth and Jacqueline S. Palmer's *Ecospeak* (1992), while the latter, "ecosee," comes from Sidney I. Dobrin and Sean Morey's edited collection *Ecosee* (2009). Both works analyze rhetorical patterns in environmental discourse with specific attention to particular modes of communication. Killingsworth and Palmer examine discourses about environmental politics, while Dobrin and Morey focus on the visual rhetoric of ecological issues. The latter text builds on the former, and ecoplay continues their discussions of the rhetorical patterns and practices evident in environmental texts with a specific focus on video games.

Ecoplay operates in a similar manner to Killingsworth and Palmer's ecospeak. Ecospeak, a notion inspired by "Newspeak" from George Orwell's *1984*, is both an emergent discourse and a framework for analyzing rhetoric. As a discourse, ecospeak defines "novel positions in public debate" (Killingsworth and Palmer, 1992: 8) and represents "several distinct ethical and epistemological perspectives on environmental issues" (11). On its surface, ecospeak appears to oversimplify environmental politics into two opposing factions: environmentalists and developmentalists.[1] As a framework for studying discourse, however, ecospeak performs its own rhetorical analysis, which Killingsworth and Palmer use to demonstrate that environmental discourse is multifaceted rather than simply dichotomous (10). Killingsworth and Palmer claim that, through ecospeak, environmental discourse occurs on a continuum of perspectives shaped by distinct discourse communities, each with their own unique set of values and beliefs. Killingsworth and

Palmer's study contributes to a larger conversation focused on how ideas about ecology, environment, and nature are formed through discourse and its study. Similarly, ecoplay investigates how *play* and its study can contribute to ideas about ecology, environment, and nature. Ecoplay is at once play that is contextualized by environmental perspectives as well as an analytical tool for examining how play formulates concepts of environment and ecologies.

Ecoplay is also developed from Dobrin and Morey's concept of ecosee. Dobrin and Morey's theorization of ecosee responds to Killingsworth and Palmer's *Ecospeak* nearly two decades after its publication. In their edited collection, Dobrin and Morey (2009) argue the importance of adapting a concept of ecospeak to address our ever-changing multimedia landscape. They explain how *Ecospeak* provides a groundbreaking approach to environmental discourse, and note the framework's unforeseeable shortcomings regarding multimodal media—a product of the text's inception well before the technological booms of the late twentieth and early twenty-first centuries. To ameliorate the gap in visual analysis that ecospeak leaves behind, Dobrin and Morey propose ecosee to address the proliferations of both visual media and digital technologies. They describe ecosee as follows:

> Ecosee, then is the study and the production of the visual (re)presentation of space, environment, ecology, and nature in photographs, paintings, television, film, video games, computer media, and other forms of image-based media. Ecosee considers the role of visual rhetoric, picture theory, semiotics, and other image-based studies in understanding the construction and contestation of space, place, nature, environment, and ecology. Ecosee is not (only) an analysis of existing images, it is a work toward making theories that put forward ways of thinking about the relationship between image and environment, nature, and ecology, as well as a theory (or, more accurately, a number of theories) of visual design for those who make images.
>
> (2009: 2)

Ecosee demonstrates how images in various media play a significant role in studying, theorizing, and composing representations of nature. Dobrin and Morey emphasize that ecosee is also bound to the processes of producing and interpreting written discourse, including those of ecospeak, amplifying the scope of rhetorical ecocriticism. Ecoplay follows in this tradition by extending the work of *Ecosee* and *Ecospeak* to account for both the rhetorical and multimodal qualities of play. In the decade since *Ecosee* was published, there have been significant developments in software applications, computer hardware, mobile and streaming technologies, augmented reality, virtual reality, and social media platforms that are fundamentally changing the landscape of rhetorical ecocriticism. While *Ecosee* anticipates some of these developments, its framework is somewhat limited for addressing the rhetorical complexity of digital games.[2]

Game studies scholars, however, have highlighted several rhetorical qualities of games, such as their interactivity and their ability to model alternative possibilities, that require specialized frameworks for rhetorical ecocriticism. As Chang and Parham have observed,

> This is where, ecocritically speaking, game studies comes into its own: games possess an affective quality, engendered by their uniquely interactive basis, which is captured in many of the key concepts of this still youthful field: immersion, interactivity, incorporation, identification, and agency; the ludic, ergodic, algorithmic, and machinic; play, platform, and procedurality; and so on.
>
> (2017: 10)

This list of game aspects is useful for generating methods that can analyze various forms of environmental rhetoric in games. Any of these concepts might serve as a foundation for understanding how games make arguments about nature (e.g., eco-interactivity, eco-ludics, eco-procedurality). Among these, the concept of play is particularly productive as an ecocritical framework because of play theory's broad scope and its applicability in a wide variety of media and contexts. Linking play theory to rhetorical ecocriticism offers a way to at once attend to a vital component of digital games while also situating digital games in wider media ecologies.

Play theory is useful for rhetorical ecocriticism because it considers the interactions between players' beliefs and the values presented to players through game systems. Broadly, play is defined as a player's experience of a game. It is a dialectical relationship between the player and the game system, and in many cases, other players as well (DeKoven, 2002). Through the dialectics of play, players appropriate, create, and express themselves, at times abiding by game rules and at others negotiating with them (Sicart, 2011). Recent play theory privileges play above other rhetorical forms found in games—notably, procedural rhetoric—because play attends to players' contributions to the game experience in addition to the rhetorics of the game system itself. As Miguel Sicart argues,

> Play does not only include the logics of the game – it also includes the values of the player. Her politics. Her body. Her social being. Play is a part of her expression, guided through rules, but still free, productive, creative. Without the openness of play, the player cannot express or explore their ethics, their politics.
>
> (2011: n.p.)

Sicart's description of play acknowledges players as "value-driven agents" who are not only creative and appropriative, but who also configure their experiences of games through their unique values. Play, then, is useful for ecocritical thinking because it accounts for players' explorations of distinct ideologies underpinning various approaches to environmental thinking represented in games. Players identify specific ecological or environmental values, practice them, and even challenge them during gameplay. Thus, play should be a central component of developing an analytical framework for considering computer games as ecomedia because it supports their function as rhetorical artifacts while also acknowledging players' values.

Additionally, a concept of ecoplay can connect analyses of digital games to other forms of ecomedia. While games may be the most culturally and economically pervasive form for play, play is used for expression in a variety of contexts and objects. Play is used to express politics, aesthetics, and other aims through interactive art, sports, toys, etc. (Sicart, 2014: 4). Through play, games are connected to a rich ecology of media that may persuade individuals of similar or different beliefs, values, and practices. Therefore, ecoplay is more than simply playing games with an environmental focus. To *play ecologically* is to consider the broader rhetorical ecosystems in which play is embedded. To perform ecoplay is to consider the relations (or inter*play*) between gameplay and other rhetorical modes and media to identify how these elements inform and interact with one another. This perspective is especially important for multimodal digital games where ecoplay is linked to ecospeak and ecosee so that all three are inextricably bound to one another's meaning-making.

Given the plethora and diversity of computer games, there are many instances where ecoplay might occur; however, this chapter will focus on a few specific examples. The chapter adopts Hans-Joachim Backe's (2017) perspective that it is important to take mainstream games into consideration more frequently in ecocritical studies because of the nuances they might offer. Backe's eco-ethical analysis framework is used as a guide for selecting specific popular and independently developed games (as opposed to serious or educational games) that might serve as productive examples of ecoplay. Backe's descriptive matrix relies on several criteria that select games for their engagement with environmental and ecological topics as well as their capacity to create dissonances between players' behaviors and procedural design. This tension between game goals and player values encourages players to critically engage with the game's themes during play (Sicart, 2011). The games discussed below have been selected using Backe's framework, and their rhetorical elements are representative, though not necessarily comprehensive, of ecoplay.

Diving into ecoplay: ABZÛ

Some games facilitate ecoplay through an emphasis on environmental themes and tension between gameplay and game goals. ABZÛ, a short single-player adventure game, exemplifies how ecoplay can be encouraged in this manner. In the game, players assume the role of a diver who explores different ocean environments while discovering submerged ruins and ancient technologies. The game places few restrictions on players' ocean explorations, forgoing the limitations on oxygen availability, environment visibility, and air pressure that are typically found in diving simulations. Instead, the game opts for an idealized representation of diving and ocean environments (Nava, 2016).

Despite eschewing conventional diving simulation designs, ABZÚ curtails gameplay in other ways, specifically through its linear narrative, limited non-player character (NPC) interactions, and closed-world design. As in most adventure games, players may explore the digital world (discovering collectibles and unlocking exploration achievements), focus solely on progressing the game narrative, or perform a combination of these behaviors. These options create opportunities for diverse gameplay experiences through which players may practice distinct environmental perspectives in a simulated environment. The tension between explorative play and narrative-driven play along with the game's thematic emphasis on marine ecosystems allows ABZÚ to facilitate the emergence of ecoplay.

ABZÚ supports ecoplay through scripted events and interactions that players must perform to make progress in the game's narrative. Gameplay in ABZÚ is often momentarily interrupted by cinematic sequences, or cutscenes, that temporarily suspend players' control of the diver character. During these cutscenes, players observe moments in which the diver encounters a great white shark, and over the course of the game, these scenes establish a peaceable relationship between diver and shark where neither is hunted or harmed by the other (Fig. 2.1). The repeated depictions of amicable diver–shark encounters build towards the climactic ending of ABZÚ in which players must direct the diver as she rides the shark's spirit, destroying the undersea mines that ended its life and that continue to harm other marine creatures (Fig. 2.2). Players cannot bypass this gameplay if they intend to complete ABZÚ and must actively practice the cooperative actions of diver and shark, controlling their connection and direction, to preserve

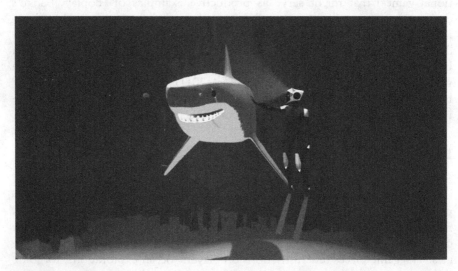

Figure 2.1 Cutscene from chapter four depicting a moment of peaceful interaction between the diver and the great white shark by Matt Nava at Giant Squid Studios; ABZÚ. Microsoft Windows, 505 games, 2016.

Figure 2.2 The player-diver and the great white shark's spirit swimming together to destroy undersea mines in chapter seven by Matt Nava at Giant Squid Studios; *ABZÛ*. Microsoft Windows, 505 games, 2016.

the game's ecosystems from technological destruction. During this instance, players must comply with the rules of the game to progress, and by doing so, they confront and participate in the game's environmentally conscious narrative that advocates for befriending and protecting marine life.

ABZÛ also facilitates ecoplay through achievements that incentivize players to explore and interact with the game environment. The game includes several achievements that players may pursue but that have no impact on the game's narrative. For example, scattered throughout the environments in *ABZÛ* are large animal NPCs that the diver can swim up to and ride, as well as objects referred to as "hidden pools" that award players' exploration achievements (Fig. 2.3). By finding and directing the diver to interact with these pools, players release several creatures of a single species (e.g., pufferfish, orcas, sharks, anglerfish) into the immediate environment, ameliorating a dearth in its biodiversity. Players may choose to seek out hidden pools, reintroducing ecological diversity into the ocean habitats, or ignore them entirely. Discovering and interacting with the twenty hidden pools in the game rewards players with the "Ecosystem" achievement, providing players incentive to complete the task. Likewise, interacting with whales, giant squids, and other large animals to traverse the environment also awards achievements. Aligning the mechanics of hidden pools and animal NPCs with achievements suggests that playing through without interacting with the ecosystem and its inhabitants is an incomplete experience of the game. It also suggests that nature is a resource for reaching anthropocentric goals, the game's achievements. Striving to complete the game's achievements is a form

Figure 2.3 The player-diver interacts with a hidden pool in chapter one that produces
           leatherback sea turtles by Matt Nava at Giant Squid Studios; ABZÛ.
           Microsoft Windows, 505 games, 2016.

of ecoplay that sutures a concept of nature as resource to the practices of
restoring biodiversity to endangered marine ecosystems. Playing without
interacting with the hidden pools and animal NPCs might also be considered
ecological play by having the player-character's impact on the environment
remain minimal; however, the game's achievements and narrative suggest that
active and direct intervention in marine ecologies is the preferred course of
action. Regardless of which style of gameplay they choose, players perform
different approaches to humans' environmental practices when playing *ABZÛ*.

ABZÛ also offers players unique options during gameplay through which
they encounter ecoplay working in tandem with ecosee and ecospeak to
make meaning. Images are integral to gameplay in *ABZÛ*, and the game's
visual designs were inspired by actual environments and sea creatures from
around the world. The game's creative team studied how specific organisms
look, move, and behave to build the game's stylized representations, which
attempt to capture the "iconic" characteristics of each species while accom-
modating the game's technical limitations (Nava, 2016). Given this emphasis
on *ABZÛ*'s visual experience, ecosee plays a prominent role in the game's
rhetoric. *ABZÛ*'s imagery represents an idealized ocean, a romanticized
depiction of nature, which is further complicated by gameplay.

Throughout *ABZÛ*, players may find and interact with twelve unique
"meditation" statutes that facilitate ecoplay through an emphasis on practicing ecosee. These large sculptures of quadruped shark creatures are found
in each of *ABZÛ*'s chapters and overlook the game's diverse ocean environments (Fig. 2.4). Clicking a meditation statue enters players into a cutscene

Press View button to meditate

Figure 2.4 The player-diver sits atop a meditation statue in chapter two by Matt Nava at Giant Squid Studios; *ABZÛ*. Microsoft Windows, 505 games, 2016.

in which they temporarily lose control of the avatar as the diver perches atop the sculpture. The cutscene then switches to a disembodied camera that autonomously follows various sea creatures in the area as they swim and feed (Fig. 2.5). Players cannot control how or where the camera moves, but they can cycle through streams of different organisms with each species name appearing in the bottom right corner of the screen. There are no limits

Press enter to exit   Five-Lined Snapper

Figure 2.5 A player's view of a five-lined snapper from one of the meditation statues in chapter one by Matt Nava at Giant Squid Studios; *ABZÛ*. Microsoft Windows, 505 games, 2016.

to how long and how often players visit meditation statues, but there are game achievements that incentivize players to use them.[3] Players may bypass all or some of the meditation statues during play or spend considerable time visiting them. Ignoring the meditation statues has no effect on the narrative presented in ABZÛ, while engaging the meditation statues presents a unique moment in which the game communicates multiple concepts of nature through ecospeak, ecosee, and ecoplay.

The meditation statues in ABZÛ introduce players to environmental rhetorics that negotiate between different ideas of nature. The game option to "meditate" on the sculpture, as opposed to "observe" or "watch," aligns these moments of play with discourses of deep ecology that envision "nature as spirit" (Killingsworth and Palmer, 1992: 14). At the same time, viewing the digital animals in meditation mode takes on attributes of scientific observation through the traveling, disembodied (rather than first- or third-person) camera perspective, and cataloging of distinct species through name tags that appear in the bottom right-hand corner of the screen. This representation of marine life aligns with rhetorics of "nature as object" (14). Gameplay during meditation is strikingly different from the rest of ABZÛ. While play largely relies on players' control over the game's diver and her interactions with environmental elements, during meditation, players can only control when they enter and exit meditation mode and when they switch between which species they view. In these moments of play, the game seems to suggest that nature is something that can be communed with and observed, but it is not something to *play with* or control. Being unable to enact conventional avatar controls in meditation mode is a rhetorical feature of the game that affords players the opportunity to explore alternative ideas of nature that challenge its presentation as a resource. Juxtaposing meditation moments with other acts of gameplay in ABZÛ demonstrates how the game offers several forms of ecoplay that allow players to appropriate and challenge different perspectives of nature as resource, object, and spirit.

Ecologies of ecoplay: Jurassic World Evolution

Ecoplay, through its connections to ecospeak and ecosee, can situate the rhetorics of computer games within broader media ecologies. At the same time, attending to the embeddedness of digital games in extensive media ecologies can reveal how ecoplay amplifies or augments existing discourses about environmental issues. Generally, game designers often construct gameplay experiences using rules, strategies, narratives, and other forms of representation observed in actual systems or depicted in other media. These representations carry with them specific ideologies about environments and ecological issues. Incorporating elements from beyond the game into its constructed world affords players opportunities to play with and against the specific knowledges, practices, and beliefs that these elements reference, making play rhetorical. The popular PC game *Jurassic World Evolution* (2018) exemplifies this process through its apparent connections to forms of ecos-peak and ecosee found in other media within the *Jurassic Park* franchise.

Ecoplay in *Jurassic World Evolution* adopts some of the rhetorics of its predecessor texts. Scholars studying the *Jurassic Park* franchise claim that the novels and films, in part, attempt to assuage viewers of their concerns regarding ecological issues. W. J. T. Mitchell (1998) describes the speculative fiction of the *Jurassic Park* series as a persuasive attempt to convince contemporary audiences to dismiss their apprehensions about losses in biodiversity. Ursula K. Heise, expanding on Mitchell's points, claims that the *Jurassic Park* films use a "visual rhetoric of excess" (2003: 62)—expressed through dinosaurs' monstrous sizes, insatiable appetites, relentless persis-tence in hunting, as well as profuse and uncontrolled bodily secretions—to present the return of extinct species as ecological glut rather than as a problem that requires rectifying (64). Moreover, Heise argues that the unpredictability and uncontrollability of dinosaurs in *Jurassic Park* imagine nature with the ability to contest the efforts of "a human civilization that leaves little that is 'natural' in place" (65). The *Jurassic Park* films rely on visual rheto-rics of excess, unpredictability, and uncontrollability to persuade viewers that recuperating losses in biodiversity is unnecessary, if not disastrous. These rhetorics are also evident in the gameplay of *Jurassic World Evolution*.

Jurassic World Evolution also suggests that recuperating lost biodiversity is a practice of excess through its gameplay, which combines genre conventions from business simulations and life-management games. In the game, players are charged with building a successful dinosaur theme park similar to those depicted in the films. When the game zooms in on the digital dinosaurs, their visual depictions reproduce much of the excessive qualities that Heise describes. The game, however, is predominantly played from an overhead, third-person perspective, making the park, its patrons, and the dinosaurs appear significantly small compared to the imagery offered by the films. What *Jurassic World Evolution* lacks in visual excess, it makes up for through excesses in play, specifically through systems, tasks, and statistics that play-ers must track and manage simultaneously. The game requires players to operate various park systems and procedures, including power, construc-tion, fossil procurement, genome research, dinosaur creation and care, and the asset containment unit (ACU), each of which has its own set of mechanics and is susceptible to various kinds of failures that may affect the overall park. At the same time, players must track their financial resources, often dealing with monetary sums in excess of thousands of dollars, and the statistics of their facilities and living assets, which range from details about their power consumption to information about dinosaurs' health, popularity rating, and environment suitability. Managing all these aspects of the game while simultaneously tracking an abundance of information demonstrates how a rhetoric of excess might be characterized through gameplay mechan-ics. Here, excess is represented not through bodies, but by activities and data that players must engage with to achieve a successfully operating park.

Contrasted against games that rely on relatively simple gameplay, such as ABZÚ, *Jurassic World Evolution* emphasizes that recuperating losses in biodiversity is a complicated and expensive process, demanding a significant amount of time, attention, effort, and resources. In offering a complex gameplay experience, *Jurassic World Evolution* supports a style of ecoplay that echoes the rhetorics of excess presented in the *Jurassic Park* films.

Through ecoplay, *Jurassic World Evolution* also offers players opportunities to appropriate and negotiate between three distinct perspectives of nature. During the game, players must complete tasks that serve three different divisions in their park: Science, Entertainment, and Security. Each division views nature (the dinosaurs, their genomes, and their enclosures) as an object that, with skillful management, can be used to achieve anthropocentric ends, such as knowledge, spectacle, and control. To emphasize the distinctions between each division, the game adopts discourses from the books and films through character voice lines and dialogue. New characters and popular characters from the franchise, such as Dr. Ian Malcolm, Dr. Henry Wu, Owen Grady, and Claire Dearing, define each of the divisions through their unique perspectives on the park project. Moreover, for each division, players can choose to complete specific contracts that will directly impact the park as well as their reputation with the remaining divisions. For example, a Security contract for "Asset Sales" requests that players, "Use an ACU Transport Team to sell at least 3 Ceratosaurus specimens" to private owners for a cash reward of $500,000. The contract's description reads, "That we have a valuable commodity is obvious. That we should consider making a profit on said commodity is obvious. That there's a contract about this should be more obvious still." Despite the contract's insistence on the obvious benefits for players, specifically the influx of a significant amount of money and boosted reputation with the Security division, the contract has drawbacks for gameplay as well. Completing the contract results in reputation losses with both the Science and Entertainment divisions, from which players can infer that these divisions do not value selling dinosaurs to private owners. In these instances, players must strike a balance between catering to the needs of each division, accepting or declining contracts based on their resources as well as their own personal values and the game's goals (the overarching mission of running a successful park). Knowing when to accept or decline a contract is crucial, since the game penalizes players for failing contracts and for spending too much time and resources serving one division through events that threaten to destroy players' parks (e.g., escaped dinosaurs, declining park reputation) Thus, players must understand each division's goals and appropriately choose when to ignore, adopt, or compromise between their objectives to be successful in the game. Through gameplay, players learn to appropriate and negotiate distinctly anthropocentric approaches to recuperating lost biodiversity.

The different game modes in *Jurassic World Evolution* further complicate its ecoplay, affording players opportunities for free play where they might explore their own values with few restrictions. Specifically, the game's sandbox mode allows players to build parks without the parameters and limitations found in the career and challenge modes. In sandbox mode, players have access to unlimited resources and need not worry about their reputation with the park's three divisions. Here, players can choose which beliefs, values, and practices they appropriate or ignore during play, allowing for endless possible explorations of how to manage, or not manage, their parks. As a player and writer at *Polygon* observed about *Jurassic World Evolution*, "If you want to feel the *Zoo Tycoon* rush of building a huge pen of carnivorous beasts only to unleash them on your unsuspecting guests, you can do that. The game not only allows for it, the sandbox mode encourages fun without the risk of penalty" (Gilliam, 2018). Sandbox mode, then, offers players freedom from the perspectives of nature lodged in science, entertainment, and security that guide gameplay in the career and competitive modes. Players might choose to focus only on one division, or to entirely subvert the conventions of career mode, finding ways to challenge the game's anthropocentrism through various means, including releasing predatory dinosaurs on park guests. This kind of free play can enable ecoplay that experiments with politics and practices not predominantly featured in the game, but that are brought to it by players, allowing for opportunities to imagine and explore radical alternatives.

Conclusion: Beyond ecoplay

These brief analyses of *ABZÛ* and *Jurassic World Evolution* demonstrate that a concept of ecoplay can be used to understand how different types of games make arguments about "nature." In each game, play designed around environmental themes engages players in moments where they might practice or resist distinct approaches to understanding and interacting with environments, ecologies, and related issues, albeit through simulation. Examining *ABZÛ* and *Jurassic World Evolution* also illustrates how ecoplay is deeply linked to and informed by ecospeak and ecosee embedded in the games and in broader media ecologies. Through these specific digital games, we can see practical applications for ecoplay in helping us understand how both indie and popular games operate as ecomedia.

In addition to considering how play participates in formulating concepts and arguments about environment, ecoplay requires critical reflection on how we design, play, and study games. If we consider the environmental criticisms produced by ecoplay as inherently connected to activism, then game designers, players, and scholars should evaluate how they approach environmental issues through play. For designers, this might mean a deeper attentiveness to how games are constructed so that players are given opportunities to explore a wider range of perspectives and practices related to environmental topics along with their potential effects. For players, ecoplay requires critical awareness and reflection on choices made during play and how these choices support or challenge existing systems for engaging with ecological issues. This specific point is becoming increasingly important considering trends towards publicizing private play sessions on streaming platforms such as YouTube and Twitch, where the rhetorics of play are being circulated to a wide audience (Taylor, 2018). For scholars studying games and play, analyzing the various ways ecoplay is performed and co-opted within and beyond game spaces, and to what ends, is crucial if we are to better grasp the connections between game rhetorics and those found in other forms of ecomedia.

Finally, ecoplay is only one proposed framework for examining games as ecomedia, and its application may be more effective if used in combination with other analytical approaches. As demonstrated here, ecoplay alone can enrich our study of games as environmental or ecological media by focusing on the rhetorics of play. Combining ecoplay with ecospeak and ecosee, however, nuances how we understand the meaning-making of rhetorical play by contextualizing it in relation to other rhetorical modes and media. Examining the complexity of games—their multimodality; their embeddedness in rich media ecologies; their interactive, affective, and ludic qualities—demands a thorough attentiveness to detail and context, a process that can be served by connecting methods in green game studies to existing ecocritical frameworks.

Notes

1 Killingsworth and Palmer define these perspectives as follows, "On one side are the environmentalists, who seek long-term protection of endangered environments regardless of short-term economic costs. On the other side are the developmentalists, who seek short-term economic gain regardless of the long-term environmental costs" (1992: 9).
2 For example, see Tom Tyler's chapter "The Test of Time: McLuhan, Space, and the Rise of *Civilization*" in *Ecosee*.
3 Such as the "Zen Master" achievement for finding all of the game's meditation sculptures, or the "Food Chain" achievement for witnessing predation while meditating.

References

Abraham, Benjamin and Jayemanne Darshana. "Where Are All the Climate Change Games? Locating Digital Games' Response to Climate Change." *Transformations: Journal of Media, Culture & Technology* 30(2017): 74–94.

Backe, Hans-Joachim. "Within the Mainstream: An Ecocritical Framework for Digital Game History." *Green Computer and Video Games*, special issue of *Ecozon@: European Journal of Literature, Culture and Environment* 8. 2(2017): 39–55.

Barton, Matt. "How's the Weather: Simulating Weather in Virtual Environments." *Game Studies* 8. 1(2008). http://gamestudies.org/0801/articles/barton

Bianchi, Melissa. "Rhetoric and Recapture: Theorizing Digital Game Ecologies through EA's The Sims Series." *Digital Environments*, special issue of *Green Letters: Studies in Ecocriticism* 18. 3(2014): 209–220.

Bohunicky, Kyle. "Ecocomposition: Writing Ecologies in Digital Games." *Digital Environments*, special issue of *Green Letters: Studies in Ecocriticism* 18. 3(2014): 221–235.

Bohunicky, Kyle M. and Melissa Bianchi. "Introduction." *Trace: A Journal of Writing, Media, and Ecology* 2(2019). http://tracejournal.net/

Chang, Alenda. "Games as Environmental Texts." *Qui Parle* 19. 2(2011): 56–84.

Chang, Alenda and John Parham. "Green Computer and Video Games: An Introduction." *Green Computer and Video Games*, special issue of *Ecozon@: European Journal of Literature, Culture and Environment* 8. 2(2017): 1–17.

DeKoven, Bernie. *The Well-Played Game. A Playful Path to Wholeness.* Writers Club Press, 2002.

Dobrin, Sidney I. and Sean Morey. "*Ecosee*: A First Glimpse." *Ecosee: Image, Rhetoric, Nature.* Eds. Sidney I. Dobrin and Sean Morey. New York: SUNY Press, 2009. 1–19.

Gilliam, Ryan. "*Jurassic World Evolution* Becomes Two Games for Two Different Players." *Polygon*19 June2018. https://www.polygon.com/2018/6/19/17476666/jurassic-world-evolution-sandbox-unlimited-mode-missions. Accessed 26 February 2019.

Heise, Ursula K. "From Extinction to Electronics: Dead Frogs, Live Dinosaurs, and Electric Sheep." *Zoontologies: The Question of the Animal.* Ed. Cary Wolfe. Minneapolis, MN: University of Minnesota Press, 2003.

Killingsworth, M. Jimmie and Jacqueline S. Palmer. *Ecospeak: Rhetoric and Environmental Politics in America.* Carbondale, IL: Southern Illinois University Press, 1992.

Milburn, Colin. "Green Gaming: Video Games and Environmental Risk." *The Anticipation of Catastrophe: Environmental Risk in North American Literature and Culture.* Eds. Sylvia Mayer and Alexa Weik von Mossner. Heidelberg: Universitätsverlag Winter, 2014. 201–219.

Mitchell, W. J. T. *The Last Dinosaur Book: The Life and Times of a Cultural Icon.* Chicago, IL: Chicago University Press, 1998.

Nava, Matt. Interviewed by Kirill Tokarev. "Interview with the Creative Director of ABZÚ." *80Level*9 December2016. https://80.lv/articles/interview-with-the-creative-director-of-abzu/. Accessed February 26, 2019.

Sicart, Miguel. "Against Procedurality." *Game Studies* 11. 3(2011).

Sicart, Miguel. *Play Matters.* Cambridge, MA: MIT Press, 2014.

Taylor, T. L. *Watch Me Play: Twitch and the Rise of Game Live Streaming.* Princeton, NJ: Princeton University Press, 2018.

Tyler, Tom. "The Test of Time: McLuhan, Space, and the Rise of Civilization." *Ecosee: Image, Rhetoric, Nature.* New York: SUNY Press, 2009. 257–277.

Games referenced

ABZÚ. Microsoft Windows, 505 games, 2016.

Jurassic World Evolution. Microsoft Windows, Frontier Developments, 2018.

3 Visualizing ecocritical euphoria in *Red Dead Redemption 2*

Steve Holmes

On October 26, 2018, Rockstar released its third-person action-adventure videogame *Red Dead Redemption 2* (RDR2). Designed by Christian Cantamessa and Imran Sarwar, RDR2 is the sequel to *Red Dead Redemption*, set at a later time in the same western-themed narrative world. The player controls Arthur Morgan, who is a long-time member of Dutch van der Linde's outlaw gang. Set on the American frontier circa 1899, Dutch schemes to maintain his gang's autonomous lifestyle in the face of impeding encroachment by urban industrialization and civilization (law and order). RDR2 was the most popular multi-platform AAA-rated videogame of 2018. Rockstar earned close to $US725 million by October 29, 2018, which made RDR2 the highest-grossing entertainment release in any commercial medium—including film—to date (Tassi, 2018).

Among the many factors that explained its widespread appeal, RDR2 offered players one of the largest open-world terrains ever designed with over sixty hours of gameplay in its single-player story mode. Crossing the entire map of five neighboring regions (Ambarino, New Hanover, New Austin, Lemoyne, and West Elizabeth) on horseback at full speed without stopping would take around sixteen real-life minutes (Fischer, 2018). While this time range is similar to other massive open-world videogames, such as *The Witcher 3: Wild Hunt*, RDR2 differs in that it offers players meaningful forms of environmental interactivity on nearly every square inch of its playspace. Almost every building on the map can be entered and players can interact with virtually any non-player character (NPC) in the game. Industry blogger Tyler Fischer put it well: "There are a ton of open-world games on the market that are huge, but empty and shallow ... [RDR2, by contrast, is] a big world, but it's also more importantly a world that feels alive and bursting with potential for player stories."

As is often the case for any eagerly anticipated commercial release, players' initial enthusiasm was swiftly followed by more critical responses. January, 2019, for example, featured one of the first major public criticisms by a high-profile member of the videogame industry. Representing the frustrations of many players, Naughty Dog's Bruce Straley, who was the lead designer of *Uncharted* and *The Last of Us*, complained in an interview that RDR2's story missions were too scripted and failed to offer players the ability to meaningfully impact in game outcomes (Cooper, 2019). Having completed RDR2's single-player story mode in February, 2019, I can attest to the accuracy of Straley's complaint. The pivotal moments of the game, such as the death of Arthur Morgan, made me feel all too often like I was passively watching a cinematic scene unfold and being prompted to click a button at the appropriate moment, as opposed to actively participating by overcoming complex in-game obstacles.

Nevertheless, when I was writing this chapter in March, 2019, both players and industry media commentators remained in consensus about one particular strength, which relates directly to the subject matter of *Mediating Nature*: the visual rendering of the natural and physical environment. When the player navigates Arthur Morgan around a country town with dirt roads, his individual footsteps are marked and retained in the highly textured dirt. The dirt also retains impressions of the wheel ruts of randomly-spawned horse-drawn wagons. Long gone in RDR2 are the days of static and largely-pixelated 2D overhead skies and clouds like those seen in the Nintendo Entertainment System console's *Super Mario Bros.* Each 3D cloud in RDR2 is animated, voluminous, and unique. Thicker clouds across the open world's varied terrain will block out the sunlight proportionate to the direction Arthur Morgan faces. Randomly generated weather patterns, like rain or lightning, strengthen and weaken the sunlight depending on the rain volume and time of day. For these and countless other types of microlevel visual rendering, critics labeled it the closest manifestation to a "living game" achieved by videogame industry to date (Wills, 2018).

In this chapter, I want to use this "living game" description to revisit a debate about the role of realistic visual representations of nature in ecocritical approaches to videogames. As the poststructuralist philosopher Jacques Derrida noted in various critiques of logocentrism, humans are always in search of (never achievable) Truth (presence) in the mediating sign systems that we use to construct meaning in our daily lives. Decades later, game designer Ian Bogost (via Derrida) dubbed "simulation fever" as the player's anxiety of experiencing a proportionate drive by the videogame industry to produce ever more realistic visual and procedural simulations of reality that never actually map perfectly onto reality (2007, 111). Countless game studies scholars have similarly critiqued the "rhetorics of 'realism'" in which attaining more realistic graphics are equated to better immersive forms of play (Abraham and Jayemanne, 2017: 87). To offer one reason, the presupposition of immersion achieved through better visual realism ignores the role that a player's body plays in a videogames' cultivation of affect (Ash, 2013; Shinkle, 2005; Holmes, 2017).

At the same time, ecocritical approaches to videogames need to remain open to more realistic visual representations of nature in commercial videogames. A number of ecocritics have argued that rendering natural actors like weather patterns as a passive background that never actively impedes player progress can reinscribe an unproductive nature/culture or Cartesian subject/object split.

Alenda Chang rightly complains that most videogames "[relegate] environment to background scenery [...] predicating player success on extraction and use of natural resources" (2011: 58). Matthew Barton (2008) similarly queries, "how can games acknowledge the threat of global warming when game characters fail to take notice of a torrential downpour on their heads?"

However, ecocritics are not interested in visual realism as much as they are in forms of *procedural realism* which shift nature—however it is visually rendered during play—to an active and agentive presence. As a case in point, ecocritics have lauded David O'Reilly's videogames like *Mountain* and *Everything* (and Keita Takahashi's *Katamari Damacy*) because they work from a "flat ontology" (Kazemi, 2012). In *Everything*, firm divisions between playful active human subjects and passive nonhuman objects are undone even though the behavior of many in-game natural actors—like the black bears who tumble instead of walk upright to move—is not visually realistic in the same sense as RDR2's exacting simulations of over 200 species of fish, birds, and animals "which behave and respond to their environment in a unique way," as Rockstar bragged in one press release.

In my reading, a great deal of ecocritical approaches to videogames privilege what I think of as a form of metaphorical proceduralism. It actually is not more hyperrealistic simulations of weather patterns that are desired—indeed, they exist in RDR2—but instead better figurations of how nature's agency is figured as an active presence. However, in a comment that I intend as suggestive and not an indictment of past work in this area, I suspect that the critique of realistic visual renderings of nature may actually indicate something of a blind spot in that it causes us to overlook some of the acknowledged ecocritical potential in hyperrealistically simulated videogames like RDR2. With no small degree of irony, RDR2 and *Everything* actually employ similar 3D animation techniques such as parallax occlusion mapping. As a result, the ways in which objects interact in these respective videogames share intriguing points of ontological overlap in their implications for nature/culture divisions.

Thus, I suggest that ecocritics can benefit not only from *metaphorical* forms of proceduralism, but also by better understanding *literal* forms of the ways in which visual rendering technologies themselves figure and unfigure nature/culture divides. Here, I want to connect ecocritical interests in videogames more directly to platform studies and software studies approaches to videogames (see e.g., Jones and Thiruvathukal, 2012) but with a specific interest in visual rendering. To this end, I start by using Benjamin Abraham and Darshana Jayemanne's (2017) heuristic for evaluating nature's simulated agency in a videogame, which is grounded in past and present ecocritical treatments of videogames, to examine RDR2. I want to demonstrate the ways in which RDR2 both succeeds and fails to avoid many common nature/culture oppositions in videogames despite its high level of visual realism.

In turn, however, I note that similarities in how *Everything* and RDR2 render object-relations may signal new ecocritical dimensions to evaluating how videogames simulate the environment through platform dynamics. To demonstrate this point, I show how both *Everything* and RDR2 benefit from an animation rendering technique called parallax occlusion mapping (POM), which demonstrates several implications for subject/object interactions. However, since my interest is primarily in redeeming RDR2, I spend more time examining the visual rendering technique common to the Rockstar company: the Euphoria game engine. The Euphoria game engine achieves more realistic looking visual collision reactions for the player's avatar in response to collisions with the player, other NPCs, and other objects like buildings or moving trains. Euphoria creates a simulated gravity field and then allows collision reactions to be calculated randomly so that no two collisions— even with the same NPC in the same space—will be exactly identical.

By digging a bit into how the game engine operates as well as the Greek roots of the word "euphoria" (*euphoros*), I locate a form of emergent subject–object, human–nonhuman behavior occurring at the microlevels of play. *Euphoros* is a kind of well-being produced by drugs in a human with illness. Similarly, by rendering 3D relationships in a way to force objects in a simulated gravity field to constantly be grappling for firmer environmental handholds, which themselves can decay and erode over time, we find an uncanny or precarious form of *euphoros* in RDR2's simulated environments, in the way the avatar controlled by the player interacts with objects in the world in euphoric ways—both as governed by the rendering platform, and in the existential sense of *euphoros*. In other words, I want to encourage ecocritics to explore not just nature's representation per se, but also the commercial *game mechanics* of the sublime (*à la* Timothy Morton's 2007 work on hyperobjects or rhetorical-poetic figures) which can serve to undercut visually subject–object relationships which, in a hyperrealistic videogame like RDR2, can seem all the more powerful.

Rendering nature in ecocritical videogames

Unlike many literary or cultural figurations of the environment as a distant pastoral "over there" opposed to non-natural urban spaces (Morton, 2007), ecocriticism, as the Introduction to this volume has reminded the reader, often strives to map complex entanglements of human and nonhuman agency undergirding what many of us would consider to be the non-environmental practices of our daily lives, such as driving to work in a personal vehicle or throwing away a plastic grocery bag. Fiction and aesthetics in any medium can play a key role in how nature and culture are figured as belonging together in the same ontological substrate.

In turn, ecocritics across literature, game studies, and rhetoric and writing studies have started to explore how "computer and video games present a rich limit case for the claims of environmental scholarship—a place where the natural and the digital collide and prompt careful reexamination of our assumptions about nature, realism, and the visual" (Chang, 2013: 1). Deborah Jordan, for example, calls for videogames to explore an "ecocentric perspective" that "recognizes our interdependence with the non-human world, and our position within ecological systems that need to be maintained and protected for our future survival"? (2014: 8). The problem, of course, is that commercially successful (i.e., widely played) videogames do not address climate change or environmentalism. Thus, ecocritics are often relegated examining "the underlying ideas, conceptions and narratives of human environment relationships that have been a part of games since their earliest incarnations" (8). This process is not an easy one, as much of a player's interactions with the environment, such as the weather, are limited to the visual background or, at most, instrumental or means–ends goals to achieve in game tasks.

As a result, ecocritics often have to read against the grain in a videogame like RDR2 for the ways in which a player interacts with the environment procedurally. To help situate RDR2 as an ecocritical game, I use Abraham and Jayemanne's four-part heuristic for identifying how nature is figured in a videogame: environment as backdrop; as resource; as antagonist; and as text. I have no intention of offering a comprehensive reading of RDR2, which is a massively complex game world, in this chapter. My goal instead is to establish some heuristic benchmarks for RDR2 that are common to ecocritical readings of videogames, which I will in turn use to highlight how different visual rendering technologies in RDR2 work within, and yet exceed, some of these categories.

1. Environment as backdrop

This category is a direct cause of Barton's expressed frustration with how the weather is typically figured in videogames. As backdrop, the environment is an unchanging or static visual and interactive background space. Prime examples occur in sidescroller videogames and their flat 2D spaces. Players move avatars past static objects with no in-game acknowledgment of any object depth or reciprocal agency to background environments. While there are countless older examples, Playdead's *Limbo* is a good example of an inert background and an active foreground. If the background matters for this first heuristic category, it is as an aesthetic backdrop for human contemplation (which Morton has noted is a classic literary trope that maintains a nature/culture dichotomy).

How RDR2 fares

In many ways, RDR2 avoids the environment as backdrop category. Across its massive world, physical objects like houses can be entered and physical structures like mountains can be scaled. As a point of comparison, Abraham and Jayemanne locate a version of the environment as backdrop trope in a previous Rockstar title, *Grant Theft Auto V* (2017: 81). While GTA4 allows the player to run around and steal cars in a large urban environment, very few buildings in this urban space can be entered. By contrast, every single building with a doorway in RDR2 can be entered. Mountains can be climbed, flowers can be picked, fish can be caught, trains can be boarded, rivers can be ridden through or accessed by boat, wild wolves attack, and barnyard cats can be petted. When Arthur Morgan rides his horse in the country, he and the horse both get dirty. Arthur has to brush his horse to keep it clean, and the failure to do so impacts the horse's vitals and stamina. Arthur's appearance generally becomes unkempt if he is not bathed or dunked (by the player) in a flowing river.

2. Environment as resource

Since their inception, most videogames require players to collect, maintain, or craft resources from the environment, such as mining for ore in *World of Warcraft* or, more recently, scouring a *Fortnite* map for consumables like mushrooms to maintain health. Since many in-game resources in a videogame are fixed or finite, it is tempting to think that environment as resource is a productive model of actual human/nature relationships. If we kill too many deer, then we run out of deer. However, this stance ignores the largely instrumental relationship players have with environmental resources, which "presents the relation between human and environment in fairly instrumental terms, with certain things necessary to continue, and often in quite transparently 'economic' ways" (Abraham and Jayemanne, 2017: 82)

How RDR2 fares

Arthur is procedurally encouraged to hunt and fish, to collect meat to cook and eat. He can also collect herbs and flowers to build resources to aid survival. The land is a finite resource. One quest interestingly involves chasing down and confronting buffalo killers who are killing buffalo and leaving the entire unskinned bodies to decompose for sport. Overhunting certain areas actually depletes access to local game in these areas. It is true that a great deal of Arthur's interaction with the environment is an instrumental form of resource collection. However, when Arthur hunts an animal, he has to track it, or lure it in the case of bears, by expending some of his depletable Dead Eye function, which slows down moving human and animal targets to make a shoot easier. Once an animal is shot, a separate and time-consuming process has to be initiated to skin it. He then has to decide whether to carry the pelt and the carcass on horseback, which is often a tough decision given limited horse saddlebag space and carrying capacity. Finally, a player has to determine whether to individually cook and eat a piece of meat at a campfire, which also has to be set up and torn down each time, to covert the meat into a consumable object. The same laborious processes occur for fishing and herbology as well. Thus, it is true that the environment exists as a sort of "standing reserve," as Heidegger might call it, for human consumption (i.e., means–ends extraction). However, the game does build in some impediments to call the player's self-conscious attention to the laborious nature of these tasks. Arthur also has the ability to craft collected in-game items into food, equipment, and other elements to aid his survival.

3. Environment as antagonist

This category examines the extent to which the environment thwarts player movement or progress as "something to be overcome" (Abraham and Jayemanne, 2017: 83) and, in particular, in a way that is interactive. RDR2, for example, allows Arthur to rob any passing stagecoach in the world. However, he has to be careful in taking a stagecoach because if he damages it during transit or robbery (i.e., receiving bullet holes) or by driving too fast on country dirt trails, it cannot be returned for full value. As an example, Abraham and Jayemanne mention the notoriously difficult *Dark Souls*, in which the physical environment itself is often as punitive as the NPC enemies that player has to defeat (83).

How RDR2 fares

If Arthur falls from a high cliff, he will die. If he is falls off of a fast-moving train or takes too many bullet wounds during a daring train robbery, then he will die. There are sufficiently meaningful in-game punishments for trying to act in ways beyond what a normal Earth gravitation field and human body will tolerate (save for being able to take twenty bullet wounds, heal oneself on the spot, and still be able to fire back). When aiding a nature photographer to take photographs of wolves in the wild, the hungry photographic subjects unsurprisingly do not cooperate, and instead attack the photographer and Arthur.

On many accounts, RDR2 does make the environment fairly antagonistic. There are meaningful in-game consequences in relationship to Arthur's interaction with the environment. As mentioned above, Arthur's clothes have to be adjusted depending on the weather (snow, sunshine, winter, fall) in order to maintain optimal bodily conditions. He also has to eat continually to maintain energy. Furthermore, certain consumables impact Arthur negatively and positively. Snake oil, for example, or tobacco products will grant Arthur temporary Dead Eye replenishment so that he can slow down enemies' movements to improve his aim. However, consuming these products reduces his core agility and health since tobacco products in real life are not amazing for human long-term health. Simply put, Arthur exists in part as an ecological subject in which his agency exists in direct relationship to antagonistic constraints. The animals dwell in particular habits and travel in groups. As in real life, hawks float on randomly gener-ated thermal updrafts in the sky, pronghorns and bison roam the landscape in herds, sockeye salmon struggle to swim upstream, and animal remains that Arthur cannot carry are attacked by scavengers. In terms of simulating an ecosystem, a player can readily appreciate the level of detail across the entire openworld landscape of a simulated food chain.

4. Environment as text

But are RDR2's visual and ecological realisms enough? The fourth heuristic category answers my question in the negative. "Environment as text" is a form of environmental creative interactivity, but also one in which the environment itself takes on narrative role. As opposed to random drops or mere instru-mental attribute addition, certain objects in *Dark Souls* 3 have stories behind them for the player to uncover. Some in-game objects have histories. Yet, this category of environment as text can also be metaphorical. For example, Kyle Bohunicky (2014) has observed that *Minecraft* enables an ecocritical perspective because the environment can be discursively composed by the player. Dirt, biological matter, trees, and water all form the building blocks to help the player write the environment. Another important feature of this fourth category is emergent play, in which the environment records traces of itself on the player and vice versa, much like an organism in a complex adaptive system or a writer in an emergent ecological assemblage.

How RDR2 fares

I already noted that Arthur's hair grows, and his horse becomes dirty. However, RDR2 is not *Minecraft*. It is not a sandbox game where players can alter the environment with high degrees of creativity. There are some build-ing and construction capacities in RDR2, especially in the final stage when Arthur dies and the player becomes John Marsten, who Arthur had saved, to complete the revenge plot. John buys a small homestead and has to build a customizable ranch from scratch. Yet, these structures, once built, are not really manipulable or changeable to the degree of *Minecraft*. However, this last component—emergent gameplay—is one that I circle back to in the next section. RDR2 does not have nearly enough emergent ecological effects in the visible sphere. However, in terms of object relations and platform dynamics, we can, I will suggest, find a few.

To sum up, RDR2 does embody many of Abraham and Jayemanne's cri-teria, which means that it largely simulates a nature/culture divide. In fact, they are the first to caution that these four criteria themselves are often more useful for categorizing how most videogames fall short of realizing a true ecocritical perspective: "In all four design modes, the environment is largely subject to the activity of more lively entities that inhabit it: either an index of their movement (background) or subject to their extractive (resource), militarist (antagonist) or cognitive (text) gameplay" (2017: 85). In this regard, RDR2 is an unexceptional. Many commercially popular videogames may embody certain ecocritical dimensions but not others. Indeed, even *Minecraft* falls short some regards. Bohunicky comments,

> Minecraft's model of ecocomposition, like many models that quantify nature and ecology, does slip into a reductive Cartesianist [sic] treatment of matter that greatly reduces ecological complexity. Much like the blocks in Minecraft, Cartesian matter is controllable and predictable, bound to laws of Euclidian geometry and Newtonian physics, bequeathing human subjects a sense of mastery over the land rather than truly positioning them as a member of its wild, untouched or untamed space of non-humanness which has been enclosed, harnessed and drawn upon as part of the long process of the emergence of capitalism. (2017: 17)

Both RDR2 and *Minecraft* also reinscribe a Cartesian subject/object dichotomy. In fact, the avatar in most videogames encourages an egocentric identification with the landscape as a puzzle to be overcome and tamed. Indeed, one could speculate that *Minecraft* might even work against ecocriticism in certain ways because it figures nature as a "blank slate" for an infinite number of human creative and cognitive projects. Resources are perhaps *too infinite* in *Minecraft* to the point where nature itself doesn't even matter any more as part of the play space.

The ontology of rendering platforms in ecocritical games

To sum up, if the goal of an ecocritical analysis of a videogame is to privilege videogames where nature has an active presence in the game *procedurally* and not just visually, then it is true that RDR2 does not fare very well. However, it is worth noting that Abraham and Jayemanne conclude their essay by describing how *Everything* actually "escapes the four environmental modes" by which agentive subjects manipulate passive objects (2017: 88). *Everything* is a game that places all actors (human and nonhuman) on a flat ontological plane (Kazemi, 2012). The player is dropped into a procedurally-generated universe and can control larger animals like bears. Eventually, the player can control smaller and smaller animals and organisms down to the microscropic level. Players can shift back to any form that they have previous occupied, and so the purpose of the game is to explore the multifaceted, complex, and emergent macro- and micro-systems that comprise reality, but that we humans lack the ability to perceive. The Alan Watts philosophical voiceover can be distilled down to his comment, "What is chaos at one level of magnification is harmony at a higher level of magnification." The game procedurally simulates a Spinozist monad in which all entities participate in the same material ontological substrate.

What is interesting about *Everything* is that it doesn't exactly strive for visual or even procedural realism in the same way as AAA-rated titles like RDR2. O'Reilly's bears tumble instead of walk. The graphics are stunning, yet cartoonish by design. What ultimately makes this videogame an ecocritical masterpiece is precisely its metaphorical simulation of a monad. A better example lies in O'Reilly's *Mountain*, in which the player's typical role as Cartesian knower and manipulator of reality is inverted. *Mountain* embodies the genre of a "non-game" in which the meaning occurs through the player's lack of interactivity. The player sits and watches random objects spawn in the procedurally-generated mountain which just hovers in space. It's a woefully unrealistically visual or procedural simulation of how a mountain actually functions, as opposed to how Arthur Morgan has to navigate snowfall or ease his horse up steep mountain cliffsides.

Yet, simulating an object's unknowability, as Bogost (2017) has interpreted, is precisely where the ecocritical payoff occurs: it's a metaphorical simulation of what a player cannot know about the being of a mountain. Thus, I find it interesting that the rightful suspicion of how AAA-games like RDR2 exchange visual realism for reinscribing the nature/culture divide can leave ecocritics in a position where comparatively unrealistic visual simulations of nature like *Everything* or *Mountain* take on more ecocritical significance despite failing to offer a *visually realistic* (or even procedurally realistic) view of nature.

Elsewhere, I have previously discussed metaphorical simulations in relationship to simulating the object's withdrawal from a subject in the context of object-oriented videogames (Holmes, 2019). To add something new, I want to use this distinction in *Mountain* to highlight in this chapter the visual *rendering* elements that RDR2 and *Everything* share despite having different visual and procedural simulations of nature. O'Reilly as well as his lead designer Damien di Fede used the Unity game engine. The Unity game engine was released primarily for Mac OsX in 2005, but has since expanded to include every major operating system. While other game engines included visual user interfaces, Unity functions like the Mac video-editing software Final Cut in terms of allowing designers to compose distinct scenes and then combine them like a series of film clips.

In 2013, Unity (as well as Unreal or CryENGINE) emerged as a gold standard for animation due to its ability to incorporate complex animations within its internal rendering processes. Prior to 2013, designers would use separate 3D digital content-creation programs like Blender and then add these animations to their game engine in a process akin to having to hit the "pause" button while waiting for a video clip to load (Wiltshire, 2017). By contrast, Unity streamlined the process by being able to generate real-time animation within the system itself in a few unique ways. *Everything* seems like it is an entire world that a player can effortlessly scale up and down without ever leaving it. Each new object a player controls contracts or expands up until an abstract geometric dimension about the galaxy scale (before circling back to the microscopic).

Everything, as an interview with di Fede confirmed, is not an entire world. Rather, it is designed from seven pre-designed stages (particle, tiny, human, landmass, planet, galaxy, and collapse) (Wiltshire, 2017). What achieves the visual effect of the monad is, ironically, a simple game mechanic that tricks the Cartesian player: a camera swoop. "It's basically just a magic trick, where we distract your attention to one place while doing stuff in another" (di Fede, quoted in Wiltshire). It is precisely in these forms of real-time visualization that support the sort of immersive feel, even in a videogame that procedurally seeks to simulate a subject/object erosion.

To achieve this real-time simulation while preserving highly textured environments, both Rockstar and *Everything* utilized techniques such as POM (Linnemann, 2018). Common approaches to 3D textured surfaces in videogame design are often limited by the computer's processing cycles, because they must create effects by calculating and creating new geometric patterns each time a player's avatar shifts a visual perspective. By contrast, POM employs a displacement map which alters objects' appearance relative to a player's perspective by self-occlusion (i.e., object subtraction) in real time. POM therefore enables even more realistic environmental traces of the perception of simulated embodied activity and environmental emplacement. This in part is how RDR2 can simulate such small ecological details as a cat's footprints in the dirt, or muddy tracks versus non-muddy trains of a wagon wheel in the dirt depending upon the weather. In other words, this particular rendering technique frees up processing power. Interestingly, as this image shows, the technique works by never fully making an effort to render an entire object. Phenomenologically speaking (from Arthur Morgan's perspective), he never encounters the (simulated) "world-as-such." Rather, like the many sides of a Husserl-ian house, Arthur only ever sees small partial disclosures of his simulated environment.

Shared points of overlap like POM highlight the need to connect ecocritical analysis to the visual rendering technologies' role in figuring or dis/figuring subject/object and nature/culture dichotomies—a claim that I believe supplements and furthers the type of work that ecocritics like Abraham and Jayemanne are after. O'Reilly stated of *Everything*: "I wanted to create a kind of philosophy you can experience" (quoted in Mufson, 2017). There is actually a bit more metaphysical or ontological experience to be had in the platform itself. As a case in point, consider Rockstar's Euphoria game engine, which is actually built with the same physically-based rendering models that *Everything* and Unity are built upon. They actually both utilize similar, albeit distinct, rendering techniques and platforms.

Like Unity, Euphoria is compatible with all major game design engines. As an illustration, I would advise the reader (trigger warning: simulated cruelty to animals) to go and watch user Grandos's "RDR2 Epic Horse Crash Compilation" demonstration on YouTube (2018). I've picked this example deliberately. Keep in mind: once we have entered the realm where "visual realism" does not matter as much as the metaphorical simulation of nature–culture relations, it is actually the implications for horse crashes that hold insights for ecocritical approaches to videogames. (As a related case in point, no substantial research has found that playing violent videogames makes one violent, since a videogame is first and foremost about puzzle-solving.) What is uncanny about viewing these horse crashes is that each one is unique. A player can ride the same horse over the same cliff and each crash will be slightly different because the weather is different, the environment is different, because another horse is present (as the second cut scene in the videoclip displays).

It is the Euphoria game engine that helps make these uncanny moments possible. Let us peel back the blackbox on this visual rendering technology for a moment. Created by NaturalMotion, Euphoria uses a proprietary technique called Dynamic Motion Synthesis (NaturalMotion). Similarly to POM, Dynamic Motion Synthesis does not attempt to animate or control in advance all possible object interactions. Rather, most major object interactions occur in a simulated field and then the objects adjust to the localized conditions. Each individual body—human and animal—is simulated down to the motor nervous system and muscles in terms of what is able to respond to environmental stimuli. What is key is that Euphoria is not actually an animation platform. Instead, it creates a simulated environment and then gives each 3D component—both the human avatar and the other objects around it—a reflexive ability to act in real time and, particularly, in *emergent* relationships to the local and unique configuration of local actors.

Animator and YouTuber JediJosh920 offers an excellent introduction to Euphoria physics on YouTube. At the 25-second mark, he starts throwing storm trooper ragdolls (from Star Wars *Battlefront*) at a wooden ceiling beam in a simulated physical room with high ceilings. The storm troopers are tossed at a wooden beam at the top of the ceiling. They flail and actually reach out—*with no player input or prompting*—for the beam because they realize that it's a kind of empty space that they're falling through and they will die until they can find a stable surface. The key here is that these reactions are not pre-programmed like a typical animation. Rather, reactions are simulated. The Euphoria game engine offers a different micro-level form of visual-interactive-procedural environmental realism.

With full consequences for a flat ontology, the nonhuman actor—the beam—also registers the aleatory activities of the stormtrooper. The beam will splinter under the player's weight and stress will visually render and then cause it to break, just as the dirt in RDR2 knows about the cat's paw prints. Here's the kicker: the animator does not know in advance or control what will occur. JediJosh920 describes:

> you can imagine how difficult it would be for an animator to animate all this because you never know what's going to happen. You'd have to animate every possibility. Here you can see we made it a little more difficult and we're throwing rocks so you'd have to animate him falling forward, falling backwards, and he winds up repeatedly protecting himself from the rocks.
>
> (2015, 1:38)

To tie this anecdote back to my horse example: it is not as if human actors in a Euphoria engine are ontologically distinct from horses. The perhaps sadistic desire of a human player to crash animals off of cliffs in RDR2 may also designate a repressed (if we wax Freudian) reality: the human avatar is similarly subject to a constrained Spinozist monad flailing motion. The horse–Arthur Morgan assemblage tumble emergently together.

The name "Euphoria" for this game engine is quite appropriate given these emergent flat ontological relations. The German philosopher Martin Heidegger inspired a still highly relevant mode of what he called "etymological clearing," wherein he observed that modern understandings of contemporary Greek terms often obscure ancient (Greek-Western) primordial meanings. For example, the word "euphoria" we commonly associate with an experience of intense joy or excitement. According to the *Oxford English Dictionary*, however, the late 17th-century Latin roots of this word actually connoted a particular kind of well-being—a feeling of comfortableness produced in a patient with an illness by a result of taking a medication (OED). While our modern English definitions miss this connection, the ancient Greeks were the ones who likely inspired the Latin meaning. *Euphoros* meant "borne well, healthy" but in this sense of a mode of bearing (*eu*—"well + *pherein*") or undergoing something while producing healthiness (and, of course, there's likely a comparison to be had to Jacques Derrida's famous *pharmakon*—poison/cure—discussion) (OED). A(n admittedly self-serving) translation might be more akin to the ability to endure easily while under conditions that seek to impinge upon a normally healthy body. With respect to thrown horses or stormtroopers as well as the emergent responses of nonhuman actors like beams, I can think of no better term for this euphoric striving proper to the existential and gravitational. There is no Cartesian master or instrumental (*gestell*) enframing moment for the subjects, objects, and natural environments caught up in RDR2's Euphoria engine. Instead, it animates actors of equal ontological weight—materially speaking—who will always interact in emergent and unpredictable ways that the player cannot fully account for or control.

It is worth noting that in rhetorical studies, Victor J. Vitanza (2000) has noted that computer-simulated aleatory generation is precisely how we get at the absence of human control over language. It is a metaphorical simulation—an intuition of the uncanny or the unspeakable. However, to tie this back to Abraham and Jayemanne's heuristic, emergence is something that does help game designers avoid nature/culture binaries. Organisms are produced by their environments (beams, rocks, and cliffs), but, at the same time they help to create them, and therefore what an environment is cannot be characterized effectively except by assessing the presence of the actual organisms—simulated or "real." Thus, I'd suggest that Europhia can help make a game ecological not just by producing rain on the face of the avatar, but also when "the act of externalising and objectifying the environment as other is broken down by insisting on the mutuality of production, the interaction of multiple users to produce an evolving rule-set" (Abraham and Jayemanne, 2017: 93).

Conclusion

My analysis in this short chapter is meant to be suggestive: there is a world of simulated (and actual, for Arthur Morgan and the horse he rides) object reflex and interaction that is uncanny. It is a world, in my opinion, worth better exploring, particularly when emergent human–environment interactions can be found and located through a consideration of the visual rendering platform's roles. Is this claim new? Hardly. Abraham and Jayemanne point to Walter Benjamin's interpretation of the animated short films and cartoons of his time, like Mickey Mouse, as "radically challenging anthropocentric hierarchies" (Hansen, quoted in Abraham and Jayemanne, 2017: 93). In turn, contemporary videogame animations with even a tiny NPC like a cat and its paw print in the dirt do have something of a flat ontological ring to them, even if we still largely see this view from a Cartesian perspective of Arthur Morgan.

Such a mode of ecocritical analysis of the visual helps to avoid what Jason Moore (2015) critiques as "green arithmetic," which just adds nature to a given ideological worldview or critical perspective that occluded it without fundamentally rethinking why the latter ignored it to begin with. Moore uses another Greek term, *oikeios*, which is this state of touching and being touched by the relations through which we are able to act upon nature. These smallest ecologically emergent differentiations, borne on the humbled avatar–object interaction of embodied touch in RDR2, offer per-haps a more accurate form of ecological realism despite—and not because of—their visual realism. In any case, my arguments here—again—are not critical but suggestive. Once ecocritics shift from visual realism to privilege procedural realism (or metaphorical realism), then we have no good reason not to pursue this line of thinking to include the ontological implications of the visual rendering technologies themselves.

References

Abraham, Benjamin, and Darshonna Jayemanne. "Where Are All the Climate Change Games?" *Transformations* 30(2017): 74–94.

Ash, James. "Technologies of Captivation: Videogames and the Attunement of Affect." *Body & Society* 19. 1(2013): 27–51.

Barton, Matt. "How's the Weather: Simulating Weather in Virtual Environments." *Game Studies* 8. 1(2008).

Bogost, Ian. *Persuasive Games: The Expressive Power of Videogames*. Cambridge, MA: MIT Press, 2007.

Bogost, Ian. "The Video Game that Claims Everything is Connected." *The Atlantic*23 March, 2017. www.theatlantic.com/technology/archive/2017/03/a-video-game-abou t-everything/520518/ Accessed March 1, 2019.

Bohunicky, Kyle. "Ecocomposition: Writing Ecologies in Digital Games." *Green Letters: Studies in Ecocriticism* 18(2014): 221–235.

Chang, Alenda. "Games as Environmental Texts." *Qui Parle* 19(2011): 56–84.

Chang, Alenda. "Playing Nature: The Virtual Ecology of Game Environments." PhD Thesis, 2013. http://escholarship.org/uc/item/9ch2w332#page-1. Accessed March 1, 2019.

Cooper, Dalton. "*The Last of Us* Director Criticizes RDR2." *GameRant*1 January, 2019. gamerant.com/red-dead-redemption-2-the-last-of-us-criticism/ Accessed March 1, 2019.

Fischer, Tyler. "RDR2: Here's How Long It Takes to Cross the Map." *Comicbook* 27, October, 2018. comicbook.com/gaming/2018/10/27/red-dead-redemption-2-ps4-xbox-map-how-long-to-cross/ Accessed March 1, 2019.

Grandos. "RDR2 Epic Horse Crash Compilation." YouTube 27 October, 2018. www.youtube.com/watch?v=sCcDdFjQBKE Accessed March 1, 2019.

Holmes, Steve. *Procedural Habits*. London: Routledge, 2017.

Holmes, Steve. "The OOOculus Rift." *Rhetorical Speculations*. Ed. Scott Sundvall. Logan, UT: Utah State University Press, 2019. 174–202.

JediJosh920. "Euphoria Physics Engine." YouTube 25 September, 2015. www.youtube.com/watch?v=c7fJGAK7EbQ Accessed March 1, 2019.

Jones, Steven E. and George K. Thiruvathukal. *Codename Revolution*. Cambridge, MA: MIT Press, 2012.

Jordan, Deborah. *Climate Change Narratives in Australian Fiction*. LAP Lambert Academic Press, 2014.

Kazemi, Darius. "The Prince of Objects: Katamari and Ontology." *Tinysubversions*May 4, 2012. http://tinysubversions.com/2012/05/the-prince-of-objects-katamari-and-ontology/index.htm Accessed March 1, 2019

Linnemann, John. "RDR2 Analysis: A Once-in-a-Generation-Technological-Achievement." *Eurogamer*25 October, 2018. www.eurogamer.net/articles/digitalfoundry-2018-red-dead-redemption-2-tech-analysis Accessed March 1, 2019.

Moore, Jason W. *Capitalism in the Web of Life*. New York: Verso, 2015.

Morton, Timothy. *Ecology Without Nature*. Cambridge, MA and London: Harvard University Press, 2007.

Mufson, Beckett. "A Panda? An Office Building? A Galaxy? You Can Become Literally Anything in this F*cking Incredible Video Game." *Vice*22 March,2017. www.vice.com/en_us/article/534qax/everything-video-game-david-o-reilly-interview Accessed March 1, 2019.

NaturalMotion. "FAQ." 1 January, 2019. www.naturalmotion.com/faq.htm Accessed March 1, 2019.

OED. "Euphoria.". en.oxforddictionaries.com/definition/euphoria Accessed March 1, 2019.

Shinkle, Eugenie. "*Corporealis Ergo Sum*: Affective Response in Digital Games." *Digital Gameplay: Essays on the Nexus of Game and Gamer*, edited by Nate Garrels. Jefferson, NC: McFarland & Co, 2005. pp. 21–35.

Tassi, Paul. "RDR2 Sales Revealed." *Forbes*30 October, 2018. www.forbes.com/sites/insertcoin/2018/10/30/red-dead-redemption-2-sales-revealed-725-million-in-three-days/#5254415355d7 Accessed March 1, 2019.

Vitanza, Victor J. "From Heuristic to Aleatory Procedures; Or, Towards 'Writing the Accident." *Inventing a Discipline: Essays for Richard Young*, edited by Maureen Daly Goggin. Urbana, IL: NCTE, 2000. pp. 185–206.

Wills, John. "RDR2: Can a game be too realistic?" *The Conversation*12 November, 2018. theconversation.com/red-dead-redemption-2-can-a-video-game-be-too-realistic-106404 Accessed March 1, 2019.

Wiltshire, Alex. "How Everything Conjures Infinity with Camera Tricks." *Rock, Paper, Shotgun* 25 August, 2017. www.rockpapershotgun.com/2017/08/25/how-ever ything-conjures-infinity-with-camera-tricks/ Accessed March 1, 2019.

Games referenced

Everything. David O'Reilly. Double Fine Presents. 2017. Video game.
Grand Theft Auto V. Rockstar Games. 2013. Video game.
Katamari Damacy. Namco. 2004. Video game.
Minecraft. Mojang Studios. 2011–2017. Video game.
Mountain. DavidO'Reilly. Double Fine Presents. 2016. Video game.
Red Dead Redemption 2. Christian Cantamessa and Imran Sarwar. Take 2 Interactive's Rockstar Games, 2018.
Wildlife. Rockstar Games. 2019. www.rockstargames.com/reddeadredemption2/fea tures/wildlife Accessed March 1, 2019.

4 Stereoscopic rhetorics

Model environments, 3D technologies, and decolonizing data collection

Shannon Butts

Natural disasters, war, human development, and climate change are affecting cultural heritage sites around the world. In 2016, Bagan, an ancient city in Myanmar, experienced an earthquake that damaged many temples and made the surrounding area inaccessible. In 2017, ISIS nearly decimated the Syrian city of Palmyra, targeting 2,000-year-old temples and monuments with "dynamite, fire, bulldozers, and pickaxes" (Domonoske, 2017). In 2019, the world watched Notre-Dame de Paris burn, the fire destroying the spire and centuries-old rafters, and collapsing part of the roof. However, before damage, each of these sites was scanned using 3D technologies to capture accurate measurements and create photo-realistic 3D models that preserved the sites in digital form.

Increasingly, scientists, archeologists, and museum curators are using 3D scans to document artifacts and study at-risk areas. The technologies are often heralded as a non-invasive method for preserving cultural legacies and educating people about the natural wonders of the world (Smithsonian, 2016). For example, capturing 3D data from an environment such as a coral reef enables biologists to study the complex tubular structures of coral without damaging them. Similarly, scans of historic temples or war-torn areas can help track deterioration or rebuild damaged sites. Nonprofits and heritage organizations such as CyArk are also scanning areas to "save the collective treasures" of global heritage by creating a "digital archive of the world's heritage sites for preservation and education" (CyArk.org). CyArk—the name a combination of Cyber and Archive—has partnered with Google Arts & Culture and scanned over 200 locations including Angkor Wat, Mesa Verde, Pompeii, and Mount Rushmore.

Yet, as 3D technologies measure and remediate select sites, they create models dislocated from the complex ecology of the surrounding environment. The resulting 3D models inscribe a way of seeing cultural heritage that isolates the physical structures of a location, creating *ex situ* archives. As such, in digitally preserving historic structures we often lose local context or marginalize the voices of Indigenous communities. 3D technologies might offer mathematically accurate data for understanding structures or landscapes, but the current collection practices invoke concerns about digital colonialism. As we measure and model, we must also consider how our making practices inscribe meaning. To preserve the local heritage as well as the land, scholars need to pay attention to how they capture, curate, and disseminate data, and actively work to create more decolonial data practices that collaborate with local communities to create knowledge.

In this chapter, I examine how 3D technologies create "model environments" that dislocate sites from culture and context in favor of accuracy and archives. Digital platforms such as Google Earth and CyArk offer 3D renders to the public, but limit how viewers can understand and interact with the digital data. Preservation can generate reference points for memory, identity, and cultural change—and 3D technologies create opportunities to understand structures in more detail than ever before. However, 3D imaging technologies also remediate environments and author new ways of seeing filtered through archives and ownership. Who owns the 3D data, and who has access? What determines which sites are scanned, whose heritage matters, and what environments are protected (and how)? Drawing from a history of stereoscope devices, I first examine how 3D technologies are linked to colonial practices of collection and dislocation. Historically, 19th-century stereoscopes reframed how viewers understood mass-marketed images, proclaiming a more accurate, educated, and immersive experience of landscapes and people. However, stereoscopes also proliferated many stereo-types dislocated from context, and trained users to value a western perspective of mediated vision. I use the concept of stereoscopic rhetorics to examine how 3D scans rewrite cultural heritage sites and engender similar ways of seeing that dislocate local landscapes in the name of global heritage preservation.

Stereoscopic rhetoric, or "rhetoric in 3D," is a strategic approach to evaluating the practices of digital data collection and reframing how 3D technologies mediate natural and built environments. Stereoscopics is a process for creating depth where two photographs of the same image are taken at slightly different angles and then viewed together. The different angles, the different perspectives, create a fuller picture that presents the details of depth. Digital 3D technologies use thousands, millions, even billions of angles to measure and then model environments, but often fail to contextualize the data from multiple angles or local perspectives. Many 3D scanning methods privilege mathematical accuracy over humanistic inquiry, creating a surface-level, one-dimensional picture of cultural heritage and environments.

Isolating landscapes from their surroundings reinscribes some of the same problematic collecting practices that historically "dislocated" physical artifacts from archeological sites and into far-off museums. Once complete, a 3D data file becomes part of a collection, usually created, curated, and archived by research organizations or private companies, and held in an institutional repository or behind paywalls. Kimberly Christen (2018) reminds us that modern archives are linked to colonial practices of collection that often work to standardize knowledge from a specific perspective while negating local actors and ontologies. Many stereoscopic technologies employ a rhetoric of experience and authenticity, a rhetoric of depth, while promoting one vision or version of a site. I close by discussing the need for more decolonial methods of data collection that can contextualize 3D scanned sites and promote local engagement. Instead of simply cutting and pasting a digital render, stereoscopic rhetoric offers one way of considering the many dimensions of heritage sites in order to promote more ethical, and more accurate, decolonial data practices.

Seeing in stereoscope: how 3D technologies mediate environments

Before virtual reality or digital renders, the hand-held stereoscope reframed visual images as an immersive 3D experience. Introduced in the 19th century and released again as the View-Master in the 1950s, stereoscopes became a staple of parlors and classrooms, and offered participants the chance to see foreign lands and experience new scenes without having to move at all. By refocusing optical input, the stereoscope used depth perception to create a 3D experience. The device arranged two images at varying distances from the viewer's eyes so that when looking into the viewing window, the images seemed layered and projected a sense of being there that was touted as more realistic, even more natural, than a flat photograph. Stereoscope producers such as the Keystone View Company praised the device as a technological power that "provides the perfect space for the eye and mind—not merely a suggestion of space as in ordinary pictures; objects stand out in all three dimensions, or as solids, as in nature" (Hanson, 1923). Oliver Wendell Holmes even named the type of imagery a "stereograph," from the Latin roots for *solid* and *writing*. [1] The images, alongside the apparatus, inscribed a new way to see that "captured, segmented, and standardized visibility" (Fowles, 1994: 92). Wrapped in a rhetoric of authenticity and visual accuracy, the stereoscope packaged a better version of vision that enabled viewers to consume culture conveniently from the comfort of their own home.

Yet, as Kristie Fleckenstein discusses, the stereoscope cut the viewer off from the lived experience of an environment by creating a sense of disembodied vision (2016). Instead of travelling to Tahiti and smelling the salt of the sea or hearing the local music and language, the experience of Tahiti became locked in the authenticity of an image—made three dimensional by the placement of photos. With standardized card formats and easily consumed content, the material rhetoric of the stereoscope inscribed "a new way of seeing that substituted lived experience with mediated vision" (Bak, 2012: 164). The stereoscope also suggested a hierarchy of "authentic" experience where seeing is believing. As the viewer looked into the hood of the stereoscope to learn about far-off places, the apparatus suppressed other senses. The "physical design and everyday use" of the stereoscope, Fleckenstein argues, "persuaded into existence a new way of seeing characterized by disembodiment and hyperattention" (125). Extending Fleckenstein's analysis, I argue that stereographic images not only limited the experience of places, they also dislocated sites from their specific context by promoting a myopic rhetoric of education and accuracy. Through the stereograph, Holmes proclaimed,

> form is henceforth divorced from matter. In fact, matter as a visible object is of no great use any longer, except as the mould on which form is shaped. Give us a few negatives of a thing worth seeing, taken from different points of view, and that is all we want of it.
>
> (1859)[2]

Alongside a disembodied hyperattention, the stereoscope created an archive of dislocated images that mimicked many of the colonial practices of documentation, collection, and dislocation.

The rhetoric of stereoscopic experiences did the work of dislocating and reclassifying images by linking the technology to western perspectives and emerging visual literacy. Early advertisements promised "laughable, interesting, and exotic scenes from every land" and "a tour of the world for only 75-cents" (1906; see Fig. 4.1). Although some pictures came with educational materials to accompany the slides, most stereoscope images had only a cursory explanation of the expected view. In fact, as Fleckenstein highlights, a series of images was usually designed to be seen quickly, when one had a spare moment, almost like casually scrolling through a social media feed. Stereographs played on an early form of the attention economy, training viewers to see and consume images in a particular way to educate themselves about the world.

The device also instilled a type of visual literacy and aesthetic that conditioned viewers to recognize difference as exotic commodities. As Edward Said (1979) has noted, mass-produced pictures of the exotic were often westerners' first exposure to cultural, racial, or even topological difference, and thus conditioned a certain way of seeing non-western sights as other. Scrolling through images of "exotic" places taught viewers to privilege western perspectives and created flashcards of culture lacking critical complexity. Similarly, stereoscopic adverts sold slides as "some of the most noted places in the world" alongside "famous natural phenomena" and "places that we all should know about" (1906). To be "in the know," one could use a stereoscope and see the world, or at least a mass-marketed version of it. Disconnected from the body and dislocated from context, the pictures became what W.J.T. Mitchell describes as an image—a site of imagined recognition. According to Mitchell, a picture "appears in material support" while an image is "a ghostly, fantasmatic appearance that comes to light or comes to life (which may be the same thing) in [such] material support" (2009: 18). The disembodied, dislocated experience of the stereoscope brought images "to life" as viewers developed a new way to see visual media and learned to recognize mediated environments.

The stereoscope operates as a colonial apparatus by inscribing an authoritative view of the world that repositioned users as educated spectators. Despite dislocating both the viewer and the scene, visual literacy initiatives

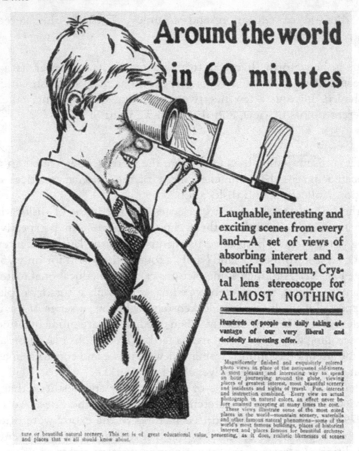

Figure 4.1 Late 19th-century advertisement for a stereoscope in *Amador Ledger*, May 25, 1906.
Source: New Orleans Museum of Art (public domain).

praised the technology for cultivating an "accurate" view of the world. Companies even partnered with academics to publish promotional materials and record testimonies to endorse the educational value of the stereoscopic viewing process. According to Charles Eliot, President-Emeritus at Harvard University, stereoscopic:

> material provides the means of training children and adolescents to see accurately, to make mental note of what they have seen, and then to put into language whatever has impressed them. It is this combination of visualization with training of the memory, and practice in accurate reproduction of language of what has been pictured in the eye which so strongly commends the method which the Keystone apparatus makes available.
>
> (Hanson, 1923: xvii)

The immersive experience of the scope replaced contextual knowledge of sites as the technology emphasized affect and immersion as a part of cultural education. The images and the apparatus were the emphasis, not the context, so that the viewer could develop an accurate experience marketed as on-the-ground knowledge. Through the stereoscope, members of the general public could say they had "seen" the Eiffel Tower, the wilds of Africa, and the latest celebrities up close and personal. Middle- or lower-class viewers were able to attain a sense of culture or enlightenment by experiencing travel and tourism through the 75-cent lens. In addition, the available scenes or topics instituted a value system of what was important. Common stereograph cards included expeditions and expositions, portraits of Native Americans,[3] cities and towns around the world, national parks, presidents, celebrities, and disasters. Views of the 1906 San Francisco earthquake, the Chicago fire, and images of the American West were particularly popular (Library of Congress; see Fig. 4.2). The stereoscope's emphasis on 3D visual experiences

Figure 4.2 View-Master advert (1962).

made even simple portraits or landscapes part of a dislocated collection of culture that empowered viewers to take ownership of each scene.

However, the reductive images of "exotic scenes from every land" gave the user a stereo-type view that was, in fact, a carefully arranged and curated illusion to promote cultural heritage. Cut off from local context, the images were framed by corporate agendas and a mythos of American citizenship. Mass market stereoviews were almost exclusively distributed by companies in the United States, with a few producers in Europe. As a result, the images privileged western perspectives where the "exotic" depictions of foreign lands or iconic vistas of national landmarks only further inscribed the superiority of American interests and ways of life. Collecting images became a collection of experience and cultural capital. In her discussion of colonial photography and exhibitions, Anne Maxwell posits that stereotyped spectacles of people or lands created malleable images ready to be deployed for social and political agendas. Detailing the monoscopic photographs of empire, Maxwell argues that:

for many people these images constituted a precursory glimpse into the world's least traversed regions, an experience hitherto confined to intrepid explorers and those who could afford a Grand Tour. For others they were a part of the Victorian passion for collecting, an activity that strengthened colonialism because it enabled participants to possess the whole world, if not literally then at least visually.

(2000: 11)

Maxwell's description of imperial photos extends to stereography in terms of continuing an imperial practice of looking, defined by collecting, archiving, and ownership. Similarly to photographs, stereographs delivered to viewers the peoples, places, resources, and even virtual spaces of empire. Dislocated from context, the landscapes could be reframed and rhetorically rewritten to fit the desires of the masses or the needs of the market—extending colonialism through a type of visual literacy that purported immersive ways of seeing defined by education, accuracy, and heritage.

3D archives of impression

Digital technologies continue to draw on the stereoscopic rhetoric of immersion, education, and accuracy, but also promote collecting digital data as a way of preserving cultural heritage. While historic stereoscopes trained viewers to collect idealized visions of environments and cultures, contemporary 3D technologies promote mathematical accuracy and "model environments" as a way of preserving places. By model environments, I mean the digital renders produced to record a specific site. More than merely looking, technologies such as 3D scanning and photogrammetry create three-dimensional environments where viewers can rotate, zoom in, and even walk through digital landscapes. However, 3D scans of cultural heritage sites create an archive of environments cut off from the dynamic nature of place. The technology measures structures, or maps the topography of a site, but the resulting experiences occur in a digitized vacuum curated by corporations and panels of academic experts. As a result, 3D experiences offer a limited impression of a place—a surface-level scan of cultural heritage. Digital preservation and data collection have a great value, and can help scientists, scholars, and local communities learn more about places, people, and artifacts. However, as digital scans are remediated into archives, dislocated from context, and curated according to corporate agendas, the images become part of a model environment that reduces cultural heritage to mathematical accuracy and authors another mediated version of history. To understand how 3D technologies can isolate landscapes and reduce sites to a one-dimensional view of cultural heritage, we should understand how 3D tech works to scan, capture, and save historic areas.

Digital 3D technologies survey an object or landscape and record precise, reproducible measurements, translating math into a three-dimensional model. The technologies scan, measure, and model through a variety of techniques, each compiling images, light, or laser data to render a 3D replica. A 3D method called photogrammetry stitches together images, documenting color and texture, while light or laser methods measure rates of refraction. Similarly to a bat's sonar that measures distance and shape, the refractions from the light or laser measure surface and dimensions by tracing the topography, curves, distance, etc. Then, computer-aided design (CAD) programs translate the geometry into 3D models using a series of xyz coordinates known as a point cloud. The 3D modeling process works like playing connect the dots in three-dimensional space—you put together an image, but you build a cube instead of a square by adding (many) additional points for reference.

3D scans are considered some of the most accurate methods for reproducing objects or scenes because of the sheer amount of data collected. Regardless of the specific type of input (image, light, laser), the process of creating a 3D scan and then a model involves documenting an object from all angles, capturing millions or even billions of data points, and then processing the data to create the 3D model. With accurate data measurements down to the centimetre, 3D models can help track changes over time, or map surface areas by creating a digital record of structure, topography, and detail often undetectable by other methods. Capturing sites in such detail is an impressive accomplishment, but a 3D model offers only a limited impression of an actual place. Aesthetically, the models are usually cut-out images with jagged edges or blurry boundaries, a feature that only emphasizes the contextual disconnect of 3D renders.

For example, the Google Arts & Culture scans of Mesa Verde in Colorado (Fig. 4.3) offer an extremely detailed render of the Pueblo "Balcony House" cliff dwellings, but only limited information about the features of the actual site, and no information about whether American Indian communities

Figure 4.3 Screen capture of Balcony House cliff dwellings, Mesa Verde, Colorado. Source: Google Arts & Culture.

contributed to the data collection. Instead, the CyArk website notes that the textured model was completed in two days because CyArk wanted to "understand the resolution possible given a limited amount of time" (2019). Reducing a landmass down to coordinates and angles is another way of rewriting a space and dislocating an image from context. Focusing on the technology, the digital scans and three-dimensional models merely scratch (and scan) the surface.

The scans of many heritage sites provide only a surface-level view of the location, carefully documenting form and structure while the contents and context are neglected, lost, or inadvertently marginalized through this one-dimensional focus (Rico, 2017. The idea that heritage can be saved by documenting a select portion of the environment ignores the multivalent components of cultural heritage. The zeros and ones of computer-generated data recode a space as a mathematical model, dislocated from the local culture and communities that contextualize the very heritage the scans are meant to save. In addition, as accurate as 3D collection methods are, the technology is not a point-and-shoot camera. Stitching together millions of data points is a collaboration between CAD and human experts. Scans often require editing by technicians who smooth out errors and sculpt the models to represent as accurately as possible the physical structures of the site—that accuracy is political and rhetorical, and affects the final product. 3D scans begin with data points but become models through human computer composition. Captured by computers, sculpted by humans, and archived into repositories, the models gain institutional authority marked by a particular perspective, especially with institutions such as Google and the Smithsonian mapping and archiving sites. As another incarnation of the stereoscope, 3D models mediate natural and built environments through the digital process of capturing, editing, and making.

As historic sites are remediated into 3D virtual environments, the technology becomes a key part of the rhetoric of preservation. 3D models are data visualizations—a way of assembling measurements and images to create an accurate (and thus authentic) digital render. As with any data set, "data visualization amplifies the rhetorical function of the data" (Gitelman, 2013: 12). The data-driven models of historic sites communicate a larger concern about the dangers threatening human history and heritage—climate change, war, natural disasters, etc. The models also communicate a way to save this heritage—3D technology. Trinidad Rico cautions that emphasis on the positive futures of digital technologies only "obscures the reality of the way these methods are being put to work, and, by association, obscures ... the establishment of a powerful new order, a technocracy in heritage construction and management" (2017: 227). 3D technologies use accuracy to develop technological authority, which in turn promotes an ideological perspective—that the technology will save us all. Scholars and scientists need to think about how 3D technology initiatives deploy rhetoric of heritage to collect data, and how the practices of digital data collection not only mediate nature, but also instil ways of seeing that reify positions of power and privilege.

Archives of oppression

As digital technologies continue to author new ways to see landscapes and curate experiences, we also have to recognize how 3D technologies dislocate landscapes and rewrite space through practices of data colonialism. Couldry and Mejias argue that data colonialism mirrors many of the historic features of colonialism—resource appropriation, ideology, and corporate concentration of knowledge (2019). Digital technologies have created new types of user-generated archives that encourage the curation of content through search, clip, and share practices. A quick Google search enables users to find a photo, download it from a website, generate a meme, and post the new image to social media. The process is considered neutral or even creative. Social media sites thrive on uploaded photos, meme generators, video clips, and tag-and-share tactics designed to circulate data. However, digital curation methods can also reinscribe colonial collecting paradigms that position content as dislocated from people or places of origin and free for the taking. Kimberly Christen describes the term "data mining" as a "telling example of how colonial legacies of collecting physical materials from local places and peoples are grafted onto digital content. Content is imagined as open, reusable, and unhinged from communities, individuals, or families who may have intimate ties to the materials" or locations (2018: 405). As 3D technologies "capture" land and reorganize space, the technologies dislocate data, create corporate archives, and rewrite specific sites through colonial practices of collecting.

Like the historic stereoscope viewing experience, 3D technologies write, record, and rhetorically reinscribe a place by first dislocating data from context. Stephen G. Brown and Mary Louise Pratt explain how early travel writers and cultural tourists inscribed places and thus helped industrial nations take possession of a place through a "linguistic-sleight-of-hand" (Brown, 2001: 122). Describing an area as "barren, empty, undeveloped, inconceivable" and even "needful of European influence and control" isolated the land from the people who inhabited it and cast the colonizer as a benevolent force that would develop or save the area (Pratt, 1992: 35). To the engaged reader at home, the land is "reinvented rhetorically as a 'new world' or as a 'last frontier'—as a precondition for transference of ownership from colonized to colonizer. The native's land is given a face-lift whose aim is transference of 'title' to the land" (Brown, 2001: 122). As 3D technologies document the many (sur)faces of cultural heritage sites, the scans create a data record dislocated from local context and communities, performing an act of erasure. Reframed, the location then becomes part of a larger narrative of loss and reconstruction, and 3D technologies become the benevolent force of a new frontier that can save sites at risk.

The preservation focus also extends colonial practices of collecting by positioning makers, as well as viewers, as saviors of nature and culture. Most recently, technology companies have used the rhetoric of "save" and "share" to inscribe the value of 3D scanning for the global good. For example, the 3D scanning firm CyArk claims in its "About Us" video that its mission is "to capture and protect these gifts to share with the world" because "terrorism, looting, and natural disasters are wiping out the cultural symbols and stories we share as human beings." Thus, CyArk must "protect these sites but open this global library to the world" (CyArk.org). The focus on "capturing," "saving" or "preserving" heritage sites, for the good of all, insinuates a type of ownership by humankind. Organizations such as Google Arts & Culture rhetorically reinscribe locations as part of a collective global heritage while taking ownership of digital data and transferring it into their archives. But just as no land is barren, no data is raw. Lisa Gitelman argues that, like photographs, "data too need to be understood as framed and framing, understood, that is, according to the uses to which they are and can be put. Data is never raw, but always framed, always in use. The question is, who is doing the framing?" (2013: 12) Complex ecologies and cultural systems play out across landscapes that often escape a quick scan or surface-level view. Many cultural heritage sites are sacred to local communities, with a local meaning and purpose. Without collaborating with the local communities, corporate data scans and digital archives participate in a type of data colonialism that erases local activity and once again takes land away from Indigenous groups. In addition, data scans are the property of the companies that do the scanning. Google, CyArk, the Smithsonian, and several other 3D scanning initiatives publish 3D renders on their websites, but the sites are carefully curated with only a select portion of the "global library" accessible to the public. Even when scanning UNESCO World Heritage Sites, individual countries have to petition to gain access to the 3D models—and historically, those petitions are not always granted. Data capture and collection then becomes another repatriation battle for local people and Indigenous communities. By controlling the records of sites, 3D archives not only dislocate images, but oppress local sources of knowledge in favor of institutional authority.

Archives can help preserve and inform, but archives can also privilege specific perspectives and obscure marginalized voices through how they *mediate* knowledge. Google (in partnership with CyArk) and the Smithsonian are only two of the many companies working to create digital renders of environments. Yet, their websites and rhetoric offer a window into how corporate entities shape the archival knowledge presented to the public. Each organization has an online 3D viewer and archive of scans framed by claims they are "preserving our shared heritage" and "recording our most recognizable landmarks" as "sites worth seeing" (https://artsandculture. google.com/project/openheritage). Both institutions advocate for 3D experiences as educational, and both institutions mediate the user experience to privilege technological accuracy and institutional authority. Through Google's *Open Heritage* 3D platform, users can explore 3D models, collect artifacts, and listen to audio clips from scientists, conservators, and archaeologists as the "world's leading experts" guide a journey through history. However, the narratives that accompany 3D experiences, the metadata, also produce a version of history that often silences local voices.[4] Featured experts include people with institutional authority, but rarely offer a perspective of someone from the local community or culture. In the archived web exhibit of the Mesa Verde pueblo site (see Fig. 4.3), the captions state only that the structure "remains an important place for American Indian communities today" (https://artsandculture.google.com/exhibit/AQICXBsd ZeHfLg). The website neglects to detail any specific relevance, feature stories from the local community, or offer sources for the information. What is worth scanning and who curates the data authors a hierarchy of heritage.

Archives are not just read or accessed; they are materials that perform. Chakrabarty argues that the creation of archives is part of a wider project to create a public sphere (2010). Historic archives promoted a white, western, heteronormative perspective that marginalized alternative viewpoints and thus perpetuated western ways of seeing. (Trouillot, 1995; Christen, 2011; Jimerson, 2007). Similarly, 3D archives author new ways of seeing heritage sites that prioritize dislocation, capture, and monoscopic perspectives. While some 3D projects do mention collaborations with local communities, many models present an idealized or even gamified version of a heritage site. Collectable artifacts are often digitally added to the models to enhance the authenticity of the virtual environment or represent a specific aspect of history or culture. To illustrate, when zooming around the 3D model of a temple in Bagan, users can pick up Buddhist relics to learn more about the art and area. However, taking control of an item propagates a western system of ownership that not only removes artifacts from context, but also positions objects as remnants of supposedly lost traditions. The experience also implies that the people who

would use the object or inhabit the area are no longer present, effectively eras-
ing local relationships in favor of academic authority (Cushman, 2013; Genovese 2016). The model environments of 3D experiences already dislocate
landscapes. Encouraging users to collect artifacts only further models colonial
acts of collection onto these digital environments. In remediating sites through
digital archives, 3D technologies can also displace a colonial past in favor of an
educational experience.

As cultural heritage institutions and benevolent corporate giants work to
save and preserve at-risk sites, they rewrite sites and rhetorically deploy data
for their own uses. Digital archives often publish a privileged perspective of
a site that encourages accessibility while appropriating data as one would
historic stereoscope cards or images of empire. For example, Google claims
that its online 3D experience "provides users with access to sites in far flung
locations across the globe" and to "sites that are not open to the general
public" (Ristevski, 2018). For a viewer at home, the digital archives become a
model for how 3D technologies can save cultural heritage, and a way of
seeing the wonders of the world. Open access might sound empowering, but
what about displaying burial remains or sites sacred to specific cultures?
How are digital archives and corporate education initiatives controlling digital data while neglecting local customs? In dislocating and redistributing the
3D models, the archives present sites as open to all without considering
cultural significance or local practices of sharing. The work of CyArk and
Google Arts & Culture provides valuable information for conservation
efforts and public education initiatives; however, the scans also dislocate
sites from the local ecologies that shape meaning. The digital data and
careful curated archives present a model, dislocated environment that again
re-enacts many of the colonial practices of collection.

Decolonial by design

To decolonize data collection, technology firms and educational institutions
must work with local communities to document, store, and share, and
develop a set of practices that actively work against the structures of colonialism. If dislocation is the issue, then relocating 3D content might offer one
way to decolonize digital heritage. Thus, decolonial data methods should
analyze context and encourage collaboration—designing digital archives that
reflect the many layers of meaning at work within any location. Jentry Sayers
argues that "technologies are constructed, maintained, preserved, and
consumed, and they are intricately interlaced with labor and knowledge
production" (2018: 2). Collecting data, in some sense, will always dislocate
and mediate—but by practicing collective curation, emerging technologies
can also disrupt some of the colonial methods imbedded in traditional
archival practices and technology use. By better understanding how 3D
technologies dislocate heritage sites, we can also model new curation strategies that work to reconnect landscape data within the local environments

that shape cultural heritage. Environments are complex, ecologies are complex, cultures are complex. The way that digital archives represent heritage sites should also illustrate that data is complex. What would a multi-dimensional, decolonial approach to 3D scanning and archives look like?

Recent Indigenous scholarship holds that decolonization must involve the "repatriation of Indigenous land and life" (Tuck and Yang, 2012: 21). To better account for both land and life, digital archiving methods must consider the local. Instead of merely capturing places with emerging technologies, collectors should curate data with local communities. 3D technologies offer new, less intrusive ways of studying land; but without context, the models are merely data, not discourse, and another form of digital colonization. The idea of "capturing" an environment—image capture, data capture—evokes a colonial rhetoric of mining resources or the scientific acquisition of specimens. But places are inhabited. Even crumbling ruins are inhabited, by animals, insects, stories—imbued with layers of movement and meaning that construct a place—both rhetorically and physically. Simply capturing data without accounting for context ignores the dynamic nature of place. To decolonize methods of collection, emerging methodologies of 3D scanning, modeling, and archiving need to understand the relationships between land and life. Places are not just geographic locations, or clouds of data, but collections of meaning. Nedra Reynolds calls this a "sense of place," where places, "textual, material, or imaginary, are constructed and reproduced not simply by boundaries but also by practices, structures of feeling, and sedimented features of *habitus*" (2004: 2). Like the striations on sedimentary rocks, places are layered with multiple histories, stories, memories, and physical attributes. A place is also an archive. Merely measuring the surface fails to account for the relationships at work on the ground and the many layers of meaning passing through.

3D scanning technology creates a more accurate image by considering multiple (even millions of) angles—so too should archival practices consider the multiplicity of place, layers of meaning, and multiple perspectives. Instead of merely archiving records, Kimberly Christen advocates for cultivating relationships. According to Christen, "curation implies a conscious effort to put materials in relation to one another to form something new—whether it be for commercial, academic, entertainment, or other purposes" (2018, 405). Collecting data, curating information, and arranging an archive are all acts of writing and assemblage. Even 3D scans are assemblages—a weaving together of data points to make a new whole. How we assemble data and curate archives is a work of composition that occurs with computers, sites, technicians, scholars, and, if done well, the local communities and people whose land or artifacts are being scanned. Basu and De Jong assert that "the relationship between parts and wholes, disjointed fragments and imagined totalities is a fundamental dynamic in archival knowledge production" (2016: 15). Decolonial methods assemble and reassemble parts to disrupt imagined totalities and curate multiplicity, reconnecting data to local ecologies of meaning.

In addition, as Christen and Adam Arola note, assemblage offers a more ethical approach to composition that acknowledges Native people's right to articulate their own identity through diverse forms of textual production and curation (2017). Stories, maps, memories, 3D scans, location-based technologies, and material traces all offer different ways to assemble and know a place. Curation should be more of a participatory practice where technicians, scholars, and local communities collect and mediate data together. A participatory culture of collection or curation designs a system where "not every member must contribute, but all must believe they are free to contribute when ready and that what they contribute will be appropriately valued" (Jenkins et al., 2006: 7). As local communities help design 3D experiences, curation tags, and metadata, the surface scans of heritage sites gain a depth and detail that re-situates heritage sites as part of a complex ecology of a place. Working with local communities and contextualizing data from multiple viewpoints also usurps the classic white, male, heteronormative perspective and repositions curation as a more emplaced network of knowledge-making relationships.

However, decolonial approaches should also recognize what types of knowledge work archives make possible, as well as what they limit. Digital collections can balance education and preservation by designing access policies that respect Indigenous communities. Kimberly Christen calls this kind of balance "digital heritage stewardship," where local people work together with cultural institutions to develop sharing agreements that honor Indigenous knowledge systems.[5] For example, many museums, online collections, and virtual exhibits now mask or delete images of sacred items or deceased people. Other digital archives include terms of service that contextualize images and require visitors to agree to a respectful, ethical engagement before entering a site. The Plateau Peoples' Web Portal, a collaboratively curated and managed archive of Plateau cultural materials, mediates access according to specific tribal protocols and even features a statement of commitment on their website. The statement details the collaborative contract between six Plateau people groups[6] and Washington State University that addresses "project goals, partner contributions, content agreements, and project oversight and organization" (plateauportal.libraries.wsu.edu). Instituting a system of "cultural checks," Christen argues, "broadens the notion of curation beyond the individual item or collection by *locating* it within a history, social relations, and ongoing political situations that move between the past and present and multiple groups of people" (2018: 407, emphasis added).

Locating curation within a specific environment also reframes preservation as a living act. Traditional preservation methods often treat sites and artifacts as dead, barren, or leftover, but collaborative, participatory approaches look to the lived experience of heritage materials, reframing objects, belongings, and sites as part of a living ecology. As such, digital archives have created new ways for Indigenous cultures to take ownership of their data and cultural materials. Archives created and maintained by

Indigenous peoples not only offer spaces for local preservation, but also demonstrate how Indigenous practices operate in alliance with digital environments through similar knowledge-making practices, such as the hypertextuality of wampum belts, non-linear storytelling, or multimodal assemblage (Haas, 2008; Cushman, 2013; Arola and Arola, 2017). Similarly, the re-location of 3D data creates an opportunity for local communities to delink from the mechanisms of colonialism and participate in what Malea Powell and Phil Bratta (2016) call a "constellation" of meaning-making practices rooted in lived environments. Collaborative community work with 3D technologies repositions "model environments" as the dead, barren, and empty space and reframes heritage sites as living archives and thus active sites of knowledge production.

(Re)locating rhetoric in 3D

Angela Haas warns, "just as the rhetoric we compose can never be objective, neither can the technologies we design" (2012: 288). All technologies are culturally, historically, and rhetorically situated—never neutral or objective. But just as technologies can dislocate and mediate data in ways that limit knowledge or oppress communities, technologies can also open pathways for inventing new practices. Stereoscopes, 3D imaging, and digital archives are all part of assemblages that compose new ways of seeing landscapes and preserving places—influencing both visual and cultural literacy. Stereoscopic technologies might mediate land through one-dimensional analysis and dislocation, but the framework of stereoscopic rhetorics encourages data collection methods and archive designs that acknowledge the many dimensions of a place.

Place also offers a site for inventing archival practices and ways of seeing that acknowledge the many movements, layers, and relationships that create meaning. Advocating for decolonial methods, Ellen Cushman claims that "the archive might become a place-based learning center where knowledge unfolds through stories told in and on the people's terms" (2013: 132). In the same way, place can become an archive that unfolds through stories told, knowledge curated, and data assemblages. 3D technologies provide a way for writers and curators to explore the affordances of digital archives as a mode of place-based digital writing, a mode produced with a specific site and community. As scholars, scientists, and local peoples come together to assemble and preserve heritage sites, the environment becomes both the text and the archive—a living, located experience.

Scholars in archeology and anthropology have critiqued uses of 3D technologies to map landscapes as a "scan-and-dump" big data method, calling for new approaches that intertwine environmental and cultural factors and offer "a ground-based humanistic perspective" (Richards-Rissetto, 2017. In response to such criticism, technology firms and educational institutions are now starting to partner with communities to curate data and work in local partnerships. In 2019, the Google Open Heritage project partnered with the

University of South Florida and Historic Environment Scotland to create the Open Heritage Alliance. The alliance shares best practices for 3D scanning and sharing, but also works to address "concerns dealing with standards, formats, approach, ethics, and archive commitment" (https://openheritage3d. org/about). The goal is to preserve place by creating immersive 3D environments that reflect the many values of specific locations. As a result, recent 3D projects have included more local consultants and even helped train curators and site mangers to participate in 3D scans. The Open Heritage initiative has just begun to preserve and share in ways that act as a service to the community, but these initial steps do the important work of recognizing both the local and global importance of heritage sites. The focus might still be on technology and preservation, but the Alliance is (hopefully) moving the right direction and working to consider local communities as essential contributors to heritage work.

An archive is always a mediated space; however, in co-creating, collaborating, and contextualizing knowledge, communities can use new media technologies such as 3D models to curate archives that reflect a more accurate picture of locations. Instead of "model" environments, or dislocated images, curated knowledge positions 3D images as one way (of many) to understand cultural heritage by framing digital data as part of a place-based constellation of knowledge-making practices.

Notes

1 Patrizia Di Bello (2013) and John Plunkett (2013) have also argued that Holmes' enthusiasm for the sculptural aspects of the stereoscope was a type of refiguring of the Victorian sensorium. While the stereoscope conditioned vision, the device also reconfigured relationships between vision and touch.

2 Holmes believed so strongly in the stereoscopic experience that he created a smaller, handheld version and purposely did not patent his design so that stereoscopes could be mass produced more easily. In a sense, Holmes, created the first open access 3D tech.

3 The term "Native Americans" fails to describe the 500+ nations in the United States, but I use the term to demonstrate how the slides classified people groups under a general heading of "Indigenous" or "native."

4 Ellen Cushman notes that earlier imperial archives also rely on "collecting, classifying, and isolating" alongside the "expert codification of knowledge" (2013: 117). In contrast, decolonial archives disrupt traditional systems by co-creating knowledge with local communities.

5 Kimberly Christen's (2018) article "Relationship, Not Records: Digital Heritage and the Ethics of Sharing Indigenous Knowledge Online" offers several excellent examples of how specific people groups author access. The National Museum of Australia warns that exhibits "may cause sadness and distress to Aboriginal and Torres Strait Islander people" (www.nma.gov/au/history/aboriginal-torres-strait-islander-culture s-histories). The Musqueam Indian Band's online place name archive requires visitors to accept a terms of service agreement that includes being "respectful" and "not reproducing any portion of the site without permission" (www.musqueam.bc.ca/m usqueam-our-history-we-map). The Blackfoot people's Blackfoot Digital Library has a statement that reminds users that Indigenous knowledge is not freely open and

available to all people: "You are not considered a member of the Blackfoot tribe nor are you considered a Shaman/Medicine person because you learned something on this site. This site is not for recreating Blackfoot ceremony by non-Blackfoot people" (www.blackfootdigitallibrary.com).

6 Several countries and institutions have archival guidelines designed to ensure cultural values and ethical concerns are addressed at all steps of the archiving process, from collection and cataloguing to curation and sharing (The Australian Institute for Aboriginal and Torres Strait Islander Studies, https://aiatsis.gov.au; First Archivists Circle, Protocols for Native American Archival Materials, www2.nau.edu/libnap -p/protocols.html) While the protocols generally describe physical materials and collections, the concepts of best practice have been quickly adopted by many digital repositories (O'Neal, 2014; Christen, 2018).

References

Arola, Kristin and Adam C. Arola. "An Ethics of Assemblage: Creative Repetition and the Electric Pow Wow." *Assembling Composition*. Eds. Kathleen Blake Yancey and Stephen J. McElroy. Urbana, IL: National Council of Teachers of English, 2017.

Bak, Meredith. "Democracy and Discipline: Object Lessons and the Stereoscope in American Education 1870–1920." *Early Popular Visual Culture* 10. 2(2012): 147–167.

Basu, Paul and Ferdinand De Jong. "Utopian Archives, Decolonial Affordances." *Social Anthropology* 24. 1(2016): 5–19.

Brown, Stephen. "The Wilderness Strikes Back: Decolonizing the Imperial Sign in the Borderlands." *Ecocomposition: Theoretical and Pedagogical Approaches*. Eds. Sidney I. Dobrin and Christian Weisser. Albany, NY: State University of New York Press, 2001. 117–129.

Chakrabarty, Dipesh. Bourgeois Categories Made Global: The Utopian and Actual Lives of Historical Documents in India. *Utopia/Dystopia: Conditions of Historical Possibility*. Eds. M. D. Gordin, H. Tilley and G. Prakash. Princeton, NJ: Princeton University Press, 2010. 73–93.

Christen, Kristen. Opening Archives: Respectful Repatriation. *American Archivist* 74 (2011): 185–210.

Christen, K. "Relationships, Not Records: Digital Heritage and the Ethics of Sharing Indigenous Knowledge Online. *Routledge Companion to Media Studies and Digital Humanities*. Jentery Sayers, Ed. New York: Routledge, 2018. 403–412.

Couldry, Nick and Ulises A. Mejias. "Data Colonialism: Rethinking Big Data's Relation to the Contemporary Subject." *Television and New Media* 20. 4(2019): 336–349.

Cushman, Ellen. "Wampum, Sequoyan, and Story: Decolonizing the Digital Archive." *College English* 76. 2(2013): 115–135. Special Issue: The Digital Humanities and Historiography in Rhetoric and Composition.

Di Bello, Patrizia. "'Multiplying Statues by Machinery': Stereoscopic Photographs of Sculptures at the 1862 International Exhibition." *History of Photography* 37(2013): 412–420.

Domonoske, Camila. "ISIS Destroys Ancient Theater, Trapylon in Palmyra, Syria Says." *NPR: The Two-Way*January 20, 2017. https://www.npr.org/sections/thetwo-wa y/2017/01/20/510732864/isis-destroys-ancient-theater-tetrapylon-in-palmyra-syria-says

Fleckenstein, Kristie. "Materiality's Rhetorical Work: The Nineteenth-Century Parlor Stereoscope and the Second-Naturing of Vision." *Rhetoric, Through Everyday Things*.

Eds. Scot Barnett and Casey Boyle. Tuscaloosa, AL: University of Alabama Press, 2016. 125–138.

Fowles, Jib. "Stereography and the Standardization of Vision." *Journal of American Culture* 17. 2(1994): 89–93.

Genovese, Taylor R. "Decolonizing Archival Methodology: Combating Hegemony and Moving towards a Collaborative Archival Environment." *AlterNative: An International Journal of Indigenous Peoples* 12. 1(2016):32–42.

Gitelman, Lisa. *"Raw Data" is an Oxymoron.* Cambridge, MA: MIT Press, 2013.

Gurevitch, Leon. "The Birth of a Stereoscopic Nation: Hollywood, Digital Empire and the Cybernetic Attraction." *Animation: An Interdisciplinary Journal* 7. 3(2012): 239–258.

Gurevitch, Leon. "The Stereoscope Attraction." *Convergence: The international Journal of Research and New Media Technologies* 19. 4(2013): 396–405.

Haas, Angela. "Wampum as Hypertext: An American Indian Intellectual Tradition of Multimedia Theory and Practice." *Studies in American Indian Literatures* 19. 4(2008): 77–100.

Haas, Angela. "Race, Rhetoric, and Technology: A Case Study of Decolonial Technical Communication Theory, Methodology, and Pedagogy." *Journal of Business and Technical Communication* 26. 3(2012): 277–310.

Hanson, Joseph Mills, ed. *The World War through the Stereoscope: A Visualized, Vitalized History of the Greatest Conflict of All the Ages.* Meadville, PA: Keystone View Company, 1923.

Holmes, Oliver Wendell. "Stereoscope and the Stereograph." *The Atlantic*June1859.

Jenkins, Henry, Katie Clinton, Ravi Purushotma, and Margaret Weigel. *Confronting the Challenges of Participatory Culture: Media Education for the 21st Century.* Chicago, IL: Macarthur, 2006.

Jimerson, R. C. "Archives For All: Professional Responsibility and Social Justice." *American Archivist,* 70. 2(2007): 252–281.

Johnson, David. "Stereoscopes: Nineteenth-Century Virtual Reality Devices." *NOMA: New Orleans Museum of Art, News, Arts Quarterly*October 19, 2017. https://noma.org/stereoscopes-first-virtual-reality-devices/

Library of Congress. "Stereograph Cards. " Accessed June 15, 2019. https://www.loc.gov/collections/stereograph-cards/about-this-collection/

Maxwell, Anne. *Colonial Photography: Representations of the 'Native' and the Making of European Identities.* London: Leicester University Press, 2000.

Mitchell, W.J.T. "Visual Literacy or Literary Visualcy?" *Visual Literacy.* Ed. James Elkins. Abingdon, UK: Taylor & Francis. 2009.

O'Neal, Jennifer R. "'The Right to Know': Decolonizing Native American Archives." *Journal of Western Archives* 6. 1(2015): 1–17.

Plunkett, John. "'Feeling Seeing': Touch, Vision and the Stereoscope." *History of Photography* 37. 4(2013): 389–396.

Powell, Malea and Phil Bratta. "Entering the Cultural Rhetorics Conversations." *Enculturation: A Journal of Rhetoric, Writing, and Culture* (2016).

Pratt, Mary Louise. *Imperial Eyes: Travel Writing and Transculturation.* New York: Routledge, 1992.

Reynolds, Nedra. *Geographies of Writing: Inhabiting Places and Encountering Difference.* Carbondale, IL: Southern Illinois University Press, 2004.

Richards-Rissetto, Heather. "What Can GIS + 3D Mean for Landscape Archaeology?" *Journal of Archaeological Science* 84(2017): 10–21.

Rico, Trinidad. "Technologies, Technocracy, and the Promise of 'Alternative Heritage Values' in Heritage." *Action: Making the Past in the Present*. Helanine Silverman, Emma Waterton and Steve Watson, Eds. New York: Springer, 2017.

Ristevski, John. "CyArk Brings Accurate 3D Immersive Data to Life in Virtual Reality." February 15, 2018. https://www.cyark.org/about/cyark-brings-accurate-3d-immersive-data-to-life-in-virtual-reality

Said, Edward. *Orientalism*. New York: Vintage Books, 1979.

Sayers, Jentery. "Introduction." *Routledge Companion to Media Studies and Digital Humanities*. Jentery Sayers, Ed. New York: Routledge, 2018. 1–6.

Smithsonian. About the Smithsonian 3D Program. Smithsonian X3D Overview. 2016. https://3d.si.edu/about

Trouillot, M. *Silencing the Past: Power and the Production of History*. Boston, MA: Beacon, 1995.

Tuck, Eve and K. Wayne Yang. "Decolonization is Not a Metaphor." *Decolonization: Indigeneity, Education & Society* 1. 1(2012): 1–40.

View-Master Advertisement. 1962. Digital Image. Flickr. August 19, 2017. Accessed June 14, 2019. https://flic.kr/p/XAL8xq

5 If a tree falls

Mediations into and of natural sound

Joe Marshall Hardin

In his 1710 book *A Treatise Concerning the Principles of Human Knowledge*, Irish philosopher George Berkeley advanced his idea of "immaterialism" by asking readers to take part in a thought experiment: "Imagine trees, for instance, in a park, or books existing in a closet, but nobody by to perceive them." The act of imagining these trees, he argues, only proves that "when we do our utmost to conceive of external bodies, we are all the while only contemplating our own ideas" (1710, 206). "The trees therefore are in the garden," he continues, "no longer than while there is somebody by to perceive them" (218).

In 1883, Berkeley's idea would be echoed in a regular column entitled "Editor's Table" which appeared regularly in *The Chautauquan: Organ of the Chautauqua Literary and Scientific Circle*. Along with questions and answers about general knowledge, including the pronunciation of Tucson, the rotation of comets, and the birthdate of Elizabeth Barrett Browning, is the question: "If a tree were to fall on an island where there were no human beings would there be any sound?" Following Berkeley, the editor replies: "No. Sound is the sensation excited in the ear when the air or other medium is set in motion" (Editor's Table, 1883: 543). These two occasions, then, are arguably the genesis of the thought experiment that we know as "if a tree falls in the forest and no-one is around to hear it, does it make a sound?" While the question is generally regarded as "academic," as they say, several strains of thought have echoed Berkeley's idea and *The Chautauquan*'s question, including several longstanding philosophical arguments, and some startling scientific evidence about the nature and existence of reality and the role of the observer. While we may leave the very interesting question of whether objects exist outside of their perception to be argued over by others, we can take this formulation as a springboard to question the nature and constitution of natural sound and to examine how humans perceive, record, alter, and employ those sounds as markers for and as alterations to the natural world.[1] Interestingly, questions about the existence of objects outside of human perception have been generally cast in terms of the visual, as Berkeley does in his initial formulation of the issue. In this case, the question is cast in terms of sound, perhaps the only time that a question about the nature of reality has been posed in such a way as to emphasize sound instead of visual observation.

In addition to those created by falling trees in unoccupied forests, the world is full of sound waves, both observed and unobserved. Setting aside the question of whether sound exists if it is not collected and perceived, we will take here the word "sound" to signify two events: one in which propagating sound waves are created, and another in which those waves are received and understood as sound. Propagating sound waves are basically compression and rarefaction of molecules in a gas, liquid, or solid, and the character of those waves is related to the various features of amplitude, frequency, wavelength, phase, speed, and intensity. Amplitude refers to the peak pressure attained by the wave; frequency describes the rate that pressure cycles from the peak of the wave to the trough; wavelength is a measure of the distance between two cycles of compression; phase refers to the relation of the wave to other present waves; and intensity measures (in watts) the power of the wave. Propagating sound waves may be created accidentally, as when our tree falls, or purposefully by sound-producing organs or technology. As regards the reception of sound, it is tempting to suppose that only sentient beings perceive and react to sound; however, experiments have shown that plants may react to sound as well.[2] For the moment, though, we'll leave the question of "if a tree falls in the forest do the other trees hear it" and briefly turn our examination to sound-receiving and -producing organs in the animal kingdom.

Sound-receiving organs in the animal kingdom

Among animals, organs for producing and receiving sound vary greatly. Not all animals have vocal tracts or recognizable "ears," and there are many familiar examples of animals that use other organs and parts of their bodies as technologies to produce and receive sound. Most vertebrates have the familiar structures of the outer ear (pinna and ear canal), the middle ear (tympanic cavity and ossicles), and the inner ear (the utricle and saccule—which also help with balance and eye-tracking—and the cochlea). Bats, lemurs, foxes, and some other vertebrates have highly developed outer ears designed to gather an enormous volume and range of sound waves. Other vertebrates, such as horses, elephants, and rabbits, can "aim" their outer ears to gather sounds from different directions. Invertebrates, on the other hand, have a wider variety of tympanal organs, and many have no outer or middle ear at all. Some insects collect sound waves through hairs on their bodies. Gardiner's frogs have no middle ear or eardrum, and use their mouths to capture sound waves and send those directly to an inner ear structure. Such a frog may use its mouth to collect the sound waves created by a cricket which has produced that sound by scraping its legs together.

For healthy, younger humans, any sound waves with frequencies between 20 and 20,000 hertz (Hz) can be received and processed by the structures of the ear and perceived as sound by the brain, although that optimal range usually diminishes with age. Since one Hz equals one wave cycle per second, that means that humans may theoretically hear sound waves that cycle from 20 to 20,000 times per second. For reference, the lowest note on a big pipe organ is usually about 20 Hz, and piccolos can produce notes that are right at the edge of human hearing. The human body will respond to sound waves below (infrasound) and above (ultrasound) the audible range, but those waves are more felt by the body and not perceived by the brain as sound. Humans may be able to hear sounds outside of the normal range of hearing if the duration and/or volume of those waves is increased, which is why pressing a stethoscope against the chest allows one to hear the heart, which, at 1 or 2 Hz, is normally outside the human range of hearing. Within the animal kingdom, the range of human hearing is about average. Dogs, cats, and porpoises are among animals that have a greater range than humans; frogs, owls, and goldfish have lesser ranges of hearing.

Before the advent of electricity and telephonic devices, external technologies for enhancing human hearing consisted primarily of hearing "trumpets," often made from animal horns or brass, which primarily augmented the collecting capacity of the outer ear. These technologies were cumbersome and not very effective, and were often supplemented by speaking trumpets as well. Until the invention of the telephone in 1876 and the hearing aid in 1895, the only technologies available for increasing the human capacity for hearing or speaking were these listening and speaking horns, which provided only passive amplification.

Sound-producing organs in the animal kingdom

For humans, the sound-producing organ structure consists of the vocal track, which includes the lungs, the larynx, and the articulators (tongue, palate, cheeks, lips, and nasal cavity). According to the *Guinness World Book of Records*, the loudest human scream was issued in 2000 by a woman named Jill Drake of the UK at 129 decibels (dB). The sperm whale and the snapping or pistol shrimp are two of the loudest animals on the planet, and each has a unique system of sound production. A sperm whale uses the extensive muscles, nerves, and cavities of its forehead, which constitute one third of its body length and can weigh up to 10 tons, to generate sound. The whale forces compressed air through these cavities to create a variety of clicks—most at about 10 kHz—that the whale uses both for echolocation and for communication. The sperm whale's clicks have been recorded at between 188 and 230 dB. For comparison, 25 meters from a jet engine, sound waves register at about 150 dB.

The snapping shrimp uses a specialized claw to make sound, which it snaps to create a "cavitation" bubble containing a sound wave. That bubble can travel over 60 miles an hour through the water, and when it collapses and the vibration is released, the sound can reach a level of 218 dB. The collapse of the shrimp's sound bubble also produces a flash of light (sonoluminescence) and a temperature of up to 4,700 Celsius (for comparison, the temperature of the sun is estimated to be around 5,500 Celsius). As one might suspect, in addition to using this method for communication, the snapping shrimp also uses the sound bubble to hunt, stunning its prey with sound. The sound of the pistol shrimp is a major source of interference with sonar and wireless underwater communication.

In contrast to the limited early development of external hearing technologies, humans developed a wide variety of technologies external to their bodies to produce sound, and some of these were developed centuries before electricity and telephonic devices. Primitive sound-producing technologies ranged from stones and sticks beaten against other stones and sticks to early bells, cymbals, and horns. More sophisticated sound-production technologies created before the electric age include a vast array of stringed, blown, and percussive musical instruments, and complex machines ranging from musical clocks and music boxes to pneumatic and even hydraulic organs, some of which date from as early as the 9th century CE.

In addition to speech and other "human" sounds, humans have probably always imitated natural sound: whistling like birds, growling like bears, and burbling like water. In "Crickets in the Concert Hall: A History of Animals in Western Music," Emily Doolittle (2008) writes that

> Hunters and shamans of many traditional cultures incorporate ritual imitations of animal sounds into their songs; mechanical instruments for recreating birdsong date back several thousand years; canaries (the domesticated descendants of *Serinus canaria*) and bullfinches (*Pyrrhula pyrrhula*) are prized for their ability to learn human songs; human performers improvise with animal songs both live and recorded; and composers such as Jannequin, Biber, and Messiaen are known for their borrowings of bird and other animal songs.

Particularly during the Romantic era, many composers created so-called program (or programme) music, which was composed in ways that suggested the sounds of the natural world and which sometimes contain passages that directly imitated the sounds of nature. Two notable and familiar examples are Vivaldi's *The Four Seasons* and Beethoven's *Pastoral Symphony*, which includes an imitation of the cuckoo. Doolittle reports that in 1717, music publisher John Walsh published a pamphlet describing how various bird species might be taught to sing human music:

> *The Bird Fancyer's Delight* (1717) describes how this may be done with a variety of species including nightingale, bullfinch, blackbird, canary, woodlark, skylark, linnet, parrot, mynah bird and house sparrow by placing them in a darkened cage and playing a suitable tune to them over and over again on a bird flageolet or a small recorder.

From the beginning, the imitation of natural sound seems to have played an integral part in the development of human sound production.

Human sound production and reception technologies in the Industrial Age and beyond

Entering the Industrial Age, humans began to create a multitude of technologies to produce, reproduce, preserve, and amplify sound, but the first 50 or so years focused largely on amplifying, recording, and reproducing human voices. Before Thomas Edison's phonograph, several people had suggested in theory that the vibrations produced by sound waves could be translated into lines or grooves that might somehow be "played back," but it was Edison who first succeeded in both recording sound waves and playing them back. Edison's invention included a stylus that would indent the received vibrations as "up and down" grooves on tin foil wrapped around a hand-cranked cylinder. The same stylus would then vibrate, reproducing those sound waves as is was dragged back through those grooves. Edison was initially disinterested in developing his invention, though, and it fell to Alexander Graham Bell to introduce, seven years later, the wax cylinder and an engraving stylus that produced the more effective "side to side" groove. Following the advent of electricity, electric motors were introduced to the phonographic technology, replacing the mechanical cranks and springs previously used to power both the recording and the playback. Eventually, plastic cylinders replaced wax cylinders and then the cheaper-to-produce plastic "record" disk finally replaced the cylinder.

In the late 1920s, Arthur Allen, founder at Cornell University of the first American graduate program in ornithology, began to think about how recordings of bird songs would help his students learn to identify bird species. Coincidentally, this was just after the Al Jolson film *The Jazz Singer* had introduced sound to movies, and Fox-Case Movietone Corporation wanted to add more natural sounds, particularly bird sounds, to its films. The corporation came to Allen asking for Cornell's help in developing techniques for recording natural sound, particularly bird sounds. With this collaboration, the field of bioacoustics was born, as Professor Allen and his students worked with Fox-Case Movietone's technicians to develop equipment and techniques for recording natural sound.

In his article, "The Birth of Natural Sound Recording," Tim Gallagher reports that the existing sound equipment used by the movie company was both cumbersome and noisy, and it was not until Allen introduced a remote microphone to a perch where he knew that a song sparrow had been singing that they were able to record the first bird sounds—the song sparrow, a rose-breasted grosbeak, and a house wren. Interestingly, the process converted the sound vibrations into electrical impulses, which were then converted to "light of varying intensity," which was captured on the film: "after developing the film, the process was reversed, converting the light images back into electrical impulses, which were then changed back into sound" (Gallagher, 2015).

The ornithology lab at Cornell was known for its innovations and was responsible for creating many of the sound-recording devices and techniques we know and use to this day. Peter Keane, an undergraduate working in the lab, came up with the idea of using a parabolic dish to better collect bird sounds, and students began hand-making the dishes in the lab. Parabolic dishes are still the standard for collecting wildlife sounds. A graduate student in the lab, Peter Paul Kellogg, envisioned and designed the first real portable recorder: "The recorder, manufactured by the Amplifier Corporation of America in 1951, weighed less than 20 pounds and revolutionized the recording of wildlife sounds in the field" (Gallagher). Today, the field of bioacoustics focuses on biological, geophysical, as well as anthropogenic sound and acoustics and the recording and analysis of various soundscapes for monitoring biodiversity and ecosystem health.

Human mediation into natural sound ecosystems

Since the Industrial Age, humans have created a veritable din on the planet with machines, industry, wars, and the general increase in population. To say the least, the resulting racket has produced a significant mediation into natural sound ecosystems of the planet, and the results of this mediation have been profound, and in many cases disastrous. When we consider humanity's overall effect on the planet, we may be tempted to overlook the effect of anthropogenic sound, probably because we are, at least outside of the sounds made by war, largely normalized to the sounds of our machines, industry, and culture. With all the physical pollution of the air, land, and seas, it may be hard for some to envision noise pollution as a serious problem; however, anthropogenic sound has radically altered the planet in ways that are similarly ominous. Nowhere is this more obvious than in the effects of human sound on the oceans.

The oceans, by themselves, are naturally quite noisy. The sound ecosystem of the ocean minus human activity includes the sounds created by the wind, waves, and rain; the sounds created by tectonic and seismic activity; the sounds created by sea ice; and the vocalizations and other sounds created by sea life. According to a report issued by the Whale and Dolphin Conservation Society entitled *Oceans of Noise* (Simmonds, 2004), humans have introduced a cacophony of sound into the natural sound ecologies of the ocean, including:

- The sounds of transport, fishing, and leisure ships and boats (propeller sounds, the sounds of on-board machinery, and the sound made by hulls passing through the water);
- the sounds of sonar and depth sounders;
- the sounds of oil and gas exploration, including vessel sounds, construction and blasting noise, the noises made by seismic surveys, pile driving, pipe laying, pumping, and drilling; and general rig and platform noise;
- the sounds of seismic and geological surveys, which often employ arrays of air guns to generate and collect sound;

- aircraft noise;
- military noise, including vessel and aircraft noise, military sonar, military weapons' firings and weapons' tests;
- the purposeful harassment of sea life with acoustic deterrent devices, which are employed in aquaculture, fishing, whale hunting, and other activities;
- dredging; and
- marine wind farms.

The incidental effects of anthropogenic sound on the oceans have probably been even more devastating than studies show. Cetaceans, in particular, have extremely sensitive hearing, and study after study demonstrate that they have suffered enormous deleterious effects. In addition to incidentally altering the sound ecologies of the oceans, humans have for centuries used sound to actively and effectively hunt sea life. In "Hunting Cetaceans with Sound," the authors describe how humans have used sound over the centuries to hunt cetaceans:

> Fishermen around the world have used various types of low-intensity sound for centuries to drive schools of small cetaceans ashore so that they could be killed and used for food or culled. During the 20th Century, the most commonly practiced method was the use of vessels to herd the small cetaceans to the shore. The acoustic components of these fisheries varied widely, ranging from hitting rocks together underwater to the engine noise from multiple small fishing boats. Since the end of World War II approximately 500,000 small cetaceans have been killed using the drive method in various parts of the world. Also, over seven million dolphins are estimated to have been killed by herding in the deliberate incidental catches in the eastern tropical Pacific, where dolphins associate with schools of tuna.
>
> (Brownell et al., 2008: 85–6).

International law has been of minimal effectiveness in curtailing the use of herding to hunt ocean animals.

In addition to their purposeful use to hunt animals, anthropogenic sounds have had a devastating effect on the environment, and again, nowhere is this more obvious than in the harm done to the sound ecologies of the oceans. A Royal Society *Proceedings* paper (Bernaldo de Quirós et al. 2019) concludes that mid-frequency active sonar (MFAS) distresses beaked whales to the point where nitrogen in the blood causes the whales to experience "the bends," causing hemorrhaging and organ damage. In the years since this particular kind of sonar has been used, the number of MFAS-related strandings has skyrocketed. According to Nowacek et al., the incidental impacts of anthropogenic sound on sea life are "behavioural, acoustic and physiological" (2007: 81). Short- and long-term effects include damage to the animals' body and ears; changes in hearing threshold; interference with normal communication, echolocation, and normal hearing; shifts in vocalization; displacement; generalized stress with increased vulnerability to disease and debilitation; social disruption; deafness; and trauma leading to disorientation or death. Other behavioral changes include feeding changes (including reluctance to feed) and changes in diving and other swimming patterns, which may also tax these animals' "finely balanced energy budgets" (81). Other responses to the interference of human sound include changes in type or timing of vocalizations relative to the noise sources. As an example, "Worldwide Decline in Tonal Frequencies of Blue Whale Songs" suggests that "Blue Whales may modify their call frequencies to adapt to increasing anthropogenic noises." The noise made by shipping traffic is "in the same 10 to 100 Hz frequency band as blue whale songs" and so the whales may have shifted the frequency of their calls downward in tone (McDonald et al., 2009: 19). While other factors are no doubt contributing to the change in whale vocalizations, studies suggest that the frequency of blue whale calls has lowered as a result of anthropogenic sounds. Of course, these are only some of the direct effects of anthropogenic sound on the ocean sound ecologies. Each change may immeasurably alter the ocean's inhabitants' ability to survive and prosper.

This brief analysis is but a small window into the effects of anthropogenic sound on the world's ecosystems. There is no doubt that the din of our machinery and roar of our culture has had lasting effects, both good and bad, on the planet.

Human mediation of natural sound ecosystems

Representations of natural sounds currently take one of two primary modes: the scientific and the Romantic. Exemplifying the scientific mode, Professor Allen and the students at Cornell went on to create the field of bioacoustics and amass a library of over 525,000 animal sounds. The movie industry, on the other hand, has become infamous for exploiting the natural world and its sound with little regard for scientific accuracy or responsible aesthetics. The movie and television industries have also become infamous for placing random bird sounds out of context. One of the most popular bird sounds for movie-makers is the "laugh" of the kookaburra, a native of Australia and New Guinea. While the range of the kookaburra is limited, its sound appears in movie and TV settings as diverse as the African jungle (*Tarzan and the Green Goddess*, 1938), Mexico (*The Treasure of the Sierra Madre*, 1960), New Guinea (*Swiss Family Robinson*, 1960), North Carolina (*Cape Fear*, 1962), and Central America (*The Lost World: Jurassic Park*, 1997). One can even hear the sound of the kookaburra as Dorothy, the Tin Man, the Scarecrow, and the Cowardly Lion take the Yellow Brick Road through a dismal wood on the way to Oz. The sound of the dolphin on the television series *Flipper* (1964–67) is, in fact, a modified kookaburra laugh.

Many recordings and representations of natural sounds make their way into culture as Romantic fantasy meant to help with relaxation or as a way to "appreciate" or experience the natural world. Unfortunately, listening to a soundscape of waves crashing on the beach in Maui or of bird songs in the Amazon objectifies the natural world and turns it into a commodity. These kinds of soundscapes also present nature in an aesthetic that privileges the beautiful and the peaceful. Listeners are privileged to consume natural sound free from anthropogenic noise and without representation of humans at all, except as passive consumers.

In "Toward a Dark Nature Recording," David Michael discusses the genesis of the recording that began the onslaught of Romantic natural soundscapes designed for relaxation and appreciation:

> one of the most dominant forms of nature sound recording was defined by the blockbuster 1970 album *Songs of the Humpback Whale*. With a few exceptions, this style portrays a pastoral world in which the only sign of man is the recording itself. Here, songbirds are in perpetual chorus, lush rainforests are packed with exotic animals, and tranquil meadows are filled with singing insects. It is a world meticulously constructed by hundreds of recordists over many decades, who have all sought out tiny windows in time and space where man cannot be heard.
>
> (2011: 207).

The popularity of this mode, in which natural sound serves as a fantasy consumable, is undeniable. While the actual whales might not have been able to escape the interference of anthropogenic sound, the listener can enjoy the whale songs framed in isolation from any such interference, free from awareness or appreciation of the damage done by humans to the whales' sound environment. In fact, *Songs of the Humpback Whale* was so popular that 10 million copies were struck in one pressing. According to an article entitled "How Pop Music Helped Save the Whales" (Public Radio International, 2016), Roger Payne, the biologist behind the release, had obtained a tape of the whale songs from military researcher Frank Watlington, who had been trying to "record undersea dynamite explosions." Watlington recorded the sound, but wasn't sure what he was hearing and passed the tapes along to Payne, who was the first to realize that the whales were repeating phrases and thus creating "songs" in much the same way that birds do. Payne passed the tape to Judy Collins, who "sang along" with whale songs on "Farewell to Tarwathi" on her album *Whales and Nightingales* (1970). This encouraged the record company to release the whale songs without any accompaniment. The next decade saw an explosion of popular songs that included whale sounds or were dedicated to whales, and launched the contemporary genre of soundscape recordings, which fell mostly under the New Age banner and were focused on relaxation and/or environmental awareness. George Lipsitz suggests that "the songs of the whales struck a nerve because they were part of a historical moment. The US had just experienced the Kent State Shootings; the Vietnam war seemed like it would never end; Martin Luther King had been killed" (quoted in Public Radio International, 2016). The "Save the Whales" moment spawned by these recordings was part of a general feeling, fueled largely by the counterculture, that humans needed to get "back to nature." The recordings also contributed to the birth of the modern environmental movement signaled by the first celebration of Earth Day in 1970. Worth noting is that the U.S. had banned whaling and all whale products by 1972, and the awareness of the plight of the whales, helped by the popularity of *Songs of the Humpback Whale*, no doubt contributed to that change.

The problem is that, while these soundscape recordings promote an awareness of environmental issues, they also present nature as an "out there" world where humans are merely observers. The unfortunate reality is that the planet is in deep crisis and human activity is the source of most of that crisis: "Beyond global climate change driven by human action and a constant assault by industrial technologies on natural systems, there is an ongoing massive loss of biodiversity so great it is characterized as a sixth great mass extinction" (Michael, 2011: 207). While learning to appreciate nature by listening to relaxing soundscapes taken from nature might, in fact, increase awareness of nature, the Romantic aesthetic serves primarily to create a void between humans and the natural world and to promote nature as a commodity. If this aesthetic is to be challenged effectively, it will be key to promote a view of the natural world that does not frame nature as a consumable in service to individual relaxation or appreciation.

At first glance, visual artists seem to be leading the way toward this kind of representation—one that recognizes and critiques the profound effect humans have had on the environment. One might point to artists such as Brazilian Viktor Muniz, who employed *catadores* (garbage collectors) to create giant portraits of the *catadores* themselves made of garbage. This work is documented in the in the Oscar-nominated *Waste Land* by director Lucy Walker. Visual artists are also leading the way in creating art from recycled materials, and these art pieces include a valuable critique of human activity and the waste it produces. So far, equivalent public soundscapes and recordings that emphasize the darker side of human activity and its effects on the planet have been heavy handed at best. Included in these might be the use of a tape of rabbits screaming in front of Danna Karan's offices by People for the Ethical Treatment of Animals (PETA) during fashion week, or the horrifying sounds of dolphins being slaughtered in Japan, recorded and released by The Dolphin Project in 2003.

The trouble is that there is a long history of soundscapes that do not serve to isolate nature and present it as a consumable fantasy, or to engage in sensationalism, but much of that work has been displaced. In "Field Recording and the Sounding of Spaces," Michael Gallagher suggests that field recordings may once again present opportunities for representing the natural world beyond written texts, numbers, maps, and images. Etymologically, the discipline is at root a form of earth-writing, but writing is too narrow a framework to account for the diversity of geographical practices. Many other kinds of media are involved in doing geography, including audio. More fundamentally, metaphors of writing and inscription are ill-suited for understanding the functioning of contemporary digital media, including digital text. Digital data storage uses electrical currents to charge microscopic particles in magnetic materials or semiconductors. These processes are quite different to the etching of lines on surfaces. Moreover, data storage is always coupled to systems of transmission and transduction: data buses and interfaces, cables and optical fibres, power supplies and wireless networks, loudspeakers and screens. The technologies that provide the best general model for understanding these systems are not the inscriptive mechanisms of writing, printing or drawing, but those such as radio and telephony that propagate and transmit vibration through space.

(2015: 8–9)

The first step might be in recuperating the wealth of soundscapes that do not over-Romanticize nature or elide humanity's effects on the environment.

Acoustic ecology

In the late 1960s, R. Murray Shafer established the World Soundscape Project and the field of acoustic ecology (also sometimes known as ecoacoustics or soundscape studies). The most successful soundscape produced by this group was *The Vancouver Soundscape*. The project, sponsored by Simon Fraser University and the Donner Canadian Foundation, employed composers and students to construct a detailed sound study of Vancouver, Canada, and five villages in Europe. The resulting soundscapes include more than 300 tapes, and the results produced CDs, publications, and ethnographic accounts. Much of this material is still available through Simon Fraser University at www.sfu.ca/sonic-studio-webdav/. The work of this group seems a good place to start for the way it negotiates the spaces between scientific research, public critique, and creative/artistic energy in soundscape production. In 1993, another group formed: the World Forum for Acoustic Ecology. This group publishes *Soundscape: The Journal of Acoustic Ecology*, and promotes education, research, distribution, preservation, and design. Within and beyond these groups there is a wide, interdisciplinary network of soundscape recordists and theorists, and their focuses are varied. These activities point the way toward a possible resurgence in soundscape recording that embraces science and theory, is accessible and creative, and is grounded in a rejection of the objectification of the natural soundscape and the exclusion of anthropogenic sound. The current environmental crises call for just this kind of interdisciplinary work and creative response if humans are to face current environmental challenges that certainly mean the difference between life and death for many species, and this may include humans. Attention to the sounds of the world can be a powerful means to stimulate a shift in how humans live as a part of the natural world instead of apart from it. Acoustic ecology, bioacoustics, and ecoacoustic theories (and art and music grounded in the non-objectification of nature) can certainly contribute to our understanding of the problems in our world and how we might best manage them. In the end, the question "if a tree falls and no-one is there to hear it, does it make a sound" primarily indicates the problem of humanity's willingness to see itself as apart from nature. If a tree falls in the forest, somebody needs to be there with a microphone and a recorder.

Notes

1 Physicists have increasingly had to come to terms with a blurring of the lines between the objective "out there" and the subjective consciousness brought about by current thought in quantum mechanics. Recent experiments demonstrate that light, for instance, acts as a particle or as a wave based on the experimenters' expectation. This kind of experiment has forced some physicists to conclude that observation may, in fact, be somehow generative of certain aspects of reality.
2 Returning to a more philosophical mode, we might also ask, if a tree falls in the forest and a recording device captures those sound waves, does the tape recorder "hear" the sound?

References

Berkeley, George. *A Treatise Concerning the Principles of Human Knowledge*. 1710. Lippincott, 1881. Google Books. Accessed October 28, 2018.
Bernaldo de Quirós, Y.et al. "Advances in Research on the Impacts of Anti-submarine Sonar on Beaked Whales." *Proceedings of the Royal Society B* 286. 1895 (2019). https://royalsocietypublishing.org/doi/10.1098/rspb.2018.2533# Accessed January 14, 2019.
Brownell Jr., Robertet al. "Hunting Cetaceans with Sound: A Worldwide Review." *Journal of Cetacean Research and Management* 10. 1(2008): 81–88. https://digitalcomm ons.unl.edu/cgi/viewcontent.cgi?article=1086&context=usdeptcommercepub Accessed March 13, 2019.
Doolittle, Emily. "Crickets in the Concert Hall: A History of Animals in Western Music." *Trans: Revista Transcultural de Música* 12(2008). https://www.sibetrans.com/trans/articulo/94/crickets-in-the-concert-hall-a-history-of-animals-in-western-music Accessed December 18, 2018.
"Editor's Table." *The Chautauquan: Organ of the Chautauqua Literary and Scientific Circle* III.October 1882–July 1888: 543–544. Hathi Trust Digital Library. https://babel.hathitrust.org/cgi/pt?id=hvd.32044092704188 Accessed November 7, 2018.
Gallagher, Michael. "Field Recording and the Sounding of Spaces." *Environment and Planning D: Society and Space* 33. 3(2015): 560–576.
Gallagher, Tim. "The Birth of Natural Sound Recording." *Living Bird, Winter* (2015). https://www.allaboutbirds.org/living-bird-winter-2015-table-of-contents/ Accessed October 15, 2018.

McDonald, Mark A. et al. "Worldwide Decline in Tonal Frequencies of Blue Whale Songs." *Endangered Species Research* 9(2009):13–21.

Michael, David. "Toward a Dark Nature Recording." *Organised Sound* 16. 3(2011): 206–210.

Nowacek, Douglas P., Lesley H. Thorne, David W. Johnston and Peter L. Tyack. "Responses of Cetaceans to Anthropogenic Noise." *Mammal Review* 37. 2(2007): 81–115.

Public Radio International. "How Pop Music Helped Save the Whales." 2016. www.pri. org/stories/2016-03-10/how-pop-music-helped-save-whales Accessed May 19, 2019.

Simmonds, Market al. *Oceans of Noise: A WDCS Science Report.* Chippenham, UK: Whale and Dolphin Conservation Society, 2004.

6 (Re)placing the rhetoric of scale
Ecoliteracy, networked writing, and MEmorial mapping

Madison Jones

"I see the shapes I remember from maps," croons David Byrne at the beginning of "The Big Country" (1978), the final track on Talking Heads album *More Songs About Buildings and Food*. In the song, Byrne describes the experience of looking out of an airplane window and feeling abject disgust at the scene below. From such a height, Byrne looks down on the world with an elevated sense of self. On the surface, "The Big Country" is a rejection of rural, flyover America. What begins with childlike awe shifts in the refrain as Byrne sardonically jeers "I wouldn't live there if you paid me to." At scale, Byrne is able to distance himself from the places he sees. In many ways, the song grapples with the rhetorical problem of scale and the resulting production of anomie, derangement, nationalism, and isolation. The album as a whole contends with scale by exploring how remote-sensing technologies, specifically the Landsat satellite image mosaics, act as a *pharmakon* for the problems of scale in the American imagination. The Landsat images presented the United States at scale, with individual images of places patched together to rhetorically zoom up from the local to the level of nation.[1]

In this chapter, I discuss the problem of scale in environmental communication, specifically in the use of visualization technologies to promote ecoliteracy and communicate massive environmental issues (such as sea-level rise or climate change) to public audiences. By displaying topologies of place at scales beyond the individual and human perspective, geovisualization technologies present posthuman perspectives. However, these scalar technologies also produce discrete challenges for environmental communication. By presenting geological perspectives of deep time, digital technologies undermine human(ist) conceptions of place and environment. Rather than using geovisualization technologies to engage place as a topos, I demonstrate how Gregory L. Ulmer's concept of MEmorials, as discussed in *Electronic Monuments*, offers ways to engage places of change and catastrophe as networked, ecological, and emergent. MEmorial mapping allows writers to access what Zach Horton terms "thick ecology," engaging with sites of large-scale disaster beyond the rigid boundaries of scale. This approach "asks us to think with the scales of the planet in all of their interconnected complexity" (2019: 21). Rather than relying on Cartesian topologies, these practices engage place as a trans-scalar network. As technology unsettles Heideggerian notions of "world" based on scalar topologies, it also opens up new thresholds for considering how individuals relate to place in the boundary event of the Anthropocene.

Following Timothy Morton's (2015) new materialist analysis of the Toni Basil music video for Talking Heads' song "Crosseyed and Painless" (1980), this chapter turns to the example of *More Songs About Buildings and Food* in order to illustrate how scale functions in remote-sensing technologies which mediate environmental issues for public audiences. I argue that the album does the work of an electrate MEmorial, assembling individuals and collectives as relational networks (as opposed to topoi), and resisting scalar nationalism. In doing so, I will explore how the notion of scale, as well as scalar technologies, present fundamental rhetorical concerns for environmental literacy. While geovisualization technologies allow scientists to model large-scale environmental issues for public audiences (Richards, 2015, 2018), the rhetorical problems that scale presents stand in the way of how we encounter and imagine just environmental futures and inhabit sites of change. Through an Ulmerian methodology, I suggest other ways to map and visualize environmental disasters that undermine and traverse the rhetoric of scale.

Scale has become the focus of many interdisciplinary conversations across the humanities. In *Hyperobjects* (2013) and *Dark Ecology* (2016), ecocritic Timothy Morton describes the problem of scale as a fundamental concern for ecological thinking. In *Dark Ecology*, Morton describes the Anthropocene in terms of scale, where individuals cannot see their impacts except collectively as a species. Individual decisions, such as cranking up a car, are "statistically meaningless" on the micro-level yet geologically impactful when scaled up to the level of species. The resulting problem for humans as individuals is twofold: our individual actions feel meaningless; and global environmental problems seem insurmountable. In *Ecocriticism on the Edge: The Anthropocene as a Threshold Concept*, Timothy Clark (2015) terms this phenomenon the "derangements of scale," which he argues is one of the most pressing concerns for ecocriticism in the age of the Anthropocene. Building from Clark and others, this chapter frames "the great derangement" (Ghosh, 2016) as a rhetorical problem, specifically affecting the emerging relations between digital technologies and the scalar ecologies of place. Writing studies' extensive work over the past two decades with the locations, technologies, and ecologies of writing (Dobrin and Weisser, 2001, 2002; Reynolds, 2007; Edbauer, 2005; Keller and Weisser, 2007; Dobrin and Morey, 2009) prepares it for important interventions into thick, trans-scalar approaches to environmental literacy.

"The Big Country" highlights the ways that environmental communication is often rhetorically suspended in what composition scholar Derek Mueller (2017) has termed "middle altitude," oscillating between abjection and interconnection. Environmental problems are at once too vast and too mundane. Scale is a central rhetorical concern for communicators interested in promoting ways to meaningfully inhabit places of change. While new media have opened up new avenues for thinking about and writing with places, they also reify scalar metaphors for zoom and the resulting deranged relations between humans and their environments. In this chapter, I explore how Bruno Latour's concept of networks offers methodologies for place-based writing practices which function outside the bifurcated relations of zoom. Through examples of choric practices like the Ulmerian MEmorial in writing studies scholarship and in the classroom, I demonstrate ways to engage place as a network in order to connect emerging technologies and large-scale environmental exigences to the specific places of change.

Scale, zoom, and derangement

Though you may not think about it, you encounter scale every day. Whether referring to the scale in your bathroom, balancing the scales of justice, scaling a staircase, or the Great Chain of Being (*scala naturae*), scale plays a part in our sense of equilibrium and how we locate ourselves in the world. Scale (from the Latin for ladder or sequence) is also the measure through which cartographers produce ratios on maps. As we increasingly rely on smartphone applications like Google Maps and other location-based technologies for navigation, the rhetorics of scale and zoom are deeply naturalized into our sense of orientation. Technologically and metaphorically, we zoom out and in through scale to determine position in the places we inhabit. As networked writing technologies become central to our sense of place, location opens to new ways of encountering and imagining the relationships between writing and environment.

Scale and its zoom affects position writers as individuals, as members of a nation, as human, as bodies, as on-the-ground, as moments in history, as distinct, remote, separate. This produces the rift that Clark refers to as scalar derangement:

> Scale effects in relation to climate change are confusing because they take the easy, daily equations of moral and political accounting and drop into them both a zero and an infinity: the greater the number of people engaged in modern forms of consumption then the less the relative influence or responsibility of each but the worse the cumulative impact of their insignificance.
>
> (2015: 72)

In other words, mundane consumer decisions (what to eat, wear, or what mode of transportation to take) become both trivial on one scale, and of geological consequence on the other. Andrew Pilsch refers to scalar derangement as "the rhetorical problem a nonhuman rhetoric must solve" (2017: 350). Yet, while Pilsch turns to the inhuman, this chapter demonstrates that getting beyond human scales is likewise important for even humanist environmental rhetorics.

Bruno Latour's concept of actor-network theory provides useful strategies for locating rhetorics outside the abstract scalar relations of zoom. The problem, as Latour puts it in his most recent book, *Down to Earth: Politics in the New Climatic Regime*, is that "there is no Earth corresponding to the infinite horizon of the Global, but at the same time the Local is much too narrow, too shrunken, to accommodate the multiplicity of beings belonging to the terrestrial world." Networks, Latour (2018: 69) contends, allow "us to dissolve the micro- macro- distinction that has plagued social theory from its inception" (5). Instead of smaller or larger scales, networks are either longer or denser. Networks offer a means to theorize place without the problems of partitioning humans and nonhumans. Place is constituted through "the type, number and topography of connections [and] is left to the actors themselves" (1996: 5). Writing networks challenge the precise and carefully demarcated orders of magnitude from which the categories of nature/culture and human/nonhuman are bifurcated.

As scale becomes central to how we locate ourselves, the rhetorical problems zoom produces for environmental thinking likewise become a locus for ecocritical intervention. While scale has no doubt been a useful metaphor for locative technologies, it produces barriers for connecting with large-scale issues like global climate change. In his brief essay "Anti-Zoom," Latour argues that in the face of "the era known as the Anthropocene, such issues [as the problem of scale] have become increasingly urgent, since we poor humans [...] remain perplexed as to how to find our place among phenomena, which are at once immensely vaster than we are, and yet subject to our affect" (2017: 93). While the combination of photography and cartographic technologies presents zoom in digital maps as a natural means of orienting ourselves—in relation to places, regions, nations, and the entire planet—Latour demonstrates that "levels of reality do not nestle one within the other like Russian dolls" (94). Against these models, Latour proposes a networked methodology which relies on place-based approaches that at once factor the entangled relations of multiple places at multiple scales. These networks are neither local nor global, and tracing actor-networks involves crossing through these planes in order to understand how scale rhetorically shapes our methodologies and the very objects of inquiry.

Unscaling place

In many ways, the disruptions that emerging technologies present to how we map the relations between writing and environment is nothing new. When images of the Earth from space began to circulate in the late 1960s, notions of the Earth as a large-scale ecosystem arose in both scientific and public thinking. As ecosystems ecologists like Howard T. Odum began trophic mapping and modeling at the level of atmosphere and in local environments, an American environmental movement took root. Visualization technologies became increasingly important for representing the large-scale environmental concerns to the public. In *Losing Earth: A Recent History*, Nathaniel Rich writes that with visualizations of the ozone hole, "though it was no more visible than global warming, ordinary people could be made to see it. They could watch it gestate on videotape" (2019: 112). From communicating the trophic scales of ecosystems to modeling the ozone hole, visualization technologies played a major role in how publics placed themselves within ecologies and environments.

The ecocritic Lee Rozelle refers to aesthetic scale effects in environmental literacy as the "ecosublime." Working from the ancient concept of the sublime, Rozelle explores the way that the ecosublime can foster environmental literacy through feelings of awe and terror that accompany technological visualizations of environmental disasters (Rozelle, 2006). Reading the Total Ozone Mapping Spectrometer (TOMS) visualizations of the ozone hole, Rozelle demonstrates how technologies foster ecosublimity by mediating vast or otherwise invisible environmental issues. These technologies make visible phenomena which are rendered invisible either by their vast size, which eludes human imagination, or by the scientific and mathematical literacies required to grasp them. While geovisualization technologies, from *Earthrise* to Google Maps, have fostered a growing environmental literacy for American publics, they also reinforce anomie, apathy, and despair.

As they represent the systems of relations between individuals and collectives, these technologies rely on scale as a central metaphor for locating and constructing relationality. By presenting ecosublime issues like sea-level rise as scalable from the individual places to the level of Earth, geovisualization technologies naturalize topological means of imagining place. Traditions of place as a topology go back at least to Aristotelian models of place-based argumentation (Jones, 2018). As networks come to the fore of how place-based writing is theorized, following the rise of mobile and locative technologies, topological models of place are insufficient. Locative media interact with place in ways that are emergent, embodied, and distributed, and because of this, they precede and exceed topologies of place. For this reason, the philosopher Martin Heidegger feared that images of the Earth from space would disrupt our sense of the local and uproot humans from their homes, transforming humans' relationship with the world into a technological one (*Being and Time*; 2009: 84).

Thomas Rickert points out Heidegger's fear of the images of the Earth from space in his book *Ambient Rhetoric: The Attunements of Rhetorical Being* (2013: 214). Heidegger's fear of technology "uprooting" humans (2009: 325, quoted in Rickert n306) stems from a topological engagement with place that has troubling connections to his concept of "blood and soil" at the root of place-based racism towards those who are not "deeply rooted" in place. While Sonia Sikka demonstrates how Heidegger rejects racism built on reductive biologism (2018: 161), his theories about place enabled an anti-Semitism which associated "Jews with a lack of rootedness" (168). While Rickert bases much of his theories of ambience on Heidegger, this project turns away from these topologies, seeking other means of engaging place beyond the scalar, genealogical, and arborescent notions of rootedness. Instead, this project seeks to disrupt topological thinking through trans-scalar rhetorics of place.

As cartographic technologies mediate human relationships with place, zoomable scale has become a central tenet of what ecocritic Lawrence Buell (1995) has called "the environmental imagination," as well as how place has been traditionally defined in human geography, ecosystems ecology, and writing studies. The problem for environmental writers is, as Buell writes about Thoreau's *Walden*, that defining place through scale means that "nothing, however small, is small" (1995, 305). As Buell and others point out (see also Jarrett, 2008), Thoreau is one potential origin point for an American environmental writing tradition that connects emerging technology (in that case, trains) to new ways of thinking about ecology and place. While trains pose a scalar and temporal disruption to *Walden*, this essay builds from Michael Jarrett's argument that "Thoreau's ideas about listening to the railroad provide us with a 'relay' (or heuristic) for imaging place in electracy." Technologies present scalar disruptions, but these points of rupture are important sites for locating trans-scalar environmental thinking. Before turning to Ulmer's electrate MEmorial methodology, it is necessary to first understand why writing studies scholars should attend to the rhetorical problems of scale.

One of the most striking elements of the *Earthrise* photograph is its eco-sublime presentation of scale. As we look at *Earthrise*, we can imagine zooming up from our locale to the atmosphere and onward to the furthest reaches of the human imagination. In this way, scale does uproot us, but what zooms up also zooms down, connecting us to place. As scalar technologies increasingly augment the way we locate ourselves, the problems scale presents to place-based thinking come to the fore, but these problems reveal the deeper problems that place-as-topology, like those that Heidegger had in mind, produce for location-based communication practices. In an era defined by massive-scale environmental issues, this project turns to emerging technologies and ecological methodologies to move beyond topologies and to understand the relational and emergent elements of place as a network.

Mapping ecoliteracy and electrate ecocomposition

In recent years, writing studies scholars have begun to explore how locative media transforms publics (Brown and Rivers, 2013), pushes students beyond traditional classroom spaces (Rivers, 2016), and moves writing interfaces outside the desktop (Tinnell, 2015). At the same time, communication scholars have begun to explore the role of digital technologies in communicating complex environmental concerns to the public through virtual reality (Ahn et al., 2016) and geovisualization technologies (Richards, 2015, 2018). As mobile technologies like augmented reality increasingly foster engagements between the material environment and digital imaging (Greene, 2017), a public understanding of technological mediation has become central to not just coding literacy (as Vee, 2017 suggests) but also literacies of environment and place (Dobrin and Morey, 2009). These scholars are responding in various ways to a tradition of ecocriticism and writing studies scholarship that views digital technologies as a disruption for environmental literacy.

For example, in Matthew Ortoleva's "Let's Not Forget Ecological Literacy" he critiques Dobrin and Weisser's definition of ecocomposition because it "expands beyond material environments to imagined, social, and cyber environments as well and, as theorized, not always in a manner concerned with the material natural world" (2013: 69). Like Rozelle's ecosublime, Dobrin and Weisser's ecocomposition studies ecologies comprise not only the ecosphere associated with the sign of "Nature," but also the semiosphere and the technologies which mediate contact between material nature and human culture. Ortoleva distrusts the semiotic aspects of ecocomposition, which understands nature as a socially constructed sign, studies the environment as what Latour terms a natureculture, and views the relationship between digital technologies and ecoliteracy as dynamic and even productive. Ortoleva privileges ecoliteracy over ecocomposition, but his urge to separate virtual and digital writing environments (under the umbrella of ecocomposition) from material ones in his definition of environmental literacy is problematic. Such a model cleaves the dialogical relationship between writer and text, self and place. Literacy and participation are dialogic processes. As I have argued elsewhere, the tendency to separate human writers from the environments through which (and as part of which) they write stems from topological and subject-driven ways of imagining place (Jones, 2018).

Rather than thinking of environments as topics to be written about, I turn to Ulmer's (1994) concept of electracy, a term he invents to describe how digital technologies are transforming literacy, to argue that environments are emergent parts of writing which are written with/in networks that cross digital and material environments. Ulmer favors the term electracy over digital literacy because he wants to emphasize the ontological change brought on by new writing apparati, a shift he compares to the move from orality to literacy. To Ulmer, the term "digital literacy" is the contemporary equivalent of terming literacy "written orality" or science "nature magic" (Ulmer, quoted in Jones and Greene, 2017) Rather than remediate our understanding of literacy, Ulmer argues that we need a new term to describe the shift to digital media. While Ulmer's macroscopic approach to the relationship between apparatus theory and literacy produces a broad and singular narrative for understanding this shift,[2] his theories are an important influence on networked approaches to using digital technology for environmental communication.

Ortoleva's fear that notions of digital ecology will render "ecology as a metaphor with no real connection to the natural world, [removing] it from the ecological exigence currently affecting all levels of the biosphere" (2013: 69) mirrors Heideggerian understandings of world and rootedness as part of value systems connecting people, place, and literacy. Electrate practices understand technological intervention as a point of rupture, yes, but it is a productive disruption, leading to new ontological engagements with networked ecologies. While Ortoleva argues that environmental literacy is a more useful concept than ecocomposition, his bifurcated model of (human) words and (natural) world is less useful for understanding the role of technology in mediating the rhetorical problems of scale. These concerns are what Rob Nixon (2013) terms "slow violence," referring to the disproportionate ways environmental destruction affects those who are already socially, economically, and politically disempowered. These larger degrees of impact exacerbate threats already facing marginalized and disenfranchised groups. While Ortoleva considers ecological literacy as a "foundation for literate acts that seek to address the human relationship to the natural world," these models are insufficient for the large-scale problems presented by the Anthropocene. His ecological literacy focuses on humans and places environmental issues on human scales, and the rhetoric which frames these methodologies contributes to the derangements of scale and naturalizes slow violence.

Beyond these narrow definitions of environmental literacy, this chapter seeks to understand the relationship between visualization technologies and ecoliteracy as what Annette Vee terms a "platform literacy," that is, "a literacy we can build other activities and knowledge on" (2017: 3). Just as Vee asks how we can "understand the ways that computer programming is changing our practices and means of communication" (4), so this chapter examines the role of visual and digital literacies in posthuman ecoliteracy and ecocomposition. Ecoliteracy is a platform for understanding how other social justice issues are deeply enmeshed in the relations that form environments and the technologies through which we visualize those relations.

Flyover rhetoric

Like "The Big Country," writing studies is beginning to recognize the scalar problems presented by visualization technologies. Derek Mueller's (2017) *Network Sense: Methods for Visualizing a Discipline* deals with the concept of scale in relation to networks and writing studies scholarship. Mueller takes a Latourian perspective in order to understand digital networks from a "planeury" perspective, which he sets in opposition to Michel de Certeau's use of the *flaneur* concept in his influential theory of place:

> Planeury—as an everyday practice—combines the capacity of screens as digital viewports to quickly switch between the zoomed-in and the zoomed-out, to explore by these variations the specific and the general as interdependent, and to foreground the synecdochal (or part–whole) quality of visualization methods, throughout which scale is a foundational consideration.
>
> (1988: 56)

By oscillating between scales, Mueller argues that "aspects of disciplinary formation become evident at different orders of magnitude" (2017: 8). Mueller convincingly demonstrates that, "although they have been tremendously important, hyper-local, narrative-based accounts of disciplinary emergence operate more powerfully when paired with data-based accounts" (8). While Mueller suggests using both local and global perspectives to inform a networked methodology at the "aerial, middle-minded" level, his methodology leads to rhetorical derangement by placing considerations squarely on a human scale. Rather than vacillate between local and global, I argue that a networks approach, as defined by Latour, undercuts these distinctions.

The patchwork mosaic cover of *More Songs About Buildings and Food* plays with the notion of scalar nationalism. At the level of flyover, scalar nationalism becomes a formidable rhetorical problem for place-based thinking. In *The Robotic Imaginary: The Human and the Price of Dehumanized Labor*, Jennifer Rhee discusses flyover through "the scale of drone technology and policy, in which humans are swallowed up by the scale of mapmaking and individual deaths are obscured and abstracted, reduced to pins marking sites of drone strikes" (2018: 145). Because drones present the world as "not scaled to the human, but to the dehumanized, the scale at which individuals are largely indistinguishable from one another and look more like insects" (161), these technologies blur human perspectives which might otherwise produce identification with the other in their human operators. These ways of seeing are bound up in "the abject failure of the satellite image to represent the human face of drone victims, [which] gives pause and highlights the ways that drone vision itself is incompatible with the human" (161). For this reason, human ethics are one of many important considerations. Rather than confront scalar derangement through a fully inhuman rhetoric, as Pilsch describes, human perspectives must be part of the networks of considerations that unfold in these ecologies.

To return to the example of "The Big Country," Byrne's speaker exemplifies this planeury perspective and the sense of derangement it produces. Byrne wrote "The Big Country" while flying from Toronto to New York in the midst of a growing public awareness of large-scale environmental disasters throughout the U.S. Looking out the window of the airplane, Byrne offers a perspective of isolation, repulsion, and condescension toward flyover America. The album responds to the release of the 1974 Landsat 1 satellite images (Fig. 6.1) which were used to produce the 1976 *Portrait USA* photomosaic (Fig 6.2). In what follows, I will demonstrate how Talking Heads present a complex understanding of how these images would produce scalar disruptions to a sense of place, which makes sense, given that they were art school students at Rhode Island School of Design before they were a band. Building from this example, I demonstrate how this can inform a networks approach to place-based writing which counteracts the derangements of scale.

Figure 6.1 The first Landsat photomosaic of the contiguous U.S. created in 1974
         from 595 black-and-white images taken at the same altitude and angle.
Courtesy of NASA.

Figure 6.2 The 1976 photomosaic of the contiguous U.S. created by colorizing the
         Landsat images for *National Geographic*, titled "Portrait U.S.A."
Courtesy of NASA.

In the years following the *Earthrise* photograph, before the Nimbus 7
began recording data about the Earth's atmosphere, the Landsat satellites
were recording and publishing images of the Earth's surface for the first
time. These false-color composite images, like the one in Fig. 6.1, were
assembled into the first color mosaics of the United States. The *Portrait USA*

image (Fig. 6.2) contains 532 images painstakingly assembled into a map. When the map was published in *National Geographic* in 1976, they added what they called a pseudo-natural color composite.

Two years after *Portrait USA* was published in *National Geographic*, Talking Heads released *More Songs About Buildings and Food*, with the back cover featuring a version of the *Portrait USA* map but with turquoise, red, yellow, brown, and black, as if to emphasize the image as a visualization, a construction rather than a "real" image. The songs on the album, most explicitly "The Big Country," extend these lines of flight.

Through its multimodal blend of visual and auditory technologies, the album undermines Cartesian distinctions of mind/body, body/world, individual/collective, and place/world drawn (in part) by technologies of scale. The album responds to Landsat's remote-sensing technologies and considers how individuals scale to the level of national disasters.

While the album as a whole suggests a mosaic, networked approach to understanding the relationships between individuals and collectives, the song "The Big Country" demonstrates the problems with Mueller's planeury methodology for encountering scale. In the song, the higher-scale perspective from the airplane window produces a rhetorical position of superiority, allowing Byrne to literally *look down* on the distant Earth below, condescendingly embodying what Kenneth Burke called the "fantastic coefficient of power" found in transportation technologies which present the "fundamental *moral* problem [that] as individuals we are easily tempted to mistake these mechanical powers for our very own" (1973: 269). Byrne mockingly describes a bird's-eye view of the landscape that separates and distances him from the scene of disaster unfolding below. As such, the album demonstrates the rhetorical problems of the planeury perspective: vacillating between zoomed-out and zoomed-in reinforces scalar nationalism and derangement by naturalizing the drone's-eye-view that Rhee critiques, and fostering anomie by positioning individuals as distant, remote, and separate from the places which they look down on.

By the end of the song, Byrne is "tired of looking out the window of the airplane" and says "I'm tired of traveling. I want to be somewhere." Scale offers exhausting potentials for environmental thinking to confront geological impacts as the consequences of mundane actions. Zoom deranges our ability to inhabit sites of change, leading to anomie, apathy, and despair in the face of global climate change. In similar fashion, Richard Miller's 2005 *Writing at the End of the World* posed important questions about the function and purpose of writing in the dark times following disasters like Chernobyl, 9/11, and Columbine. Namely, he asks, "Why bother with reading and writing when the world is so obviously going to hell?" (16) Miller describes the lure of "apocalyptic visions, which both create and confirm a sense that despair is the only rational response to the world we have before us" (ix) and wonders if it is "possible to produce writing that generates a greater sense of connection to the world and its inhabitants" (25). Following Miller's path, I conclude by exploring a method akin to his "institutional autobiography" (136) to generate these connections: locating ourselves in large-scale disasters, connecting global to local and virtual to material, and discovering meaning in the dark times we face.

MEmorial mapping

The cover image of *More Songs About Buildings and Food* features a photomosaic of the band using 532 polaroids, replicating the Landsat flyover images of the United States. Through a distorted collage, these images connect a fragmented sense of self and collective, as if trying to piece disparate scales back together. The album was released July 1978, one month before President Carter declared a State of Emergency at the Love Canal neighborhood in Niagara Falls, NY, an event which played a major part in the creation of the Superfund list. Through its visual and ambient rhetorics, the album functions as a MEmorial confronting the derangements presented by the Landsat photographs and a growing unease toward the environmental disasters unfolding across flyover America. By putting the pieces, not together, but in agonism with one another, the album suggests networked and trans-scalar ways of imagining place.

Gregory L. Ulmer develops the concept of the MEmorial in *Electronic Monuments* as a digital writing practice which bridges the scalar divide between individual and collective in problems occurring at the level of nations and populations. MEmorials connect the individual writer (thus the ME being capitalized) to an "event of loss whose mourning helps define a community" with the ultimate goal of improving the world, or "if not to improve the world, then to understand in what way the human world is irreparable" (2005: xxxiii). Through MEmorials, writers work with digital writing environments while engaging large-scale problems beyond the rhetoric of derangement. Instead of selecting traditional tragedies for memorials, MEmorials consider the abject sacrifices made on behalf of cultural values. From gun violence to car accidents, Ulmer explores the ways that value systems enable and benefit from large-scale, national disasters. Rather than treat these problems as tragedy, which implies that they are random events, Ulmer reframes these events as abject sacrifices which are made on behalf of the values of a nation or group.

By composing MEmorials, writers orient themselves with large-scale disasters, and in doing so they call the values of a society into question. If the cost of a sacrifice is too great for the value it supports, Ulmer argues, we must then work to change that value. Ulmer's MEmorial is one networked writing practice that can counteract scalar derangement. This chapter is focused on scalar derangement in environmental thinking, but MEmorials serve to address a relationality between writer and place in ways which serve to counteract the derangement of a host of different large-scale problems. While it is beyond the scope to discuss the long history of MEmorial writing, many have discussed this subject (Brooks and Anfinson, 2009; Mauer, 1996; Mauer and Veneck, n.d.). In recent years, with a rising awareness of the vast problems we face and with the growing popularity of digital writing technologies, MEmorials have gained popularity in writing studies scholarship.

Most notably, Sean Morey's webtext "The Roadkill Tollbooth" (2017) uses electrate ecocomposition to understand the author's relationship to the BP oil spill through his personal connection to the Florida Keys. In his most recent book, Morey builds from this project to create what he calls "a map of how different identities of Key West and the Florida Keys swirl, break, mix, and network, particularly, in me" and looking "inward [only] to look outward, toward the BP oil spill and its relationship to the Keys" (2019: 25). These MEmorial projects suggest the connections between "the invention of driving" and "the remote effects created by the accidents related to this behavior" which puts "into relation one value (the right to drive) with the sacrifice needed to support that value (victims of the oil spill)." Like Byrne, Morey navigates the derangements of scale by compositing digital and narrative maps which cross scales and engage networked methodologies.

Following Ulmer and Morey, others have recently used MEmorials to negotiate who decides "official" narratives of places, such as the history of Clemson University's relationship to slavery (O'Brien et al., 2016); the connections between fossil fuel dependence, urban design, and cyclist deaths (Jones and Greene, 2017); the place of death at Walt Disney world in Orlando, FL (Crider and Anderson, 2019). These authors follow Ulmer's challenge to "promote what already exists but to produce a new kind of tourist destination" (2005: 4). For the purposes of ecoliteracy, MEmorials provide important opportunities to connect digital writing practices to what Phaedra Pezzullo calls "toxic tourism" which names relations between polluted sites and tourism (2007: 3). Through MEmorials, writers draw attention to sites of tourist *repulsion* to reorient the consumptive behavior of the contemporary tourist to something more akin to the ancient Greek practice of solonism, named for Solon, who Ulmer calls the first tourist.

MEmorials, as demonstrated in these examples, underwrite the derangements of scale by resisting the urge to view everything in relation to one scale (which is often the human scale) or to resort to oscillating between different scales in order to triangulate a location between scales (which is often a human position). Instead, MEmorials engage networks in ways that illustrate transscalar approaches to writing with/in environments and counteract the deranged subjectivities that form from viewing the world only in relation to human scales. These approaches are essential to promoting environmental literacy in the coming decades. The climate crisis we currently face doesn't scale, at least not in the simple way of previous catastrophes like the ozone hole. While the ozone hole scaled neatly from individual consumer up to the level of atmosphere, climate change is dispersed in terms of scale and time. As such, digital technologies and networked methodologies are increasingly important for communicating these issues.

Toward ground truth (conclusion)

In remote-sensing terms, ground truth refers to data collected on the ground. It is used to implement and connect data taken at a distance to local realities. The term refers to how a location exists on-the-ground, as opposed to in the abstract. Ground truth provides an excellent metaphor for thinking about how specific communities respond to the networked impacts of a changing world. The sleeve notes of *More Songs About Buildings and Food* describe the practical applications of Landsat photography, ranging from assessing environmental disasters, to observing effects of strip mining and monitoring pollution, to natural resource management. Remote-sensing technologies can be used for a multitude of purposes, from environmental protection to ecological devastation.

Today, mapping technologies enable prospects for mountain-top removal, but they can also help visualize the impacts of these practices. Through a balance of scalar and networked approaches to mapping, we can trace the networks of change faced by communities and forge a path forward together. Through localization, emerging technologies can help communities recognize and adapt to the large-scale changes they face with climate change. Emerging technologies provide new ways of looking at our place on the Earth and visualizing our impact on it, a cultural moment that I argue rivals the first photographs of the Earth from space. Through networked writing methodologies, we can see rich and complex connections between ourselves, our values, and the large-scale impacts we are collectively and individually producing. The question is, do we want to look?

Notes

1 I would like to thank the editors, Sidney I. Dobrin and Sean Morey, for their guidance and feedback on this chapter, as well as Charlie Sterchi, Lee Rozelle, Jacob Greene, and Shannon Butts, who read and discussed early drafts and ideas.
2 John Tinnell (2015) contrasts Ulmer's grammatology with Bernard Steigler, arguing that "Steigler's emphasis on grammatization processes offers a nomadic way to traverse minor technocultural shifts, and his microlevel method of inquiry seems to address a degree of fluidity and heterogeneity that may elude applications of Ulmer's macro-level lens" (137). While this is likely the case, Ulmer's models are still useful for framing the overlapping exigencies of contemporary technological and ecological issues, and his work has been highly influential on many writing studies scholars who take a choric approach to place, such as Dobrin, Rickert, Tinnell, Jeff Rice, Jacob Greene, and Caddie Alford, to name but a few.

References

Ahn, S.J., J. Bostick, E. Ogle, K. Nowak, K. McGillicuddy, and J.N. Bailenson. "Experiencing Nature: Embodying Animals in Immersive Virtual Environments Increases Inclusion of Nature in Self and Involvement with Nature." *Journal of Computer-Mediated Communication* 21. 6(2016): 399–419.

Brooks, Kevin and Aaron Anfinson. "Exploring Post-critical Composition: MEmorials for Afghanistan and the Lost Boys of Sudan." *Computers and Composition* 26(2009): 78–91.

Brown, James Jr. and Nathaniel Rivers. "Composing the Carpenter's Workshop." *O-Zone: A Journal of Object-Oriented Studies* 1. 1(2013): 27–36.

Buell, Lawrence. *The Environmental Imagination Thoreau, Nature Writing, and the Formation of American Culture.* Cambridge, MA: Harvard University Press, 1995.

Burke, Kenneth. "The Rhetorical Situation." *Communication: Ethical and Moral Issues.* Ed. L. Thayer. London: Gordon and Breach, 1973. 263–275.

de Certeau, Michel. *The Practice of Everyday Life.* Berkeley, CA: University of California Press, 1988.

Clark, Timothy. *Ecocriticism on the Edge: The Anthropocene as a Threshold Concept.* London: Bloomsbury, 2015.

Crider, Jason and Kenny Anderson. "Disney Death Tour: Monumentality, Augmented Reality, and Digital Rhetoric." *Kairos: A Journal of Rhetoric, Technology, and Pedagogy* 23. 2(2019). http://kairos.technorhetoric.net/23.2/topoi/crider-anderson/index.html

Dobrin, Sidney I. "Breaking Ground in Ecocomposition: Exploring Relationships between Discourse and Environment." *College English* 64. 5(2002); 566–589.

Dobrin, Sidney I. and Sean Morey. *Ecosee: Image, Rhetoric, Nature.* New York: State Univesity of New York Press, 2009.

Dobrin, Sidney I. and Christian R. Weisser. *Ecocomposition: Theoretical and Pedagogical Approaches.* New York: State Univesity of New York Press, 2001.

Dobrin, Sidney I. and Christian Weisser. *Natural Discourse: Toward Ecocomposition.* Albany, NY: State University of New York Press, 2002.

Edbauer, Jenny. "Unframing Models of Public Distribution: From Rhetorical Situation to Rhetorical Ecologies." *Rhetoric Society Quarterly* 35. 4(2005).

Ghosh, Amitav. *The Great Derangement: Climate Change and the Unthinkable.* Chicago, IL: University of Chicago Press, 2016.

Greene, Jacob. "From Augmentation to Articulation: (Hyper)linking the Locations of Public Writing." *Enculturation* 24. 1(2017). http://enculturation.net/from_augmentation_to_articulation

Heidegger, Martin. *The Heidegger Reader.* Gunter Figal, Ed., Jerome Veith, Trans. Bloomington, IN: Indiana University Press, 2009.

Horton, Zach. "The Trans-Scalar Challenge of Ecology." *ISLE: Interdisciplinary Studies in Literature and Environment* 26. 1(2019): 5–26.

Jarrett, Michael. "Walden + Railroad + Sound." *Rhizomes* 18(2008). http://www.rhizomes.net/issue18/jarrett/index.html

Jones, Madison. "Writing Conditions: The Premises of Ecocomposition." *Enculturation* 26(2018). http://enculturation.net/writing-conditions

Jones, Madison and Jacob Greene. "Augmented Vélorutionaries: Digital rhetoric, Memorials, and Public Discourse." *Kairos: A Journal of Rhetoric, Technology, and Pedagogy* 22. 1(2017). http://kairos.technorhetoric.net/22.1/topoi/jones-greene/index.html

Keller, Christopher J. and Christian R. Weisser. *The Locations of Composition.* New York: State Univesity of New York Press, 2007.

Latour, Bruno. "On actor–network theory. A few clarifications plus more than a few complications." *Soziale Welt* 47(1996): 369–381.

Latour, Bruno. "Anti-Zoom." *Scale in Literature and Culture.* Eds. Michael Tavel Clarke and David Wittenberg. Basingstoke, UK: Palgrave Macmillan, 2017. 93–101.

Latour, Bruno. *Down to Earth: Politics in the New Climatic Regime.* 1st edn. Cambridge, UK and Medford, MA: Polity, 2018.

Mauer, Barry J. "Electronic Monumentality." *Kairos: A Journal of Rhetoric, Technology, and Pedagogy* 1. 3(1996). http://kairos.technorhetoric.net/1.3/binder2.html?coverweb/Mauer/kairos.html

Mauer, Barry J. and John Veneck. *Making Repulsive Monuments. Textshop Experiments,* Vol. 2. http://textshopexperiments.org/textshop02/making-repulsive-monuments

Miller, Richard E. *Writing at the End of the World.* Pittsburgh, PA: University of Pittsburgh Press, 2005.

Morey, Sean. "Deepwater Horizon Roadkill Tollbooth." *Kairos: A Journal of Rhetoric, Technology, and Pedagogy* 21. 2(2017). http://kairos.technorhetoric.net/21.2/topoi/morey/index.html

Morey, Sean. *Network of Bones: Conjuring Key West and the Florida Keys.* College Station, TX: Texas A&M University Press, 2019.

Morton, Timothy. *Hyperobjects: Philosophy and Ecology After the End of the World.* Minneapolis, MN: University of Minnesota Press, 2013.

Morton, Timothy. "They Are Here." *The Nonhuman Turn.* Richard Grusin, Ed. Minneapolis, MN: University of Minnesota Press, 2015.

Morton, Timothy. *Dark Ecology: For a Logic of Future Coexistence.* New York: Columbia University Press, 2016.

Mueller, Derek. *Network Sense: Methods for Visualizing a Discipline.* Boulder, CO: University Press of Colorado, 2017.

Nixon, Rob. *Slow Violence and the Environmentalism of the Poor.* Cambridge, MA: Harvard University Press, 2013.

O'Brien, April, Brian Gaines, Stephen J. Quigley and Eric James Stephens. "Legacies of Fort Hill." *Textshop Experiments* 2(Winter 2016).

Ortoleva, Matthew. "Let's Not Forget Ecological Literacy." *Literacy in Composition Studies* 1. 2(2013). http://licsjournal.org/OJS/index.php/LiCS/article/view/25/27

Pezzullo, Phaedra. *Toxic Tourism Rhetorics of Pollution, Travel, and Environmental Justice.* Tuscaloosa, AL:University of Alabama Press, 2007.

Pilsch, Andrew. "Invoking Darkness: Skotison, Scalar Derangement, and Inhuman Rhetoric." *Philosophy & Rhetoric* 50. 3(2017): 336–355.

Reynolds, Nedra. *Geographies of Writing: Inhabiting Places and Encountering Difference.* Carbondale, IL: Southern Illinois University Press, 2007

Rhee, Jennifer. *The Robotic Imaginary The Human and the Price of Dehumanized Labor.* Minneapolis, MN: University of Minnesota Press, 2018.

Rich, Nathaniel. *Losing Earth: A Recent History.* New York: MCD Books, 2019.

Rickert, Thomas. *Ambient Rhetoric: The Attunements of Rhetorical Being.* Pittsburgh, PA: University of Pittsburgh Press, 2013.

Richards, Dan . "Testing the Waters: Local Users, Sea Level Rise, and the Productive Usability of Interactive Geovisualizations."*Communication Design Quarterly* 3. 3(2015):25–29.

Richards, Dan . "Not a cape, but a life preserver: The importance of designer localization in interactive sea level rise viewers."*Communication Design Quarterly* 6. 2(2018):57–69.

Rivers, Nathaniel A. "Geocomposition in Public Rhetoric and Writing Pedagogy." *College Composition and Communication* 67. 4(2016): 576–606.

Rozelle, Lee. *Ecosublime: Environmental Awe and Terror from New World to Oddworld.* Tuscaloosa, AL: University of Alabama Press, 2006.

Sikka, Sonia. *Heidegger, Morality and Politics: Questioning the Shepherd of Being*. Cambridge, UK: Cambridge University Press, 2018.

Talking Heads, "The Big Country." *More Songs About Buildings and Food*, Sire Records, 1978.

Tinnell, John. "Grammatization: Bernard Stiegler's Theory of Writing and Technology." *Computers and Composition* 37. 1(2015): 132–146.

Ulmer, Gregory L. *Heuretics: The Logic of Invention*. Baltimore, MD: Johns Hopkins University Press, 1994.

Ulmer, Gregory. *Electronic Monuments*. Minneapolis, MN: University of Minnesota Press, 2005.

Vee, Annette. *Coding Literacy: How Computer Programming is Changing Writing*. Cambridge, MA: MIT Press, 2017.

7   Imagining the Eastern Garbage Patch

Ocean plastics as a problem of representation and scale

Dan Brayton

Marine plastics reveal the human capacity to do immense ecological harm almost by accident. Useful in everyday life, plastic items, from empty water bottles to used toothbrushes, become insidious interlopers when we eject them into waste streams that flow, eventually, into the global ocean. An unfathomable quantity of plastic waste ends up at sea, where, unlike biodegradable waste, it fragments, disperses, and remains, year after year, at or near the surface. Myriad species of phytoplankton and zooplankton mass at the sea's surface, swept by currents that send out eddies as they move past on their immense oceanic gyres—and so do plastics. By now the staggering scale and insidious effects of this debris are widely known to the public. Schoolchildren are aware that nylon fishing nets trap marine mammals; that dolphins starve, their beaks wrapped shut by skeins of nylon, polypropylene, or dacron; that seals choke on polystyrene; and that sea turtles drown in miles-long monofilament fishing lines. Some of these destructive items were jettisoned into the sea directly, while some made their way there from the land. Some items, such as longlines and gillnets, were designed to plunder the ocean and keep on fishing even when lost or damaged, entangling marine animals of all kinds. In the regions known as the convergence zones of the world's oceans, this detritus grows denser—in terms of its sheer quantity—and swirls in a vast collection, mostly invisible, of floating micro-plastics.

Marine scientists continually advance our understanding of plastic debris in studies published in top journals, such as *Science* and *Nature*, while pundits seek feel-good stories about cleanup efforts that are either ill-conceived, ill fated, or both. Physical oceanographers map the pathways of the great oceanic gyres in rubber duckies; microbial ecologists discover ecosystems on floating debris; marine biologists pursue the effects of plastics in the food web; health scientists examine the effects of plastic accumulation on human populations. Physical oceanographers, such as Kara Lavender Law and Curtis Ebbesmeyer, have attempted to demystify popular conceptions, such as the notion of the so-called garbage patches as Texas- or Alaska-sized rafts stretching from Hawaii to the Philippines. As they point out, the sea's surface in these regions reveals little of the devastation seen in photos of seals wrapped in nylon nets or six-pack rings. Empirical science, no matter how rigorous, can only go so far in altering popular misconceptions. The dissemination of new science on ocean plastics inevitably emphasizes one or two aspects at the expense of others equally significant. Yet when it comes to the transformation of data about marine plastic debris into cultural production—into stories—a great deal is often left behind.

Amateur journalists such as Charles Moore and Donovan Hohn, writing for non-specialists, have described the specificity and scale of ocean plastics in descriptions of sea voyages through the garbage patches. Moore (2003, 2011) led the way in publicizing ocean plastics, capturing the public imagination with vivid first-person descriptions of sailing through immense areas of the North Pacific covered in plastic trash. His accounts rely on first-person narrations of close encounters at sea, employing eye-witness rhetorical strategies that tackle the hyper-object on the somatic scale of a human spectator in a sea of debris. The presence of a narrative persona who encounters and describes the perceivable dimensions of ocean plastics animates the most effective narratives of marine pollution, yet images have proven, if anything, even more effective at capturing the phenomenology of ocean plastics. Photographer Chris Jordan, whose work on ocean plastics has also attracted a wide following over the past decade, employs a visual rhetoric that emphasizes the tragic fates of individual seabirds, whose corpses, littering remote beaches on the planet, become an arresting reminder of human hubris. Moore and Jordan situate their audience as witnesses to atrocities committed against pelagic avifauna whose lives hardly overlap with humanity, yet whose deaths result from human enterprise. The corpses of dead seabirds litter beaches on some of the remotest islands in the world, the Northwest Hawaiian Islands, their skeletons encircling plastic bottle caps, shreds of net, and plastic beads. The decomposing seabird corpses witnessed by Jordan, each chock-full of plastic bottle caps and other brightly colored plastic odds and ends, bear witness to the effects of pelagic plastics as a slowly-unfolding tragedy.

Images of garbage-strewn beaches on islands where humans rarely set foot remind us of the unintended costs and consequences of our prosperity. Recent studies by marine ecologists have found that 100 percent of Pacific albatross sampled had measurable amounts of plastics in their bodies, yet the American public has until recently remained largely ignorant of these microplastics. Out of sight, out of mind, like the ocean itself, so taken for granted by humans, who spend our lives almost entirely on shore. Each dead albatross makes each of us—like Coleridge's Ancient Mariner—an unintentional transgressor. Objects invisible to the naked eye can seem to have no history, yet it is increasingly apparent that there is a massive human dimension to the ecological history of the world's oceans, and that part of this history is written in copolymers.

By now the images of marine life choked by six-pack rings or nylon netting have captured public attention to such an extent that the cultural imaginary of plastic waste has galvanized cleanup campaigns of all kinds, to little effect. Yet the growing public visibility of marine plastic debris can delude as well as enlighten, for images and sound bites teach us little or nothing about the extent of the problem. What and where, exactly, are the so-called garbage patches, and how are they generated? What are their effects on marine and avian life? What are their effects on humans? How is climate change affecting these effects, if at all? Such basic questions arise when science and scholarship encounter the kind of phenomenon described by eco-theorist Timothy Morton (2013) as a hyperobject, a phenomenon so immense in scale and dispersed over time and space as to defy conventional modes of understanding. Climate change, famously, can be understood as a hyperobject; so can ocean plastics. The reality of pelagic plastics is so immense a biogeophysical phenomenon—the signature stratum of the Anthropocene—as to defy most technologies of representation and epistemologies of scale. Like atmospheric carbon, plastic debris is distributed on a planetary scale (the garbage patches are just regions of high concentration) and affects the biosphere in complex and still-uncertain ways. Given the vastness and evolving nature of this phenomenon, it is no wonder that artists and activists have taken diverse approaches to describing its features and effects.

The arts and the humanities have much to contribute to the natural sciences in assessing the significance of ocean plastics, for to make the vastness and complexity of the phenomenon meaningful on a human scale they must enter our cultural narrative in compelling forms. This chapter makes a case for the humanities in the study of ocean plastics by approaching the topic through the lens of narrative criticism, as I recount a sea voyage through the North Pacific Subtropical Gyre, home to the notorious concentration of ocean plastics known as the Great Garbage Patch (or the Eastern Garbage Patch). In the July of 2007 I joined the *SSV Robert C. Seamans*, a modified steel brigantine owned and operated by Sea Education Association of Woods Hole, Massachusetts, in Honolulu as one of two teaching faculty on board (SSV stands for *Sailing School Vessel*, a category created by the US Coast Guard for Sea Education Association vessels). On its yearly round of the Pacific, the *Seamans* hosts college students enrolled in Sea Semester in batches of twenty to twenty-five, which generally involves a shore component and an offshore component. On board our trip were twenty-seven American college students from institutions around the country, and a professional crew consisting of a captain, first, second, and third mates, an engineer and assistant engineer, two deckhands, three assistant scientists, a cook, and two academics—an oceanographer and a humanist. Although I had spent most of my summers up to that point sailing on saltwater, I had never crossed an ocean under sail. My students worked hand-in-hand—often literally, as we hauled on lines and sifted data samples together—with a professional crew of twelve. Our cruise track lay between the one of the most isolated archipelagoes in the world, the Hawaiian Islands, and the North American continent. In just under five weeks we sailed to San Francisco at an average of about five nautical miles per hour. What follows is a narrative of that voyage.

21° 09' North, 157° 32' West

Night falls in the tropics like a curtain dropping in a theater. From the quarterdeck of the brigantine *Robert C. Seamans* the south coast of Oahu looms in the brief gloaming over a cobalt sea. Two fathoms beneath my feet, shreds of polypropylene fishing net drift past on the surface of the North Pacific. A shearwater slices past, soaring the ridges of the groundswell in search of food. Seabirds are this planet's greatest sailors, their lives suspended at the interface of the fluid media of air and water. For millennia sailors have identified with seabirds, seeing in them companions, sacred symbols, and the lost souls of drowned shipmates. The Old English poem known as "The Seafarer," which mentions several species of bird in its elegiac description of exile, captures the emotional companionship of seabirds for the lonely mariner: "The cry of the gannet was all my gladness, not the laughter of men/ the mewing gull, not the sweetness of mead" (Anon., 1993). Like gannets, shearwaters are gorgeous fliers, swooping over the surface in search of surface prey. The shearwater that wings past our ship dips low towards the waves then soars into the gloaming as Oahu burns orange and fades through the shades of the rainbow to an indigo blob on a pool of molten lead. The next morning even the highest peaks of Oahu have dropped out of sight, and we have left the northernmost edge of the tropics. The sea differs qualitatively, now, from the mellow surface that it was for the past several days, its color deepening from teal to cobalt. The dominant visual feature at this stage is the horizon, a half-round edge between shades of blue. A groundswell—the long waves of the deep ocean—causes the ship to roll and plunge slightly. Beyond the bulwarks that demarcate a tiny zone of human safety an immense blue expanse arcs the horizon, traced, now and then, by the dark zigzags of pelagic seabirds working the surface in precise dances of flight—blue-footed boobies, shearwaters, sooty albatross.

From aloft in the rigging, our ship, even with its deck lab, navigational gear, lifeboats, rigging, and sails, seems like a bauble drifting through outer space. The *Seamans* is a state-of-the-art vessel rigged for oceanography and marine biology, deploying gear to sample data and assemble it in the sophisticated science lab on the foredeck. Nearly a hundred feet on deck, with a 34' bowsprit jutting from the bow and supporting a vast array of rigging that soars aloft, our ship is a marvelous mix of technologies, old and new. The nine sails aloft are made of Dacron, a modern petroleum-based synthetic fiber, while the standing rigging—fixed stays that hold the entire rig in place—is galvanized steel wrapped in tarred hemp. The running rigging, movable cordage that controls the sails, also consists of synthetic fibers. The ship's scientific equipment is appallingly expensive, ranging from various kinds of nets that we drag along the surface to gather marine organisms to a chlorophyll/temperature/density carousel that analyzes water samples at different depths, and an acoustic Doppler resonance profiler that gives a vivid picture of the currents at work beneath us.

Our Chief Scientist, oceanographer Kara Lavender Law, oversees more than a dozen different science projects being pursued by the students aboard, in addition to collecting data for her own long-term projects. Some of these projects require gazing across the surface for avian visitors. Kara is a physical oceanographer whose interest in calculating the flows of ocean currents has led her to study marine plastics. With her mathematician's mind and the relentless curiosity of a true scientist, she plans to work with our shipload of students to learn more about the Convergence Zone, specifically by gathering data about where the highest concentrations of plastic debris can be found. At least a half-dozen student research projects are devoted to the topic, but Kara oversees many more on topics ranging from seabird populations to thermohaline circulation. Unlike Kara, I oversee no research projects and gather no data. My role on board is to offer historical and cultural contexts for topics ranging from commercial fishing to traditional navigation so students can gain some sense of the historical role of human beings in the marine environment. We are a strange team, but we are equally part of the ship's crew.

Our captain, Elliot Rappaport, fortyish, quiet, and intense, has been a professional mariner since graduating from college two decades ago. An expert on navigation with a special interest in marine weather, Elliot agreed to the voyage because he was intrigued by the challenge of transiting the North Pacific High, a vast area of calm winds and flat water occupying an elliptical high-pressure zone stretching from just east of Japan to just west of California between roughly 20 and 40° North latitude. Towards the middle of the High, in an area known as the Convergence Zone, floating objects accumulate, deposited there by forces fully mapped out by physical oceanographers only recently. Our aim is to transit a slice of the Eastern Garbage Patch a few hundred miles north of the Hawaiian Islands and to gather data pertaining to the quantity of plastics near the surface. After leaving Honolulu under sail and spending the better part of a week bowling along in the easterly Trade Winds that continually blow across the archipelago, we will reach calmer waters and lighter winds the farther north we go, until we find ourselves eventually becalmed in the Doldrums in the Convergence Zone. At that point we will start the auxiliary engine, a 500-horsepower Caterpillar turbo diesel, and steam along at seven knots due North until we start to pick up the winds that prevail on the northern side of the Gyre. When we reach the mid-to-high thirties of North latitude we will pick up the Westerlies that blow across the Pacific in the temperate zone, turn right with the wind at our backs, and enjoy the sled ride to California. By then we will know a great deal more about plastic debris in the Convergence Zone.

23° 33' North, 154° 25' West

As we approach the Horse Latitudes we come upon increasingly light and fickle winds, flying every sail on board and still too slow. Unlike the tropics, where the Trades blow hard and steady, this is no sailor's paradise. The region between the Hawaiian Islands and the North American continent is no place for a sailor. The High, a nearly stationary high-pressure system dominated by light and variable winds, is an immense, watery no-man's land. Yet we are never alone out here. Our passage north and somewhat east brings us along the edge of the High, where we see boobies, shearwaters, tropicbirds, petrels, and the sooty albatross. The seabirds seem to be in no hurry as they fly past, circle back, and light in our rigging or on the surface of the water. Blue-footed boobies congregate on the yards, the perpendicular spars from which the squaresails hang like drying towels. The birds also like to leave traces of their presence in the rigging and all over the decks, much to the chagrin of our first mate Jeremy, who was trained in the Coast Guard and does not tolerate a mess. Squawking like teenagers, they waddle awkwardly on the spars high over our heads. When they take flight, they suddenly become magnificently skilled sailors of the air, their flight a reminder that we humans are just borrowing space in a region where survival is entirely contingent on the buoyancy of our ship.

Twice a day, at noon and midnight, we tow a device called a neuston net along the sea's surface for half and hour. *Neuston* is the word (from the Greek word for the sea) for the mass of tiny creatures living on the sea's surface. Since we are far offshore for most of our voyage, the creatures we collect are mostly pelagic jellyfish and barnacles, plankton, small fish, crustaceans, mollusks, jellyfish, and even insects. We also collect inorganic matter in our tows, and most of it is plastic. In our neuston net we gather hundreds of tiny pieces of plastic of unknown provenance. Each tow turns up numerous plastic shards, which the scientists onboard term microplastics. Our microplastic counts varied from a low of fourteen pieces to a high of just under 400. In a half-hour tow. Microplastics abound at or near the surface, tiny fragments of partially broken-down floating objects that hang suspended at the top of the water column with countless aquatic life forms. Sea birds ingest small plastic particles, some no larger than the head of a pin, others microscopic, as they feed on plankton, krill, and small fish. Because they come to the regions where plastics accumulate in order to fuel their migratory lifecycles, they consume plastics of all kinds in their search for calories, drawn no doubt by the bright colors of the debris. Some of this dangerous flotsam passes through their systems, but some does not, accumulating in the digestive tract and poisoning organs such as the stomach and liver.

One day we count over 300 small particles after a tow. Another day we have only six pieces of plastic in our net, the smallest quantity of the entire voyage. Most days the number is closer to 200. In the sink of the deck land, the tiny plastic pieces resemble jewelry, their bright blues and yellows and reds like colorful pebbles and grains of sand. Microplastics are produced by larger plastic objects breaking down—but only partially—and continuing to float on or near the surface, intermingled with phytoplankton, zooplankton, and larger life forms. Their copolymers take centuries, even millennia, to degrade to a level where they would not interfere with the organisms living on the surface, many of which photosynthesize in order to live. The mid-Pacific, like all deep-sea regions around the world, is a relative desert in comparison with the waters above the continental shelf that rims the coastlines of the continents. There isn't enough surface mixing—of air and water, cold water and warm water, oxygen-rich and oxygen-poor water, particles and liquid—to sustain much life in the great blue briny. But at the convergence zones there is an upward spike in biomass, the sheer quantity of living things. Yet here, too, our plastic counts spike as well. Surely this is an instance of what Bill McKibben described in a 1989 book of that title, as *The End of Nature*, for no part of the Pacific is free of floating plastic. The ocean is awash with uncountable tiny shards that record the presence of human lives thousands of miles away.

28° 11' North, 151° 03' West

This morning on dawn watch I see a sooty albatross (*Phoebetria*), with a wingspan of about seven feet, soar under our bowsprit. Approaching from the west, it drafts off the leach (leeward edge) of the mainsail, and then angles forward, checking us out. Larger and more magisterial than the shearwaters and boobies who have been our constant companions thus far, this superb pelagic giant seems at once otherworldly and familiar. An unaccommodated bird, just feather and blood and muscle and bone, entirely at home here, where our welded steel hull intrudes. How much plastic does it have lodged in its system? Will the plastics it has (unquestionably) ingested kill this animal? Will it unwittingly kill its own chicks when it returns to the nest and regurgitates the food it has captured over hundreds of square miles of open ocean? It seems the height of profanity that these beings, so innocent of humanity, should have to eat—and be killed by— garbage cast off thousands of miles away by unseen humans.

A whale suddenly spouts only half a mile to the east, and those of us standing on the quarterdeck jump and exclaim. The bioaccumulation of toxins in animals at the top of the food chain is a well-known phenomenon; less known are the effects of plastics ingested by feeding baleen whales such as the humpbacks and grays we see playing at the surface our first week out from shore.

We are aware that we are in a new place, qualitatively different from the high-energy tropics where we embarked. Wave heights are low; the surface is dull. Flotsam of all kinds floats past: torn nets, lifejackets, mooring buoys and net floats, balloons, rubber balls, buckets, crates, barrels, styrofoam coolers, and even the occasional rubber ducky. Pelagic seabirds are particularly susceptible to plastic waste, their beaks catching in six-pack yokes, fine-mesh seine nets, and the mouths of one- and two-liter plastic bottles. Plastic oil drums, polystyrene coolers, coils and coils of polypropylene rope, huge vinyl mooring buoys and fishing net floats, and countless two-liter and one-liter soda bottles float past on the surface of the sea. Each of these items will gradually break down into smaller pieces, becoming more and more insidious as they do.

32° 19' North 149° 58' West

In the sultry, calm waters at the middle of the North Pacific High, a shred of a teal-colored plastic gillnet drifts by, a piece of polypropylene flotsam that sticks out in the marine landscape like a sore thumb. Our engineer, Seth, who hails from the mid-Maine coast, curses at the gear, which may go on ghost-fishing for years. Seth knows a lot about human waste, the disposal of which is one of his chief hassles on board the ship. He knows how to work every gadget in the vessel (there are many) and likes to explain our ethical relation to waste in great detail at various points of the voyage. Paper and food products go over the side at midnight with the sewage, both legally okay to dump beyond 12 miles offshore (along with gray water and other biodegradable solids, like table scraps). But the cardinal rule of shipboard waste is that no plastics go over the side. The carefully separated plastics will eventually be taken off the ship and dumped in a landfill, where they will sit, inert and separate from nature's workings, for thousands or millions of years. They will break down slowly, so slowly, and eventually they will become microplastics. Better in a landfill than at sea, says Seth with a rueful look, where they would do untold damage to marine life.

The tropics, far astern, seem more and more like a half-forgotten dream. Ahead are the mainland and the world of cellphones, iPods, and the Internet that have only temporarily relinquished their grip on our lives. In *The End of Nature*, published more than a decade before marine plastic debris was identified as a global phenomenon, the writer and activist Bill McKibben argued that anthropogenic climate change spelled the end of the idea that nature is what remains unaffected by humans. A different kind of evidence for McKibben's argument floats by us at all ours of the day, every day, in the many forms of human junk: half-empty water bottles, blue bait barrels lost by some fishing boat, a life jacket bearing only itself. The excess of carbon molecules in the air is mirrored in the water.

35° 11' North, 144° 07' West

One balmy morning in mid-ocean our captain decides to divert our ship from her course. I climb aloft to the fore-topsail yard, an immense aluminum pole suspended by wire and chain lifts, which runs perpendicular to the mast about sixty feet above deck, and scan the horizon in an arc. A nimble shipmate climbs aloft all the way to the truck, the very top of the mast. About two miles off to windward an orange object appears, disappears, and reappears. The waves are about ten feet high, but they are long and easy and predictably regular. Everyone on deck wonders the same thing: is it a life raft adrift? Could some castaway be drifting way out here? Could this be another Steve Callahan, who in 1982 drifted for seventy-six days across the Atlantic after his small sailboat hit a semi-submerged object and sank? Callahan survived in a rubber life raft, living off stray fish and rainwater. Could this orange plastic object, not micro but macro, house a human life? Always waiting in the wings, the idea of shipwreck takes center stage as we gaze at the floating piece of man-made orange flotsam.

At a quarter-mile off, the bobbing life-raft takes shape as an immense orange plastic ball, probably a mooring buoy from some fishing port far to the northwest. It has broken free and drifted south in the California current, then west in an eddy. When we come alongside it, we can see that the ball is too massive to take up on deck, perhaps 500 pounds, and covered beneath the waterline with heavy organic build-up. Hanging on its plastic underside is a minor ecosystem of pelagic barnacles. For a while, at least, this piece of flotsam will act as a nursery for marine organisms, providing shelter and habitat for several kinds of organism, such as the gooseneck barnacle. Eventually, however, it will break into ever-smaller pieces until it becomes just another splatter of invisible surface microplastics.

In his book *Shipwreck with Spectator*, the philosopher Hans Blumenberg (1997) argued that shipwreck provides a ubiquitous "metaphor for existence" in European culture, an idea that gives form to contingency and disaster in human life. For the ancient Greeks, crossing the seas was an act of transgression. Now the ocean itself is being wrecked or, as Charles Moore (2003) puts it, trashed by human beings. "The Titanic of modernity," quips Morton, "hits the iceberg of hyperobjects" (2013: 19). Yet at what point does the a massive, ineffable phenomenon lose its sublimity and take the form of a watery dump? Our constant search for economic growth and a higher standard of living creates dead zones, destroys marine ecosystems, and has even begun changing the pH of the ocean itself. "Shipwreck is not something to prepare for, something that is about to happen," writes the literature scholar Steve Mentz. "It is happening. Now. We are inside it, not waiting for it" (2015: 163). For Mentz, shipwreck serves as the most appropriate, and ubiquitous, metaphor for modernity—a sort of nautical unconscious that haunts the past 500 years of human history. Yet shipwreck is more than a metaphor for global modernity; it is a cultural unconscious.

Blumenberg's universalizing account never broaches the ecological devastation of Western powers on the archipelagoes of the Atlantic, Pacific, and Indian Oceans. From the first European conquests in the eastern Atlantic, the Canaries, Madeiras, and Azores, to Polynesia, invasive species and human industry have cut a broad swath. Alfred Crosby's pioneering study, *Ecological Imperialism* (2004) details the immediate effects of deforestation, erosion, and siltation that were made permanent by the extensive grazing of European sheep and cattle on mid-ocean islands that were once heavily forested. As grazing prevented second-growth forests from taking root over much of the terrain, islands became bald and less biologically diverse. Cash-crop plantations created monocultures where once a much greater biodiversity prevailed. Invasive species inflicted drastic damage to frail, insular ecosystems, in many cases devastating indigenous flora and fauna. In Oceania, native songbirds and many plant species have been pushed to the mountainous interior regions or wiped out entirely—whole islands shipwrecked by history.

37° 46' North, 140° 01' West

Just before dawn on a cold, gray morning I am on bow-watch, standing just abaft the bowsprit where the deck ends. The superstructure that supports the bowsprit, which in turn anchors the forestaysail, jib, and jib topsail, is called the head rig. Standing on it, the sensation is one of flying as we bowl along under all plain sail (the five "lowers"), rising and sinking over the easy Pacific seas. All is inky black ahead except for a few celestial bodies, brilliant and strange here, high in the night sky. Because the horizon is invisible, as is any distinction between sea and sky, I can see neither the waves caused by the wind nor those caused by our bow cutting the surface at eight knots. Everything changes when we bang a right about a thousand miles due East of San Francisco, north of the thirty-fifth parallel. Suddenly the quality of the light and the colors of sea and sky feel like home. Born and raised in New England, I am at home around the fortieth parallel. There is a nip in the air, and the sea has grown murky, with a gray surface entirely unlike the turquoise hues of the tropics or the cobalt of the deep ocean.

Just before the first breakfast sitting, the second mate discovers a tiny Wilson's petrel, paralytic and shivering, in one of the small boats on deck. Apparently it has collided with something solid in the night—a spar, one of the deckhouses, or even a taut sail. After a short lifetime of almost miraculous flight over the surface of uncountable waves, this superb navigator has wrecked on our ship. The ruin of its little spirit strikes many of us on deck as unfathomable, a cruel twist of fate that our presence—unusual, unnatural—should cause its destruction. Now that it cannot fly, we can do nothing to help. One of the assistant scientists mercifully breaks its neck and commits its tiny body to the sea. I imagine the little bird's body sinking into the water column, beneath the rich upper layer which holds more heat than the Earth's entire atmosphere, to the darkness below.

The next night I am awakened from a sound sleep by a bustle in the doghouse, where the navigational instruments are located. The captain and third mate are looking at the radar screen along with members of the watch, plotting the course of an immense ship coming our way at four times our speed. It burns barely refined oil known as "bunker fuel" that can be smelled long after the ship disappears over the horizon. It passes at about three miles off, an enormous mass of steel and glass and stench, resembling a city with its enormously bright spotlights trained on deck suspended from a superstructure several stories high. After more than three weeks at sea, my eyes are unaccustomed to the brightness of its running lights. We are now in the shipping routes of North Pacific, where the industrial powerhouses of Asia ship to the markets of North America, and over the next few days we encounter several more ships—container-ships, tankers, and one "Ro-Ro" (short for "Roll-on, Roll-off) carrying cars from Japan to Mexico.

One morning an immense container ship, its anonymous cargo piled impossibly high in brightly colored metal boxes, crosses our bow scarcely a mile away. From afar it resembles a dark metal island with Lego mountains. It might be carrying shoes, teddy bears, coffee, or my daughter's next winter coat. Over eighty percent of the world's manufactured goods travel by sea at some point, including the sneakers and rubber duckies that, washed off the decks of container ships in heavy weather, attract the attention of oceanographers and journalists as they circulate the Gyre. At a mile off, the container ship's piled metal boxes and superstructures evoke an immense piece of amorphous wrack. Its vast bulk looks lethal, impossible to stop and utterly unconcerned with something as tiny as our 300-ton sailing vessel. As it moves by like a surfing island the crew goes silent. In its wake swirl innumerable plankton mixed with the vestiges of old cargoes that have run their course.

38° 17' North, 123° 00' West

Standing at the helm one morning, my hands on the spokes of our wooden steering wheel and the ship plowing along with a fine northwesterly breeze behind, I have the feeling of being watched. I glance over my left shoulder and there, off the port quarter, swimming in the leading edge of a ten-foot wave, is a dolphin. Its snout forms a bulge in the surface of the water as it streaks down the wave, eyeing me as it surfs. I see the texture of its mottled skin, and for a moment I feel that I am on stage, as if I were the dolphin in the aquarium and he or she, a marine mammal at home, were checking me out. Suddenly the field biologist's phrase *charismatic megafauna* makes intimate personal sense. I am so moved that I completely forget my course ordered or steered. Looking forward, I see more dolphins catching a free ride on our bow wave, using the waves made by the displaced water to soar faster and freer. They leap beneath the bowsprit with a wild grace, as if our presence here were a rare gift to them.

The foggy waters off Northern California teem with life. About ninety percent of sea creatures—the world's marine biomass—inhabit the relatively shallow waters above the continental shelf. The most productive waters, then, are those adjacent to the majority of humans. In the daylight, sea lions pop their heads above the surface to have a look. Murres wing their way at high speed across our path. Whales are once again in evidence, their spouts greeting us like the calls of old friends. Off to starboard, a lookout spots the Farallones, stark bald rocks emerging suddenly from cold, rich waters. *Carcharodon carcharias*, the white shark, stalks seals and sea lions in the neighborhood, but in vastly diminished numbers. They are far more threatened by humans than the other way around. Even as we witness the teeming life in the water, I am reminded of the anthropogenic casualties of the Pacific Coast kelp bed ecosystem: Steller's sea cow, eaten to extinction by Russian trappers in the 18th century; the sea otter, nearly wiped out a century later; and the overfished abalone, sheepshead, and spiny lobster that all perform key functions in their food chains. We are tantalizingly close to the end of our voyage.

Suddenly the fog unveils the features of a bold coast that rises dramatically from the sea. The breathtaking heights of the Marin Headlands emerge from the fog two miles off the port bow, strikingly similar in their grandeur to the Hawaiian highlands we saw four weeks ago. Mount Tamalpais looms above the sea like an immense statue looking out to sea. The raffee, our highest sail—which the mates refer to as a "kite"—flies aloft the foremast for the only time on our voyage, pulling our ship forward like a team of draft horses. Our spirits surge with the shelving swell, soaring forward with the strong onshore wind. Wide grins cross the faces of captain, crew, and students alike. The massive expanse of sea behind us fades in the mist, yet the shore remains shrouded by the California fog. Behind us in the blue, countless seabirds ply the surface of the sea in their unceasing quest for food. Ahead lie all the comforts of shore in a world where our companions, the seabirds and marine mammals that have kept us company throughout our trip, scarcely cross the minds of people on their daily rounds the grocery stories and pharmacies where each purchase is individually wrapped in plastic—plastic that lasts forever. In the brightening rays of the sun a lone raptor, our first land bird in a month, soars over Bolinas to the north as the swooping arches and gossamer stays of the Golden Gate Bridge materialize from the fog like the rigging of an immense ship, wrecked on a hazy shore.

References

Anon. "The Seafarer." Kevin Crossley-Holland, Trans., Jonathan Raban, Ed. *The Oxford Book of the Sea*. Oxford and New York: Oxford University Press, 1993.

Blumenberg, Hans. *Shipwreck with Spectator: Paradigm for a Metaphor of Existence*. Trans. Steven Rendall. Cambridge, MA and London: MIT Press, 1997.

Callahan, Steve. *Adrift: 76 Days Lost at Sea*. New York: Mariner Books, 2002.

Crosby, Alfred. *Ecological Imperialism: the Biological Expansion of Europe, 900–1900*. Cambridge, UK: Cambridge University Press, 2004.

Ebbesmeyer, Curtis and Marc Scigliano. *Flotsametrics and the Floating World: How One Man's Obsession with Runaway Sneakers and Floating Ducks Revolutionized Ocean Science*. New York: HarperCollins, 2009.

van Franeker, Jan A. and Kara Lavender Law. "Seabirds, Gyres and Global Trends in Plastic Pollution." *Environmental Pollution*, 203, 89–96. doi:10.1016/j.envpol.2015. 02. 034.

Hohn, Donovan. *Moby-Duck: The True Story of 28,800 Bath Toys Lost at Sea & of the Beachcombers, Oceanographers, Environmentalists & Fools Including the Author Who Went in Search of Them*. New York: Penguin Books, 2012.

Jordan, Chris. "Midway: Message from the Gyre." http://chrisjordan.com/gallery/m idway/#CF000313%2018x24

Law, Kara Lavender. "Plastics in the Marine Environment." *Annual Review of Marine Science* 9(2017): 205–229.

Law, Kara Lavender and R. C. Thompson. "Microplastics in the Seas." *Science* 345 (2014): 144–145.

Law, Kara Lavender, S. Morét-Ferguson, N. A. Maximenko, G. Proskurowski, E. E. Peacock, J. Hafner and C. M. Reddy. "Plastic Accumulation in the North Atlantic Subtropical Gyre." *Science* 329(2010): 1185–1188.

McKibben, Bill. *The End of Nature*. New York: Anchor Books, 1989.

Mentz, Steve. *Shipwreck Modernity: Ecologies of Globalization, 1550–1719*. Minneapolis, MN and London: University of Minnesota Press, 2015.

Moore, Charles. *Plastic Ocean: How a Sea Captain's Chance Discovery Launched a Determined Quest to Save the Oceans*. New York: Penguin, 2011.

Moore, Charles. "Trashed: Across the Pacific Ocean, Plastics, Plastics Everywhere." *Natural History Magazine* 112. 9(2003): 1–11.

Morton, Timothy. *Hyperobjects: Philosophy and Ecology after the End of the World*. Minneapolis, MN: University of Minnesota Press, 2013.

8 Meaning in the growing, the harvest, the weaving, the making

Indigenous technologies at Plimoth Plantation's Wampanoag Homesite

Lisa King

It's the last day of April, and springtime is coming slowly this year to the chilly Massachusetts coastline. The sky is overcast, the maple trees are red with tiny flower buds, the Eel River is running high, and a steady wind off of Cape Cod Bay means the winter jacket and scarf I'm wearing are warranted. I'm firmly in Wampanoag territory here, at Plimoth Plantation, and while I'm here to visit my Wampanoag friends who live and work in the Boston area, I'm also here to learn, to see, and to seek out expertise in the ways in which museum and cultural centers can best teach about Indigenous knowledges and technologies in relationship to the land.[1]

Plimoth Plantation (or Plimoth) calls itself a "living museum," and endeavors to tell the story of the 17th-century Plymouth settlement on Wampanoag territory (Plimoth Plantation, "About Us"). Founded in 1947 by Henry Hornblower II and at first only focusing on the story of the English colonists as "a memorial to the Pilgrim Fathers" (as quoted in "Presenting the Story of Two Cultures"), Plimoth began with the idea of attempting to teach U.S. history by embodying it. The idea was that visitors would learn by encountering reconstructions of the colonists' fort and town, and later it was populated with actors/cultural interpreters who would take on the identity of recorded colonists and interact with visitors through that historical frame. Under pressure from Wampanoag communities in the area, Plimoth added the Wampanoag Homesite section in 1973 ("About Us") and began a more earnest effort to present a "bicultural historical perspective" ("Presenting the Story of Two Cultures"). Unlike the English Village, the Wampanoag Homesite is populated by actual Wampanoag and other Northeastern Woodlands Indigenous people, not actors, and while they do dress in period-appropriate clothing and engage in day-to-day activities that reflect that moment in time, they purposefully engage visitors as themselves and as Indigenous people who embody living knowledge, not past knowledge, that continues to bind them to their home territories.

When most people think about their most recent visit to a museum and what technology they encounter, most likely they will think of two things: either the objects or phenomena under study when they are classified and labeled as "technology," or the actual exhibit interface systems themselves—

perhaps videos, recorded sound effects and narrations, interactive digital tablet kiosks, recorded guided tours, QR codes and smartphone apps, and printed labels alongside the framing websites and brochures. Plimoth has some of this, including a cinema with an orientation film in the Visitor Center, a website with a basic overview, a printed map for visitors to carry, and a few introductory labels outside the entryway of to each section of the site. Yet it differs in one significant way in that it relies far less—almost not at all—on the cutting-edge electronic trappings of interpretation, and instead places its emphasis on human demonstration and interaction to teach. In this place the emphasis is on bodies of knowledge as demonstrated and observed.

Of particular interest for this edited collection, however, is the combination of the reliance on seeing and interacting with the way in which knowledge about the land is foregrounded at the Wampanoag Homesite part of Plimoth. All the demonstrated "crafts, trades, domestic skills, husbandry, horticulture, and the maritime arts" throughout Plimoth are framed as "pre-industrial" in the information section of the website ("Who We Are"), and in that sense they are part of a "preservation" effort documenting historical human activity. While the English Village, the *Mayflower II*, and the Grist Mill parts of Plimoth may embody this focus on past human activity as something *of the past*, the Wampanoag Homesite interprets traditional Indigenous (Wampanoag) knowledges, lifeways, and technologies as ongoing, living, and still deeply connected to a vision of and relationship with the land that is unique to Wampanoag peoples. In this chapter, I share the experience of visiting the Wampanoag Homesite as a way to think through the process by which interaction with those Indigenous technologies mediates a specific kind of relationship to and vision of the land.

A note on methods here: as person of both EuroAmerican and Indigenous (Delaware) descent, and a researcher with a background in rhetoric studies, museum studies, and Native American and Indigenous studies, I am drawing on the intersection of these fields and experiences to tell this story—and like all theorizing, it is a story (Riley Mukavetz, 2014: 108–109). I am deliberately framing my work here (1) on the assumption that good research, from an Indigenous perspective, is a series of relationships that requires care, respect, and reciprocity (Wilson, 2008); (2) on Indigenous understandings of "technology" as a meaning-making, communicative practice (as I will discuss further);[2] and (3) on Indigenous framing of human relationship to land and to place (Kimmerer, 2013; LaDuke, 1999) rather than to the "environment," a term that tends to rhetorically divide humans from all other beings, the land, the air, and the water. It's not that the term "environment" is bad, but rather about my desire to foreground terminology with the rhetorical resonance in English that most closely aligns with both trans-Indigenous understandings and specific Indigenous community understandings of place. Or as Kathleen E. Absolon (Minogiizhigokwe) observes, "rather than adding Indigenous perspectives to eurowestern [sic] theories and methods, we need to ground our research frameworks and methods in Indigenous ways of knowing, being, and doing" (2011: 54–55).

Recognizing Indigenous technologies

Before going further, I want to acknowledge the myriad ways in which Indigenous peoples have always used an array of technologies, and still do in ever-shifting ways. Too frequently Indigenous peoples are imagined as pre-technological or without technology at all in their most "authentic" forms, which presupposes a EuroWestern frame for understanding what technology is. That is, the non-Indigenous public frequently imagines Indigenous peoples as without "real" technology before contact with Europeans, and contaminated by it afterwards. I would argue instead, as many already have, that Indigenous peoples already had technologies and making practices. Furthermore, they have strategically adapted many new technologies for their own purposes, arguably indigenizing them, while turning other technologies forced on them to both intended and innovative purposes. Indigenous peoples continue to do so today.

In order to understand how this process of indigenization works, it's important to grasp how Indigenous peoples already had technology pre-contact, and how that technology was understood as part of a larger connection to other forms of life and the land itself. I'm cautious in even calling these practices technology for fear of the EuroAmerican connotation of it as detached from the natural world, spiritual understandings, and the reciprocity required of a good relationship to the natural world. "Technology" in this sense is not the same as how we mostly hear it in mainstream discourse. At the same time, I'm deliberately using it and reframing it here in order to help dispel preconceptions of a "primitive" Indigenous past when there were and remain sophisticated understandings of the land and all beings in it that EuroWestern science is only catching up to.

One way to understand Indigenous framings of technology has to do with their groundings in relationship to community and land. In "Rhetorical Powwows," Malea Powell draws on the work of master basketweaver Robin McBride to demonstrate the ways in which the very making of a Cherokee-style basket—a technology—invokes the stories that rhetorically bind and reinforce community. She writes,

> It isn't that we tell stories about a basket, or that the basket TELLS a story, it's that it is MADE of story, it IS story; and one of the reasons that things like baskets are significant for understanding Native rhetorical traditions is because *as things* they provoke, create, and prompt the stories that tell us who we are in relation to one another. They instruct us about our responsibilities to each other, and to the land. What I've come to understand is that while a thing like a rivercane basket or a mat

can certainly be textualized and "read" in the same way we "read" texts, they should not be held to the narrow affordances of texts. They are more than texts. They stand as proof of storied practices that are also performances, occasions, events, rhetorics. The "thingness" of rivercane weaving is theoretical in that it inaugurates for its practitioners a series of habitable stories that connect the land to the body to the People across artificial temporal distinctions like "past," "present," "future." These connections reveal a rhetorical relationship in which a material discourse spins out from the bodies of Cherokee women who are situated at the intersection of the spiritual and the everyday in the overlap between ancient originary events to the present moment in which they live. And this connection is there for time immemorial – it can't be broken, only forgotten and remembered.

(2010: 10–11, emphasis Powell's)

I quote Powell at length here because where she argues about recognizing the difficulty of reducing baskets to texts, I would add a similar argument about reducing baskets to mere technology. What the process of basket-weaving teaches is a way of understanding the rivercane from which the materials come, the other plants from which dyes come, the river in which you soak the cane, the land whose cycles you observe in order to harvest, the way your hands work (or don't, if you are learning), and what your obligations to the cane, the river, and land might be. It is a technology, yes, but also a performance, an occasion, and an event beyond the utility of the technology itself. To hold a finished Cherokee basket is to have the product of that technology, to be sure, but it is also to have Cherokee epistemologies and story embodied, with the imprint of its maker, in your hands.

Angela Haas makes a related argument concerning the framing of "digital technologies" and "hypertext" in her analysis of wampum, and how its making and use means that "Indians have always been hypertextual" (2007: 81). Made of white and purple tube-shaped beads derived from the quahog clam shell (a species native along the northeast North American coast), wampum has been used for adornment, trade, ceremony, and alliance-building when it is strung into strings, or made into necklaces, earrings, head and arm bands, and perhaps most famously, woven into heavy bi-color belts. The strings and belts are particularly important for Haas' assertion, as she connects relationship and reciprocity with their making: these objects "served to engender further diplomatic relations, and their presentation was a gesture that required reciprocity on the part of the recipient. Consequently, accepting a gift of wampum meant that the recipient accepted its implied message and responsibility" (80). Yet their significance extends far beyond the initial giving and affirmation of relationship, as "wampum records are maintained by regularly revisiting and re-'reading' them through community memory and performance, as wampum is a living rhetoric that communicates a mutual relationship" (80). Wampum is therefore a powerful community-driven technology that allows memory to be passed from community to community and generation to generation. Furthermore, knowing how to make the shell beads and weave them together—with one's eyes, one's hands, one's fingers, one's *digits*—represents knowledge of a digital rhetoric, particularly in how knowledge is encoded in its interactive design (84). In sum, wampum is a rich digital technology that pre-dates European colonial influence, and it lives today.

Wampum and weaving will become even more significant as I discuss the Wampanoag Homesite, as they do represent pre-contact technologies. Yet one more point needs making: how Indigenous people indigenize new technologies by incorporating them into the network of relationships to land and established community knowledge. Kristin Arola helps make this case when she discusses Anishinabe understandings of making in terms of "culturing," though the concept can apply more broadly across Indigenous communities. Based on the idea that there is no noun in Anishinabemowin for "being Ojibwe" but there is a way to describe "culture-ing as Ojibwe," Arola observes,

> by performing an act (making something, wearing something, living in a particular way) you are part of something larger which others who also perform that act are also a part. That is, by fishing in a particular way, or harvesting cedar in a particular way, or sewing regalia in a particular way, one not only *does* (that is, cultures as) Indian but also produces and sustains more life, more culture, more (in this case) American Indian ways of being.
>
> (2017: 2)

Within Ojibwe and other Indigenous understandings of making—using technology—Arola asserts "there is the acknowledgment that you produce more life, opening up new possibilities and potentials for further acts of production and analysis" (2). To make in a mindful way that is part of the larger framework of understanding and being within one's culture, then, is to perpetuate that culture and framework. But because culture and makers are alive, technologies shift, and it is possible to make use of new technologies within the cultural framework and still be Indigenous.

For example, the creation of pigments for dye and paint, the harvesting, dying, flattening, and stitching of porcupine quills, and substantial work of making bone and shell beads into elaborate decorative and ceremonial designs on clothing and basketry in North America shifted in part to the easier application of brightly colored glass seed beads from Europe. But what matters most are the ways in which this new technology was adapted into existing Indigenous technologies of ornamentation and ceremony, and into Indigenous ways of understanding the world (Dubin, 2014: 31–33). Floral beadwork as it developed in the Eastern Woodlands and Great Lakes regions of North America, could be read as something less-than Indigenous, when in fact the designs represent Indigenous worldviews and the seed beads themselves become understood as representative of the spiritual world and connected to the natural world. Even the term "seed" bead as a descriptor was so named by Woodlands peoples because of the tiny, shiny beads' visual resemblance to seeds or berries such as blackberries (39). In other words, technologies from elsewhere can become indigenized when they are applied in ways that are consistent with the epistemological frameworks of an Indigenous community, and they are no less authentic.

Innovation continues today, and we can see that in how the digital artwork and video game designs of Elizabeth LaPensée (see www.eliza bethlapensee.com) reflect the influences of Anishinabe beadwork and the contemporary Woodland School of Art and Norval Morrisseau. Or we can look at Ruth Cuthand's series online, *Trading*, in which she uses beads—noted as a European trade good—as a way of critiquing easy narratives of "trade" between Europeans and Indigenous peoples by creating beaded near-photographic images, as if under a microscope, of twelve viruses Europeans introduced into the Americas and set off mass infections among Indigenous peoples (www.ruthcuthand.ca/trading-series). Or we can look at the work of Jamie Okuma (www.jokuma.com/gallery), or the galleries of Indigenous artists and makers through the blog and online boutique Beyond Buckskin, founded by Jessica Metcalf (www. beyondbuckskin.com), to see the range of contemporary interpretations of technique into fashion for today. For all of them, as with most Indigenous artists, makers, academics, and people, the multi-layered use of technology isn't a sign of inauthenticity or cultural depletion, but rather a new manifestation of it.

Indigenous museums and technologies

Why does this matter to museums and how they use technology? In many respects, the same kinds of argument apply, though the rhetorical resonances of taking on a colonial framework of knowledge (the Museum), with its attendant technologies of seeing in an Indigenous context, presents an array of challenges. Below, I discuss some of those challenges, note some of the tactics Indigenous museums have used, then address the choices at the Wampanoag Homesite.

The history of European and North American museums' treatment of Indigenous peoples from around the world is well documented (see e.g., Barringer and Flynn, 1998; NMAI, 2000, 2012; Kreps, 2003). As a colonial affair that began with collections for European cabinets of curiosities, museums developed in tandem with centuries of colonial conquest as a means of visually interpreting colonized cultures for the colonial public. Over time, such collections became the foundational "evidence" supporting scientific racism, and while some items were acquired through trade or willing sale, many other objects and human remains were acquired through conquest, grave robbing and looting, and legal or economic duress.

The public displays of these collections were meant for mass public edification, though audiences were always kept at a kind of distance. The standard technology of display then is still recognizable today in the use of glass cases and cabinets with labels indicating age and provenance of the objects. Interaction for the most part was limited to seeing from that physical and rhetorical distance, whether that was a collection of arrowheads arranged artfully in a frame, pottery in a case, or the use of dioramas (still not to be touched) to create some semblance of objects in situ—or at least as curators imagined them to be. At times, Indigenous practitioners of these kinds of makings were brought to the museum to perform (or even set up in villages to live as an exhibit), but still the idea was to watch the work from a distance—physical distance, cultural distance, and social distance. Indigenous peoples were at best informants, but the greatest authority over display and narrative rested with curators, archaeologists, exhibit designers, and docents. As Evan M. Maurer points out in his historical overview (2000), the end result was generally that Indigenous peoples were frozen in the past and non-existent in the present.

Over the past several decades, museums have made some efforts to lessen that distance between their audiences and exhibitions as well as do better by Indigenous peoples. Today's visitors to a major museum can expect to check out an exhibit through a museum's website for some general context and perhaps a sampling of images of objects as a teaser. The exhibit itself will likely still have the standard glass cases for display, but it is far more likely to enhance the meaning-making capacity of the objects in question for many visitors with short videos of artists or makers playing on repeat on strategically placed monitors; tablet kiosks that go beyond the standard label and allow visitors to explore topics or concepts related to the objects; and sometimes hands-on interactive stations that allow visitors to touch or play with replica objects for a more direct experience. More museums are experimenting with apps for smartphones to allow a more personalized and mobile experience for visitors. Furthermore, if makers or artists visit the exhibition to do demonstrations, they are more likely to be treated as experts rather than as objects themselves. Frequently the artist/maker is asked to speak on the significance of what they do, which can again lessen the distance between the audience and maker, and introduces visitors to the practice and process of making, not just the finished object.

For Indigenous museums, particular care must be taken when choosing technologies to assist in the telling of Indigenous histories and cultures. Traditional museum display technologies have guided visitors' vision in such a way as to create perceptual and conceptual distance between the objects and the lands and cultures who made those objects, and those narratives serve colonial narratives of conquest and Progress. Decolonizing museum practices, then, includes revealing those narratives for what they are—as Amy Lonetree puts it, "telling the hard truths of colonization" (2012: 25)—and rethinking how technologies of display can relink viewers with understandings of culture and land, instead of delinking them.

In my own work, I've discussed some of the nuances of this selection and implementation process, and I argue that part of the work Indigenous and Indigenously-affiliated museums and cultural centers are doing is finding ways to self-represent that will resonate with multiple Indigenous and non-Indigenous audiences. That is, if the goal is cross-cultural communication, Indigenous self-representation and declarations of cultural sovereignty are not enough if audiences do not take up (or do not know how to take up) the teachings presented in that space. Because of the powerful precedent set by the colonial frame of museum presentation and the concomitant looking, Indigenous museums and cultural centers have to strategically take audience expectations and habits into account in order to unmake and remake them (King, 2017). How this happens depends on the culture, context, history, and audiences at each site, and so what the Smithsonian's National Museum of the American Indian in Washington, D.C. has done must vary significantly from a local tribally-owned and operated site such as the Saginaw Chippewa's Ziibiwing Center of Anishinabe Culture & Lifeways on the Isabella Reserve, just outside of Mt. Pleasant, MI. Different circumstances require different approaches, and sometimes new technologies are called for to circumvent viewing habits, or old familiar technologies can be repurposed and their meanings shifted.

At the same time, some commonalities are emerging across Indigenous institutions to help audiences "re-see" what an exhibition or a space can be and mean, particularly in relationship to land. One of those commonalities is the creation of a medicinal/indigenous plant garden as an extension of the expected building and gallery space. At the National Museum of the American Indian (NMAI), for example, the entire property outside the museum has been landscaped to be a small wetland, a hardwood forest, a meadow, and an indigenous cropland. "By recalling the natural environment that existed prior to European contact, the museum's natural landscape design embodies a theme that runs central to the NMAI—that of returning to a Native place" (NMAI, 2012: 22). Similarly, the Ziibiwing Center has a medicinal-indigenous garden planted around it to create "Bbaamoseg Gitiganing: All Will Walk About the Plants that Grow," a living "plant walk exhibit" with more than forty plants used by past and contemporary Anishinabek peoples (Ziibiwing Center, "Plant Walk Exhibit"). In such places, the direct encounter with the land is the attraction: though labels and printed guides play an interpretive and informative role, the goal of the experience is seeing the living plants themselves, in context, and in connection with Indigenous knowledges. Moreover, the buildings themselves frequently take on visually symbolic meaning. In the case of the NMAI, its sandstone exterior is meant to mimic the wind-carved face of a cliff, again invoking the landscape at large and the common respect for land across all the Indigenous cultures represented there. For the Ziibiwing Center, the main entrance and interior hall was constructed to represent a teaching lodge, again creating a direct visual link with the values of the broader Anishinabe culture and the Saginaw Chippewa community specifically.

Technology as a concept in Indigenous museums, then, reflects the traditional making practices of Indigenous peoples, the innovations and indigenization of other technologies into Indigenous worldviews, and then the mediating and interpretive technologies used to help audiences understand these practices and worldviews in a museum setting. How this constellation of technological meaning-making is constructed and enacted depends much on the site, depending on the needs of the Indigenous community at the center and then the interpretive support necessary for the audience. In the following, I discuss what this looks like at the Wampanoag Homesite, particularly in relationship to seeing, recognizing, and engaging with the land that takes the experience several steps further.

The Wampanoag Homesite: technologies of the first light

The name "Wampanoag" translates to English as "People of the First Light," as the sixty-nine original Wampanoag tribal communities that made up the nation have their traditional homelands in the Northeast coast of the United States, in Massachusetts and Rhode Island. When the colonists known now as the Pilgrims made landfall on the land of the Patuksut (also spelled Patuxet) Wampanoag, European traders had already brought yellow fever, smallpox, leptospirosis, and other illnesses to North America, and it is estimated that two-thirds (45,000) of the Wampanoag peoples had died by the time the Pilgrims arrived (Mashpee Wampanoag Tribe, n.d.; Marr and Cathey, 2010). The nearby Wampanoag communities were cautious in making contact out of fear of further disease, but eventually a working alliance was formed between the Plimoth colony and the Pokanoket Wampanoag—an alliance that later dissolved with increased colonial pressure and the resulting King Philip's War.

While it is beyond the scope of this essay to go into great detail with this history, suffice to say most people do not know even the basics, and rely rather on a kind of mythology instead. Every U.S. school-aged child now knows—or thinks they know—about the "First Thanksgiving" of 1621, and the ways in which the story of the Pilgrims is foundational to the narrative of the United States. The Wampanoag, if their name is even known, are the Indians who play the welcoming Natives in that story, and then disappear. As a result, it's not surprising that Henry Hornblower, the Plimoth Plantation museum's founder, began not with the Wampanoag but rather with a historical reconstruction of the English settlement first in 1947 "for the historical education of the public with respect to the struggles of the early settlers, the expansion of the settlement, and the influence of the Pilgrim Fathers throughout the world" (Plimoth Plantation, "Presenting the Story of Two Cultures"). Coinciding with the first major wave of tribal museum development in the 1960s and 1970s (Lonetree, 2012: 19) and under pressure from local Wampanoag communities during and after the 1970 Thanksgiving Day protest (Blee and O'Brien, 2019: 144), Plimoth Plantation opened the Wampanoag Homesite in 1973 ("About Us").

As already noted, these historical reconstructions are meant to be highly interactive, with a crucial difference that the people in the English village are actors who play an assigned role demonstrating historical technologies and ways of life brought from England, and the people in the Wampanoag Homesite are actual Indigenous people who are not treating the lifeways they interpret for visitors as "past," but rather ongoing meaning-making from a Wampanoag point of view. In the context of historical erasure, it matters that Indigenous people represent themselves and that audiences understand that this knowledge is not pretending. Moreover, the work at the Wampanoag Homesite establishes a different kind of relationship to land, from the point of view of long occupancy and relationship rather than that of recently arrived foreigners, a point I'll return to. For now, I walk through the Wampanoag Homesite itself—as much as I can, given my own technological limitations here as a writer—in order to demonstrate how this relationship to land is reinforced for both Indigenous interpreters and visitors.

When visitors arrive at Plimoth Plantation and pay their entrance fee at the Visitor Center, they have the option of going in to see the orientation film, or directly to the outdoor spaces. This is important to note, because the labeling is kept to a minimum throughout Plimoth Plantation. The website does provide plenty of background information if visitors choose to use it, and there is a page for each individual "exhibit" associated with Plimoth Plantation. For portable context, the paper map/brochure available to visitors at the front desk describes the Wampanoag Homesite as "a re-creation of the homesite of Hobbamock—a Pokonoket man who lived in Patuxet/Plymouth Colony in the 1620s" (though it is noteworthy that the website does not try to place the Wampanoag Homesite into a fixed historical frame). Both the website and the paper map emphasize that the staff are not role-players in this part of Plimoth, that they are Wampanoag/Indigenous, and though the skills they demonstrate are accurate to the 17th century, they will speak from "a modern perspective" ("Map: Welcome to Plimoth Plantation" and "Wampanoag Homesite").

If a visitor has done some looking online before their visit, they will see images of the Wampanoag cultural interpreters appear intermittently throughout the website, primarily on the "Presenting the Story of Two Cultures" page next to Pilgrim interpreters, everyone fully dressed for their roles. There is also one image on the "Wampanoag Homesite" feature page of a smiling woman wearing deerskin and wampum, sewing hides. Given the context of the museum, these images are somewhat ambiguous in their meaning. While the text itself emphasizes that the Wampanoag Homesite interpreters are not role playing, setting them side-by-side with the Pilgrim interpreters, who are, presents a challenge for a viewer. This is why actual interaction and first-hand seeing become crucial.

Once the visitor exits the Visitor Center, the Wampanoag Homesite itself is the first space the visitor will enter after walking down the trail. There are two tall labels that a visitor sees before arriving at the Homesite, the first of which directly challenges the visitor, and the second of which provides the more museum-like text. The first features a near-lifesize image of interpreter and now Director of Wampanoag and Eastern Woodlands Research and Interpretive Training at Plimoth, Darius Coombs, in full period-appropriate Wampanoag dress. The text asks,

> Do you have a picture in mind from movies or books of what "Indians" look like? Hello and welcome—My name is Darius Coombs, and I am Mashpee Wampanoag. That picture you might have in mind of 'Indians' or 'Native Americans' could be a stereotype. In the Wampanoag Home-site we may look very different from what you expect, but we are all Native People. Sometimes stereotypes are not images at all, but words. Calling us 'braves' or 'squaw;' or saying 'How, Chief' are examples of this. We thank you kindly for not using stereotypical words like that.

That a label like this is necessary at all is testament to the impact of colonial narratives about Indigenous peoples and the immediate difficulties presented by the problematic and racist expectations that many visitors may carry. The "Wampanoag Homesite" webpage also instructs visitors not to show up in "Indian" costumes, ostensibly because it will cause visual confusion for other visitors. Authority over cultural knowledge and self-representation is maintained in part by visual presentation, yet in that presentation the inter-preters know they are overlapping with a history of stereotypical imagery that visitors will know better than historical truth. In interviews with staff, Lisa Blee and Jean O'Brien underscore the emotional labor undertaken by the cultural interpreters in order to educate the non-Native public, and the efforts Plimoth has to make to help avoid creating an abusive work envir-onment for them when visitors fall back on racist stereotypes (Blee and O'Brien, 2019: 146). The standard technology of today's museum—a label and a webpage—is used in this place not only to explain factual information, but also to directly address and avert racist behavior. However, the intent is to welcome as much as it is to encourage respectful and thoughtful interac-tion. The label continues, "We are eager to meet you and share with you the stories of our ancestors, our traditions, our history and our community. Not everyone working in the Homesite is Wampanoag. Please feel free to ask us what Native Nation we are from. Welcome!"

The second label is equally as large but repeats the same framing infor-mation as the map and the website together: this is meant to be a repre-sentation of Hobbamock's home, the Native people a visitor is about to meet are not role-playing, and they can speak on Wampanoag culture and history from the 17th century to the present. This label serves both a more standard informational purpose and as a reinforcement in case the visitor has missed the message on the website, the map, and in the film.

Now the visitor is at the Homesite, and other than the information I've already covered on the map and through the website (also linkable from the map to the website through a QR code for a smartphone), there are no other substantial labels. Information now comes through talking to the cultural interpreters, through observation, and through interaction with Indigenous technologies.

On the day that I am there, the cold weather is keeping most tourists indoors, and the last of the school groups has already departed when we arrive midafternoon. I am with Dr. Joyce Rain Anderson, who has worked from her position as director of Ethnic and Indigenous Studies at nearby Bridgewater State University to build some relationships with Plimoth. Her Mashpee Wampanoag cousin, Kerri Helme, is the new Homesite manager and has been working hard this spring to oversee changes and updates to the Homesite. She meets us there and walks us through the features of the space and the kind of work she does.

Directly to the right when we leave the trail and enter the clearing, the newly-relocated Three Sisters garden is taking shape. The earthen mounds for each hill of combined corn, beans, and squash have been hoed into position in a new plot in order to allow the previous plot to lie fallow. As the annual herring run has just finished, there are fish buried in the mounds to decompose for fertilizer before the first seeds go in. Three Sisters gardening is a traditional Indigenous agricultural innovation that has deep spiritual roots in various stories across North America. As ethnobotanist Robin Wall Kimmerer describes it, it is a harmonious cultivation process that can be explained both in scientific terms and through the frame of Indigenous teachings and story (2013: 131–134), as the corn provides the central support for vining beans which in turn provide the site for nitrogen-fixing bacteria that feed all three plants. The squash vines spread out below, providing shade for the soil and protection against predators. As an agricultural technique, it is startlingly (from a EuroAmerican perspective) efficient, far more so than if the three were grown separately in rows. This is the first technology visitors will see.

Next to the garden is a round, woven mat-covered *wetu* (house), which would be a summer dwelling (Fig. 8.1). This *wetu* is relatively new, but occupied. Today two women dressed in deerskin and trade cloth, one with fur-wrapped braids and the other with wampum earrings and bracelet, sit by the center fire inside as they work on finger-weaving a sash or sewing hides. It is warm in spite of the *wetu* not having door coverings installed yet. Kerri explains how the circular shape of the house and the center placement of the fire with benches all around and a smoke hole above provide the most efficient heat distribution. I admire the finger-weaving as it progresses, and I'm tempted to sit down and take my jacket off, it's that comfortable, but our time is limited and we move on.

The next stop is the place where *mishoonash*—dugout canoes—are regularly built as part of a working demonstration for visitors. The fire has been put out for now, but the long, trimmed tree trunk is partially hollowed by the steady burning that has been going on recently. Fresh soot coats the

Figure 8.1 The summer *wetu* at the Wampanoag Homesite.
Photo taken by the author, included courtesy of Plimoth Plantation.

inside, and it's easy to imagine how this *mishoon* will take shape (Fig. 8.2).
Two more *mishoonash* are mostly sunken into the water at the edge of the Eel
River Pond a few steps away; Kerri notes that because it can still freeze, it's
safer to leave them in the water so they don't ice over and split in the air.
This seems counterintuitive to many visitors, but a good understanding of
how wood absorbs water and how and when it freezes points again to sound
Wampanoag knowledge, and it's clear to see the preservation technique
works. She also wryly observes that there will likely be a label installed in
the near future in front of the path down to the water to help encourage
visitors to stay in the designated areas and not attempt to ride in the *mishoonash* unsupervised.

As we move around the circle of the Homesite, Kerri narrates the uses of the
arbor and the construction of a fish-weir-style (another Wampanoag technology, though placed strategically to catch people here) railing that will guide
visitors in a circle around the clearing, and how the camp will be arranged as if a
visitor is moving through the yearly cycle of seasons. That way, she says, visitors will be able to see a broader scope of the kinds of activities Wampanoag
people would engage in throughout the year. In the center is space for play and
for making; here, the cultural interpreters teach visitors to make corn husk
dolls and to play a still-popular Wampanoag game called hubbub.

Figure 8.2 A partially completed *mishoon*, or dugout canoe, at the Wampanoag Homesite. Photo taken by the author, included courtesy of Plimoth Plantation.

We make the round to the large *nashwetu*, or bark longhouse (Fig. 8.3). Since it's the end of the day the fires here have also been put out, but the three fire pits inside look more than up to the task of heating the space. As a long oval, its use of round space is much like the smaller *wetu*, simply elongated and expanded. Finely woven rush mats hang partway up the walls for extra insulation and decoration. Hide- and fur-covered benches for sitting and sleeping run down the long sides of the interior. I remark that the warmth must be considerable here when the fires are lit. Kerri nods, and adds that from historical accounts there are stories about the surprise of some of the first Europeans observing Wampanoag children running nearly naked from a *nashwetu* outdoors in the winter. While the European accounts implied neglect of the children, Kerri points out that between multiple people occupying the space and the fires inside, it would have been quite warm and therefore logical not to overdress a child. Running outdoors

Figure 8.3 The *nashwetu*, or bark-covered longhouse, at the Wampanoag Homesite. Photo taken by the author, included courtesy of Plimoth Plantation.

would have been for cooling off a little. (Later, when Joyce Rain and I tour the English village, the thicker-walled English houses are surprisingly chilly, and even with a fire in each one we visit, it's still considerably cooler in those dwellings. The English cultural interpreters are dressed in multiple layers against the chill. The sharp contrast is something that wouldn't have been observable without being able to experience the two side-by-side.)

From the interior wooden frame of the *nashwetu* hang multiple woven bags filled with objects. I ask if I am allowed to touch, and Kerri smiles. "Of course, that's what they are there for!" she says, and begins to show me a bag of tools, describing the making of a club from the selection of the tree root to its final shape. Every bag hanging here has some kind of tool in it, and visitors are encouraged to handle them and ask questions (Fig. 8.4). I've seen her hand weave the twine bags before as part of her work at the 2015 Native American and Indigenous Studies conference, so I know that the bags are handmade.

I ask her about the sourcing of the materials for the *nashwetu* and the hides, as the hides on the benches are plentiful, and I wondered if there were forests old enough nearby to supply the thick bark for the longhouse. She explains that the materials actually have to be brought in from elsewhere. In the 17th century the forest would have provided what was necessary, but

Figure 8.4 One of many woven twine bags in the *nashwetu*, this one with an assort-
      ment of clubs and tools.
Photo taken by the author, included courtesy of Plimoth Plantation.

several centuries of EuroAmerican settlement along the Massachusetts coast
have taken their toll. The hides are frequently donated by hunters to Plimoth
or are sometimes purchased. Kerri touches one of the rush mats hanging on
the wall, and comments, "Back then these would have covered the walls all
the way to the ceiling and covered the floor. But I can't stand to think of
anyone walking on these. We don't have enough of them." She clarifies that
it's difficult to get the right kind of rushes now with wetlands being drained
and developed, and how time-intensive it is to harvest, prepare, dye, and
weave the rushes. In short, though the Wampanoag technologies on display
here represent sustainable practices, they currently aren't sustainable given
the land's exploitation and settlement by non-Indigenous peoples. It is a
working challenge to maintain these ways of knowing and making in substantial part because the physical resources aren't readily available.

After completing the tour of the Homesite, we follow the trail up the hill to the next stop, the Craft Center. This building houses contemporary artisans and their work, and visitors again are encouraged to talk to the staff. According to the map, "At the Craft Center, artisans create some of the items that would have been imported from England in the 1660s. Native artisans make traditional artifacts that today are used in the Wampanoag Homesite." It is worth pointing out the interactive contrast between the Wampanoag Homesite and the English village; while my focus remains on the Wampanoag Homesite for the sake of this chapter, the English village becomes a foil for Indigenous making knowledges connected to land in the sense that nearly everything the English colonists had was imported. It is true a visitor will see small gardens and cows and sheep being kept there, but the plants they are growing and the livestock represent either imports from foreign soil or knowledge (in the case of cultivating corn, beans, and squash) from the Wampanoag. Under the "Craft Center FAQs" section of the website, visitors can find answers to "Did the Pilgrims make everything they needed themselves?" (the abbreviated answer is no) and "Why isn't anyone in the English Village making baskets or pottery" (the short answer is because they were imported at that time). The English colonists did not have adequate knowledge of making these objects because of how labor was divided into trades back in Europe and because they did not have adequate knowledge of the land they settled on. Thus the myth of two self-sufficient societies side-by-side is debunked—but it takes some reading and asking to find that out. Once again, minimal labeling means seeing and interacting are key.

On this day, Sokoki Abenaki artist Bob Charlebois is the only person present in the Craft Center—the English side of the space with the pottery replicas of what would have been imported from England is unstaffed at the moment—and he is working on a porcupine headdress (or roach). Several completed roaches are on display in radiant colors of dyed porcupine hair and trade beadwork, and a long label mounted on the railing in front of his workspace explains the origin of the headdress and what traditional and contemporary roaches are made of. We chat for a little bit, and a family enters the Craft Center behind us and approaches. They are German speakers, a mother, father, and two children perhaps four and six years old. The mother reads the label and attempts to translate for her children, and then she and her partner begin a conversation in English with Bob about his work, asking about natural dyes, what plants would be used, the kinds of feathers than he mounts on top of the roaches. The exchange is halting yet one of good will. Bob can offer *Stachelschwein* as a translation for "porcupine," but there's some difficulty explaining what sumac is when he lists the plants that would be used for traditional dyes. One question causes some discomfort: why, the woman asks, has she only ever seen feather war bonnets on Indians (she makes a gesture with her hands in the shape of a Plains feather headdress). Bob answers her patiently and explains that not all Indigenous peoples wear those and it's not the tradition of Northeastern Indigenous peoples. She is surprised and thanks him for correcting her, as she admits she thought all Indians wore them. Regardless of the intermittent language barrier, Bob is able to answer their questions far beyond what the label provides by way of introduction, and the family moves on after about 10 minutes. Once again, being able to see the object in question and talk about it with an Indigenous person with the knowledge makes a significant difference in understanding, and in this case directly corrects a misperception.

While we did continue through the entire Plimoth site, the Wampanoag Homesite and the Craft Center provided the best opportunities to see Wampanoag and Northeast Indigenous knowledges at work. These technologies are alive and well, and giving visitors the chance to interact with cultural interpreters who are knowledgeable about past and present making practices creates a unique opportunity to re-see what "technology" means and what its relationship to land has been, and continues to be.

Conclusion

The Wampanoag Homesite at Plimoth, though only one part of a larger site, provides a uniquely Indigenous frame through which to understand two things: the reconceptualization of Indigenous knowledge as technology, not primitive past practices; and the power of personal interaction with these technologies to reground visitors' understanding of the land they stand on. As I discussed above with Powell, Haas, and Arola's work, these making practices are not divorced from the people from which they come. Blee and O'Brien's interviews with staff lead them to observe, "From the perspective of Wampanoag and other Indigenous staff ... programming is a deeply personal embodiment of history, representing the continuation of cherished traditions that carry the unequivocal message that 'we're still here'," and whether it is the carving of a mishoon or weaving a wampum belt, "It's recovering our culture and maintaining our identity" (Darius Coombs, quoted by Blee and O'Brien, 2019: 147). For the Indigenous people who work as cultural interpreters, they are not simply demonstrating a craft or technology. They understand these skills and this knowledge as an embodiment of who they are, and an embodiment of their relationship to the land they have lived on for thousands of years.

Translating that embodiment for visitors is a challenge, and at the Wampanoag Homesite the standard museological practices involving glass cases, isolated objects, and distance from the peoples who produced them have been exchanged for something that in this place is far more effective. By spending time at the Homesite, visitors have a chance to see Indigenous knowledges at work, whether it is the warmth of a mat *wetu*, the durability of a *mishoon*, or the promise of a Three Sisters garden. The interwoven experience of learning about these technologies by experiencing them, being able to ask questions on the spot, and understanding their direct connection to the land itself has the potential to reframe visitor understandings of

Indigenous peoples and the land we all walk on. Strategic use of labeling, website framing, and photographs can help set the metaphorical stage for visitor interaction and calling attention to stereotyping, but the most powerful potential for learning and re-seeing comes in the full experience on site.

Though it is clear the approach at Plimoth is far from perfect, its power is undeniable. The Wampanoag Homesite and its Indigenous cultural interpreters embody the meaning in the growing, the harvest, the weaving, and the making, from the present back through time, and offer visitors a vision of the land as a relation, if we are willing to take it up.

Notes

1 My heartfelt thanks—*anushiik*—to Joyce Rain Anderson and Kerri Helme for their invitation and guidance, to Bob Charlebois for his time and work, and to Rob Kluin and staff for their assistance and support on this project.
2 I do not belabor the point here that Native American and Indigenous rhetorics exist as a field of study unto themselves and also in relationship to other rhetorical traditions. It is assumed here for the sake of directing focus to discussions of Indigenous technologies as meaning-making practices.

References

Absolon, Kathleen E. (Minogiizhigokwe). *Kaandossiwin: How We Come to Know.* Halifax, Novia Scotia: Fernwood Publishing, 2011.

Arola, Kristin. "'All Things Are Alive. Everything is Related': An Indigenous Approach to Making." Presentation at the Conference on College Composition and Communication. March 2017. Portland, Oregon.

Barringer, Tim and Tom Flynn, Eds. *Colonialism and the Object: Empire, Material Culture, and the Museum.* New York: Routledge, 1998.

Blee, Lisa and Jean M. O'Brien. *Monumental Mobility: The Memory Work of Massasoit.* Chapel Hill, NC: University of North Carolina Press, 2019.

Dubin, Lois S. *Floral Journey: Native North American Beadwork.* Seattle, WA: University of Washington Press, 2014.

Haas, Angela. "Wampum as Hypertext: An American Indian Intellectual Tradition of Multimedia Theory and Practice." *Studies in American Indian Literatures* 19:4(2007): 77–100.

Kimmerer, Robin Wall. *Braiding Sweetgrass: Indigenous Wisdom, Scientific Knowledge, and the Teachings of Plants.* Minneapolis, MN: Milkweed Editions, 2013.

King, Lisa. *Legible Sovereignties: Rhetoric, Representations, and Native American Museums.* Corvallis, OR: Oregon State University Press, 2017.

Kreps, Christina F. *Liberating Culture: Cross-Cultural Perspectives on Museums, Curation, and Heritage Preservation.* New York: Routledge, 2003.

LaDuke, Winona. *All Our Relations: Native Struggles for Land and Life.* Boston, MA: South End Press, 1999.

Lonetree, Amy. *Decolonizing Museums: Representing Native American in National and Tribal Museums.* Chapel Hill, NC: University of North Carolina Press, 2012.

Marr, John S. and John T. Cathey. "New Hypothesis for Cause of Epidemic among Native Americans, New England, 1616–1619." *Emerging Infectious Diseases Journal*

16. 2(2010): 281–286. https://wwwnc.cdc.gov/eid/article/16/2/09-0276_article. Accessed June 26, 2019.

Mashpee Wampanoag Tribe. "History and Culture of the Mashpee Wampanoag." https://mashpeewampanoagtribe-nsn.gov/culture. Accessed May 23, 2019.

Maurer, Evan M. "Presenting the American Indian: From Europe to America." *The Changing Presentation of the American Indian: Museums and Native Cultures.* Seattle, WA andWashington, DC: University of Washington Press with Smithsonian Institution, 2000.

NMAI. *The Changing Presentation of the American Indian: Museums and Native Cultures.* National Museum of the American Indian. Seattle, WA andWashington, DC: University of Washington Press with Smithsonian Institution, 2000.

NMAI. *Map and Guide.* National Museum of the American Indian. Washington, DC: Smithsonian Institution, 2012.

Plimoth Plantation. "About Us." 2003–2019. www.plimoth.org/about-us. Accessed May 15, 2019.

Plimoth Plantation. "Craft Center FAQs." 2003–2019. www.plimoth.org/what-see-do/craft-center/craft-center-faqs#CCQuest4. Accessed May 25, 2019.

Plimoth Plantation. "Map: Welcome to Plimoth Plantation." 2019.

Plimoth Plantation. "Presenting the Story of Two Cultures." 2003–2019. www.plimoth.org/about/who-we-are/presenting-story-two-cultures. Accessed May 15, 2019.

Plimoth Plantation "Wampanoag Homesite." 2003–2019. www.plimoth.org/what-see-do/wampanoag-homesite. Accessed May 24, 2019.

Plimoth Plantation "Who We Are." 2003–2019. www.plimoth.org/about/who-we-are. Accessed May 15, 2019.

Powell, Malea. "Rhetorical Powwows: What American Indian *Making* Can Teach Us About Histories of Rhetorics." Hutton Lecture Series, Purdue University, November 2010.

Riley Mukavetz, Andrea M. "Towards a Cultural Rhetorics Methodology: Making Research Matter with Multi-Generational Women from the Little Traverse Bay Band." *Rhetoric, Professional Communication, and Globalization* 5. 1(2014): 108–125.

Wilson, Shawn. *Research is Ceremony: Indigenous Research Methods.* Halifax, Novia Scotia: Fernwood Publishing, 2008.

Ziibiwing Center. "Plant Walk Exhibit." Mt Pleasant, MI: Ziibiwing Center of Anishinabe Culture & Lifeways, 1998–2019. www.sagchip.org/ziibiwing/exhibits/plantwalkexhibit.htm. Accessed May 22, 2019.

9 Translating nature

Manipulation of natural landscape in contemporary digital photography

Anastasia Kozak

"The unfortunate truth of photography is that the picture we see often isn't the picture we get," writes Debbie Grossman, the senior editor of *Popular Photography*, in her 2004 article on how to use Adobe Photoshop to create properly exposed skies (52). Before the magazine ceased publication in 2017, after eighty years of continuous coverage of consumer photography trends, it regularly featured articles on how to use image-editing software to transform landscape photographs. One article provides a step-by-step guide to make a choppy lake surface appear more tranquil and "fake a reflection"; another advises readers how to "optimize a landscape" in Photoshop by "tak[ing] a few liberties with your nature shots" (Grossman 2011b).[1] Even though the speed of software development has already made many of the tips obsolete, the desire for such content and the popularity of natural landscape photography—judging by the YouTube channels and blogs dedicated to the subject—show no signs of abating. The ethos, whether in online or print publications, is that great pictures don't just happen; you have to plan for them, both before (the dictum of "shooting to edit") and after, indoors.

When it comes to digital post-editing, natural landscapes present an entirely different set of challenges from other types of photography. While we accept, and even expect, that images of celebrities are routinely airbrushed; or that hamburger buns in fast food ads feature perfect distribution of sesame seeds, there is something disingenuous about retouching nature. On learning that a landscape print we have admired in a gallery has been digitally retouched, we may feel tricked or mildly scandalized. Nature, we suspect, is supposed to be already perfect, inimitable, and beyond amelioration. How much, then, do we limit digital post-editing, and what are the ethical implications of using digital technology to recreate the "ideal" landscape visualized at the time of picture taking? And what is the price we must pay for availing ourselves of technological affordances in order to capture the perfect landscape?

This chapter attempts to answer these questions not by juxtaposing the analog and the digital photographic techniques, or by implying that the digital innovation has presented a paradigm shift in capturing and presenting nature to the viewer. I propose instead to see the analog and the digital as a continuum—with the latter inheriting and recycling the ways of seeing nature that became internalized over the course of earlier analog experiences. Thus, much of what follows—while focusing on digital landscape photo-graphy—is a tracing of certain practices of seeing and capturing nature that, in spite of Adobe Lightroom and Photoshop "magic," have not only withstood the test of time but became even more entrenched in an age that, according to the philosopher Paul Virilio, erases the chronodiversity of past-present-future and makes everything instantly updatable and shareable, the so-called age of the instant (2010: 59).

My point of departure in tackling these questions is the concept of *exposure* and its associated meanings. In photographic terms, exposure is the amount of light that reaches either the film of an analog camera or the electronic sensor of a digital camera—the amount that can be adjusted by manipulating aperture (f-stop), shutter speed, and ISO (sensor or film sensitivity). Exposure also takes place in the darkroom, when negatives are exposed to the light and projected onto chemically treated paper; the longer the exposure, the darker, more "burned," the image. In digital post-editing, this rather complicated procedure is transformed into a setting controlled by a slider bar.

Exposure is such a vital aspect of both analog and digital photography—something akin to breathing—that it is often taken for granted. Gilles Mora, French historian and former editor-in-chief of the pre-eminent journal of photography *Cahiers de Photographie*, omits it entirely from an alphabetized table of contents in his *Photospeak: A Guide to the Ideas, Movements, and Techniques of Photography, 1839 to the Present* (1998). Mora's book index jumps from enlargement to equivalents, and then on to Farm Security Administration.[2] Other reference works that aim to be exhaustive, such as *Focal Encyclopedia of Photography* (2007) edited by Michael Peres, cover the technical and historical aspects of exposure, but avoid another type of exposure that is becoming increasingly widespread in the 21st century: the circulation of digital images online. In the field of landscape photo-graphy, the circulation of iconic places—many of which are located in national parks and conservation areas that draw millions of photo-graphers—allows us to experience the places vicariously, prior to or in lieu of actual travel, whether it is via Facebook, Instagram, YouTube, WhatsApp or Snapchat. It is the increasing circulation of digital photo-graphy that was at least partially responsible for the shut-down of *Popular Photography*, the publication that ironically pioneered the coverage of digital technology.[3]

In addition to exposure through photographic processes and digital circu-lation, there is another type of exposure relevant to landscape photography—the meteorological one. The primary ingredient in exposure is light, and the best nature photographers are adept at using natural light to frame and define their subjects (Defibaugh quoted in Peres 2007: 333). This exposure, removed from the controlled conditions of a studio, extends beyond the quality of light to the changes in seasons, temperatures, visibility, flora, and fauna. There is an adventurous and often stoic aspect to photographing nature; the photographers earn their stripes by accumulating sunburns, blisters, insect bites, chapped lips, split ends, dehydration, and chills.

The exposure in landscape photography is layered, both from the point of view of equipment and atmospheric conditions, and from the afterlife of these images in the sphere of digital circulation. It begins with photographers, who make decisions regarding aperture, shutter speed, and ISO, frequently in inclement weather; continues with the transformation of the image in digital darkroom; and concludes with sharing and exposing oneself to the audience's criticisms. Exposure is as applicable to analog as to digital photographic practices, a constant that provides continuity in the field in spite of the ever-present advancements of technology.

The grandfather of "dramatic" landscape

The discussion of exposure as manipulation of camera settings begins with the master of 20th-century landscape photography himself—Ansel Adams. Even though referencing Adams's work in a piece on digital landscape photography has become common to the point of being a cliché, this cliché is a useful one: Adams's work provides a practical benchmark for comparing analog to digital. I suspect that many 21st-century landscape photography enthusiasts secretly wish to resurrect Adams from the dead: to outfit him in high-performance climbing gear; equip him with a DSLR, an ultra-light tripod, and a GoPro for good measure, and let him loose, once again, in the Yosemite National Park, the backdrop for his most famous shots. The enthusiast could tag along with Adams for hours, "looking for photos" (Adams's phrase), munching on Clif Bars, and picking his brains about what camera settings—that magical combination of aperture, shutter speed, ISO, focal depth, and filters—he would have chosen to properly expose an image given certain atmospheric conditions. That is the power Adams still exercises on the crowds of visitors who journey to Yosemite to take photos, pay homage to his work in the onsite gallery, and perhaps take a workshop or two run by his grandchildren.

Adams did nothing to de-mythologize his own work; in fact, he encouraged it. In his writing, he unabashedly stresses the physical endurance, mental recall, and visualization techniques that allowed him to take his most famous photos. Writing about his experience shooting the Half Dome, the iconic 4,800 foot monolith towering about Yosemite, Adams muses: "Those were the days when I could climb thousands of feet with a heavy pack and think nothing of it." His entourage—fiancée Virginia and two friends—is similarly undaunted in those "pre-roping times" (1983: 3). After a cold day of climbing, Adams is left with only one plate, but then experiences a sort of photographic epiphany. He clearly visualizes the picture he would like to take "as a brooding form, with deep shadows and a distant sharp white peak against a dark sky" and knows that he must use his deep red Wratten No. 29 filter to capture that image. Half a century later, Adams reflects:

> Over the years I became increasingly aware of the importance of visualization. The ability to anticipate—to see in the mind's eye, so to speak—the final print while viewing the subject makes it possible to apply the numerous controls of the craft in precise ways that contribute to achieving the desired result.
>
> (1983: 5)

Because of his advocacy of visualization, Adams comes across as a seer whose well-trained powers allow him to see the final product before it is taken—beating the affordances of the modern LCD display and its review function. His physical endurance, coupled with the will to possess the perfect shot, almost wills the photos into being—nature, like Galatea, responds to the artist's desire.

And yet, Adams is known not only for his proselytism of visualization, for his incredible recall and indomitable energy, but also for constant experimentation with photographic techniques (outside and in the darkroom) that were passed onto and equally embraced by digital landscape photographers. Michael Frye, in his practical guide to digital landscape photography, argues that, in spite of the increased power of control brought about by new digital tools, the basic principles of operation are the same as those developed by Adams and other analog masters such as Edward Weston and Eliot Porter (2009: 7). Adams famously compared his negatives to the musical score, and his prints to performance. Frye extends the analogy further by comparing RAW files stored in camera's memory card to the negatives that "need work" in Adobe Lightroom in order to transform into final products—the edited images.[4]

Few people realize the extent to which Adams developed his darkroom techniques, the specialized equipment for development he has invented and built in his home studio, the countless iterations of prints made off a single negative. *Moonrise, Hernandez, New Mexico* (1941), with its moon rising over distant mountain range, positioned in the middle of the print with top half of the image dominated by dark, cloudless sky—is just as famous as the story behind it. On Adams's own admission, it is a product of "combined serendipity and immediate technical recall" (41). As the story goes, Adams was struck by the landscape and immediately set out to photograph it; however, he soon realized that he forgot his Weston exposure meter. Fortunately, Adams recalled the luminance of the moon and was able to mentally calculate the appropriate exposure, taking just one shot before the scenery changed completely. Over the years, however, Adams made so many prints of *Moonrise, Hernandez*, often starkly different from each other, that it is easy to suspect that there must have been more than one negative. I had written to Andy Smith, of the Andy Smith Gallery in Tucson, Arizona, who said that he, too, has seen many interpretations of prints off the negative, and that when he hangs them together, "people commonly think they are from different negative" (email from Andrew Smith, November 8, 2018). In other words, the prints look so different that the audience assumes that multiple negatives were taken by Adams. In reality, Adams edited the single negative in so many different ways as if to create an illusion of a whole series. The multiplicity of interpretations of natural landscape was integrally tied up with Adams's artistic identity. Smith then put me in touch with Leslie Squyers, Senior Archivist at the Center for Creative Photography at the University of Arizona in Tucson (co-founded by Adams), who confirmed that only one negative exists, although there is photographic evidence that Adams made proof prints of Hernandez Church before 1941, which "demonstrate that Adams passed through that area several times" (email from Leslie Squyers, November 8, 2018).

As the celebrated *Life* photographer Andreas Feininger observed, a landscape photography "could never be called a 'reproduction' in the true sense of the word, regardless of how technically perfect it may be. Too great is the difference between the 'original' (the real landscape) and the 'copy' (the print)" (1953: 192). Feininger instead preferred the word "translation" for such metamorphosis from three-dimensional reality to a two-dimensional medium. And, just like a translation necessarily involves a series of choices taken by the translator (photographer), images have to be transformed "by means of controlled lies" (189). Adams's work with his negatives, which involved controlling for specific effects, is a useful story for fending off the purists who point accusatory fingers at those who fiddle with exposure settings in Adobe Lightroom. For even though objective representations of reality in photographs is a pipe dream—as the scholars of visual rhetoric have long argued—the idea of editing cannot seem to detach itself from the charges of being untruthful, fraudulent, and imprecise. In spite of the lessons from Adams regarding the power of visualization, framing, lens choice, and film sensitivity, editing nature "for effect" is a ground that must be trodden lightly. Ellen Gamerman, *Wall Street Journal* writer who covered the controversies inspired by several well-known photo contests and media outlets to include digitally manipulated images, writes that "a new wave of digital manipulation—and the blood sport of hunting for it—is roiling the world of photojournalism" (2016). There is even a new term for this, clearly borrowed from the field of project management: "manipulation creep." And the accusations of fraudulence get more severe when the manipulated subject is particularly arresting or awe-inspiring.

If the availability of enhanced digital post-editing tools, as an independent variable, is directly related to the increasing frequency and volume of online image exposure, then it seems to have an inverse relationship with the amount and quality of attention the viewer is prepared to invest in a landscape image. In order to be "attention-worthy," an image must be striking *as well as* represent "the real thing." The rising expectations of the public and the good natured, albeit competitive pressure from other photographers are powerful incentives in the digital darkroom. In a *New York Times* travel story on Yosemite Park (Story, 2008), Glenn Crosby (then curator at the park gallery, which is still managed by Adams's family) comments on the disconnect between the visitors' expectations of the park's monoliths (El Capitan, the Half Dome, Sentinel Dome, the Cathedral Spires) and their take-away experiences. Some people are "kind of disappointed," Crosby says, since "they only know the park through Ansel's eyes [...] the park is not always as dramatic as his work" (quoted in Story). We can say, with relatively high degree of confidence, that Ansel did dramatize nature, which amazed his audiences and turned out to be one of the most successful media campaigns for Yosemite. But in doing so, did he also inadvertently increase the expectations we have of "the real thing," desensitizing us to the quieter, calmer portraits of nature, those that feature tonal gradations rather than stark color contrasts, narrow angle lens rather than sweeping panoramas stitched together in Photoshop? And if Adams did, in fact, contribute to the shifting in our tastes or perceptions of nature, could it be that he was merely an agent of the inevitable changes enabled by the capture technology?

Capturing the "real"

The idea of capturing "real" landscape exercises a powerful pull, even though the "realness" itself is a politicized and rhetorical concept. In the state where I live, the phrase "Real Florida" not only represents the nostalgic desire to uncover something authentic underneath the patina of over-development and tourism, but also functions as a recognizable servicemark of the Florida Park Service that "help[s] visitors connect to ... *the Real Florida*^{SM}." Real Florida, it is implied, is contained not in the things that are human-made, but rather with something that is natural (which in some cases becomes synonymous with God-made).

The Park Service is not the only organization to extoll the power of the "real." The Florida Wildlife Corridor, which aims to protect and restore the natural habitat by creating a viable, unobstructed path from the Everglades to Georgia, effectively utilizes the power of media, photography, and video-graphy to engage greater numbers of people with natural Florida. Its first main awareness-building strategy was an eponymous expedition undertaken by a small team of founding members in 2012. During the 100-day, 1,000-mile trek from the Everglades all the way to Okefenokee National Wildlife Refuge in Georgia, the team paddled, mountain-biked, hiked, and rode horses through landscapes that ranged widely in facility and accessibility. Inspired by the literary and visual narratives of other environmentalists before them (most notably William Bartram, John Muir, and the *National Geographic* photographer Michael Fay), the expedition's progress was filmed, photographed, shared via social media networks, and finally presented to the public in a book format and as a documentary by Elam Stoltzfus ("Florida Wildlife Corridor Expedition."). In the film, the Everglades are described as "another world, the landscape as God intended;" there are references to "wild places and wild things [still] left in Florida"; and, in another telling quote, one interview subject declares that "we want to see true Florida." What complicates this labelling of Florida wilderness as "real" or "true" is the underlying assumption that such an original ever existed in the first place. Since the state's landscape is highly volatile, as a result of either natural phenomena such as sinkhole formation and shifting coastlines, or economic ones in real estate development, it is also an environment that constantly shifts and resists interpretation, making recourse to nostalgia problematic. When it comes to capturing a landscape, "real" Florida usually means a landscape that is visibly free of development, which in turn functions as an effective marketing tool for conservation, in spite of the irony that photographers pull all the stops to frame and edit the material for the most amount of impact per pixel.

Florida is photogenic, too. There is an especially mesmerizing beauty in its long, undulating coastline, the sea oats swaying in the wind, supporting the sensitive dunes. In the northern part of the state, one can still take long walks by the shore without encountering a single soul, apart from a lonely crab or adventurous tortoise. My partner and I often take photos on the fourteen-mile barrier island next to St. Augustine, a city that prides itself as "one of the oldest continuously inhabited European and African American settlements in the United States" (National Park Service), and attracts many tourists to its manicured cobblestoned streets crowded with gift shops. However, the farther one travels from the city southbound on Anastasia Island, the easier it is to imagine the evasive "Real Florida." In addition to being perfectly positioned for both sunrise (Atlantic side) and sunset (inlet) photography, the island is teeming with aquatic birds. Dolphins are often present, judging by the elegant rotation of their dorsal fins, like the teeth of oversized gears, just above the water line.

One evening, we took a tripod to the beach just after sunset to take some night shots. The outline of the beach houses above the dunes, the shaggy crowns of isolated palmettos, and the distant glow of lights at the northern end of the island "looked interesting."[5] The evening was punctured by twenty-second segments as a Canon DSLR, perched on a tripod, was taking long exposures—during which we remained reverentially silent as if even the sound waves could affect the output. As a final shot of the evening, I suggested we take a long-exposure selfie, standing with our backs to distant lights, and so we stood in the blue-purple haze, trying not to sway with the waves that licked our ankles (Fig. 9.1).

Later that evening, the following adjustments were made in Adobe Lightroom: the shot was cropped to adhere to the "rule of thirds,"[6] the horizon line was corrected, the highlights (of which there are blissfully plenty thanks to the light pollution) were made lighter. The shape of the software histogram guided this transformation—the metamorphosis from a palette of violets and blues to a background of yellows, oranges, and magenta. Our silhouettes and shadows—almost black against the saturated sky and the surface of the water—were adequately defined. When I saw the final

Figure 9.1 Ismael Iribar. Crescent Beach, Anastasia Island, Florida.

product, my first impulse was surprise, because the colors were not at all what we saw at the beach a few hours earlier.[7] This surprise and even suspicion persisted in spite of my understanding that the camera "sees" a lot more than the human eye and picks up a lot more information from the world. To this day, our family and friends default to calling that silhouette shot "a gorgeous sunset," even when told that the picture was taken at dusk, long after the sun set behind the horizon. The insistence on sticking to what one sees, rather than what knows to be true, is poignant. While many would say that post-editing landscape photography can be a conjuring trick, even in cases when the magicians are transparent the viewers refuse to abandon the illusion. There is nothing "magical," however, about post-editing, which uses the information imprinted on the camera sensor. Digital tools allow to view things with a greater precision (attention to detail) than the human eye, even though their capture of information is often interpreted as "lies." By presenting us with nature images that look different from what we have perceived, photography exposes us to our own vulnerabilities and physical limitations.

I have seen this place before

In his iconic study of the way humans perceive and interpret art images, E. H. Gombrich demonstrates how what we see depends on our previous exposure to similarly recorded portrayals of reality, what he calls our "schema" (1984: 59). The creators of images are also shackled to their own "reliance on acquired [visual] vocabularies," (128) and are often unaware how much their own work is influenced and tightly woven into that of their predecessors: the Greek notion of *mimesis*, the vanishing point of the Renaissance, the "golden" rule of thirds.

Gombrich debunks the myth of the innocent eye and argues that it is in the field of landscape painting (and landscape photography) "where sight counts for so much more than calculation, that these psychological facts were first discovered" (254). According to him, nature "could never have become 'picturesque' for us unless we, too, had acquired the habit of seeing it in pictorial terms." We look at a sunset photograph and translate it as a "sunset" because we were previously exposed to other, similar sunsets—the colors are warmer, the light is softer. Because our brains and eyes are particularly good at recognizing relationships between things, we read the spatial positioning between the heavy orange orb hanging just over the horizon as a sun. In order to make sense of the world around us and not get overwhelmed, we need to rely on the pre-existing schema and to use it to re-create the natural world—whether with a paintbrush, film, or digital code.

Perhaps that is why hundreds of thousands of photographers flock to the scenic Horseshoe Bend just a few miles south of Lake Powell, Arizona—the point where the Colorado River dwindles to a barely moving stream as it skirts the circular monolith base. An hour or so before sunset, the 1.5-mile hike from the parking lot off U.S. Route 89 looks like a pilgrimage route, with at least one in ten hikers carrying a solid tripod; DSLRs abound. And, as in a case of real pilgrimage, everyone has a very clear picture of what is to be found at the end, for pictures of the Horseshoe Bend are among the most frequently imprinted on touristic imagination in the region—on par with the stone buttes of the Monument Valley in Colorado or the dramatic arches in the Arches National Park. At any rate, pilgrimage is not so much about getting to the destination, but about bringing the boon back home—in this case, one's own, private version of the natural landscape.[8]

In terms of color balance, nature is doing the editing for you in Arizona. Atmospheric haze in the desert gives the distant rock formations a blue tint. The soil, by contrast, appears red, orange, and yellow. When the morning and afternoon sun hits the mountains, it reddens the reds and oranges the oranges, throwing the shadow side into an even deeper blue. As a result, the image looks even more dramatic, without the application of filters. The contrast between the warmth of the sun-caressed rock and the cold faces of the mountains is pleasing to the eye. In less photogenic landscapes, post-editing in Lightroom would have been used to achieve a similar effect. Instead, Arizona charms us with the seeming effortlessness of its beauty. There is just one complaint—in the dry season, the clouds are rare, the skies are too clear. As I stood at sunset next to the precipice overlooking the dark U of the water in the canyon below, I recalled reading an article by photographer Jim Zuckerman in *Petersen's Photographic* (2003), which advised readers on "dramatizing boring skies" in Thar Desert in northwestern India. In order to enhance the "cloudless, blue and boring"

Rajasthan sky, Zuckerman worked in Photoshop to replace it entirely with a picture of the sky taken in La Paz, Bolivia (37).

There are many online articles on how to photograph Horseshoe Bend for greater effect—which lens to use, how to position a tripod next to the edge (not separated from the drop by a railing or even "caution" sign in spite of the 1,000-foot drop). Some photographers lie prone on the red rocks, stretched out like lizards right next to the precipice, training their lenses directly below. Others straddle the rocks that jut out over the abyss for an adventurous selfie, using their phone to remotely control their camera. Each one will go away with their own coveted shot, apply post-editing workflow, and share the photo with others—their own, private canyon (Fig. 9.2). In the age of social media, Horseshoe Bend became a "must see" in Arizona, drawing approximately 2 million visitors in 2018 (many from China, Germany, and France) (Craven, 2018). Conducting an image search for "Horseshoe Bend" on the Internet brings up the same composition, but in a staggering array of color gradations. The ubiquitous "U" of the water can be emerald green, deep cobalt, turquoise, and even royal blue striated with green. As if denying the rule of thirds, the monolith takes up central space in the images, pushing the horizon line up. In reality, however, the rock looks different, our gaze is trained down onto the rock as our bodies struggle to adjust to the height, to keep the adrenaline levels in check as we try to ignore the nagging thought of what would happen if a gust of wind pushed us a few inches closer to the edge. Where the image of the bend is expansive if taken with a wide lens

Figure 9.2 Ismael Iribar. Horseshoe Bend, Page, Arizona.

such as a fisheye, the reality is more claustrophobic. One is reminded of the Yosemite's visitor reaction to the disconnect between the actual landscape and the one composed and edited by Adams—only this time, one is not underwhelmed but rather overwhelmed with concern for one's safety. While the image is breathtakingly beautiful and even comforting, the reality exposes us to danger, makes our body feel vulnerable when faced with the drop, the quickly setting sun, the encroaching desert cold. But there is also a strange sense of connection among the "pilgrims." Like the apprentice artists huddling around a masterpiece at a museum in order to copy the original, they are also here to recreate previous iterations of the image many of them have seen online. It is both humbling and reassuring that everyone, in spite of the lenses and software tools they use, is still sharing and is shaped by the same visual vocabulary.

Waiting for the single moment

It is very cold and dark just before the sunrise, as the earth is almost out of the heat stored during the previous day. This is the hour one must set out in order to capture a sunrise. During a late October visit to the Grand Canyon National Park in Arizona, my partner and I spent some time on the pitch black roads looking for the Mather viewpoint parking. When we finally hike to the rim in cold drizzle that is threatening to turn to wet snow, I recall Adams's descriptions of the shooting temperatures. "It was *cold* in the gulley," he writes about shooting the Half Dome in Yosemite, "patches of snow and ice remained in the recesses of the rocks, and a chilly wind flowed over us from the high regions above" (3). On his early morning drives around the park "in search of photographs" everything is cold—the solution, the film, the camera—and it not possible to process pictures even when taking shelter in the car (45). Another time, shooting a winter sunrise in Sierra Nevada, he again writes that it was "very cold—perhaps near zero" as he "waited, shivering, for a shaft of sunlight to flow over the distant trees" (164). "Cold," it would seem, or rather Adams's exposure to it, accompanies and defines the photographer's most dramatic landscapes. Photography is not for the faint hearted—like a true passion, it takes its toll.

My partner and I are also here to wait for the "shaft of sunlight" to be thrown over the east-facing canyon walls, but we are starting to get concerned about the unpropitious weather—as are the other visitors, who are gradually emerging from the shadows. Closer to the sunrise, the viewpoint is dense with a multilingual throng equipped with smartphones, selfie sticks, point-and-shoot cameras, and the well-recognizable Canon and Nikon DSLRs. It is very cold, the wet type of cold that pierces multiple layers and stiffens the joints; it is as if the canyon is breathing cold air from down below. Without the elusive shaft of light—lasting only brief moments—there will be no dramatic photo, and there won't be enough information on the camera sensor to augment the images in either Lightroom or Photoshop.

The rain shows no sign of abating, and I give up, drive back to our lodge to warm up and think about Adams, what he would have said about this failure of willpower, and faith. My partner returns a few hours later via village shuttle, barely able to feel his fingers and toes, but jubilant and bearing a boon. The sun did come out, for a brief moment its rays pierced through thick clouds, and he was able to capture the illuminated canyon—gloriously lit as if on fire. The pictures received minimal post-editing.

With Grand Canyon, the choice of lens and framing are paramount, and the weather conditions do the rest. But here the landscape photographer is faced with another limitation—the sheer vastness of the natural wonder that can never be captured. Framing a photograph with "interesting" detail in the foreground can provide some sense of perspective, or using a human figure to convey a sense of scale. In Fig. 9.3, it is a butte jutting into the canyon that resembles a moai profile from Easter Island that provides a counterbalance to the line of fire above it. But these are happy accidents, and Grand Canyon is one of those places that are impossible to overdramatize, no matter how much we are exposed to the images online.

The mirror-less future

One thing that connects all the photographic examples discussed here (apart from the fact that they deal with natural landscape) is that they all are concerned with the gap between what is seen and the "final product," what gets

Figure 9.3 Ismael Iribar. Mather Point, Grand Canyon National Park, Arizona.

lost in the translation between the real world and the digital pixels we see printed on the screen. This chapter opened with the mention of a similar gap—in the now-defunct *Popular Photography*—and continued to trace the desire for the ever more effective post-editing techniques in the age when darkroom has been replaced with Adobe Lightroom. If photography, both etymologically and literally, is "drawing with light," then it involves the same process of translation from reality as a drawn image. We are constantly registering and interpreting nature, relying on the affordances of our own biology and the inherited visual vocabularies, using our bodies and minds as transmission apparatuses. The act of seeing (whether through our eyes or optical instruments) is a complicated systematic and iterative process that is quite often taken for granted.

In a DSLR camera, we look at nature through a viewfinder that belies a simple yet ingenious contraption. If it wasn't for the mirror positioned behind the lens, and the pentaprism that reflects the image from the mirror into the viewfinder, we'd see nothing but darkness. When the shutter button is pressed, the mirror flips up, temporarily exposing the sensor behind it to the light. Similarly to the human brain, the mirror turns the image right-side up after receiving the information through the lens. Seeing (and capturing) and image is a by-product of several "translations," like a game of broken telephone. The image that is finally recognized as a landscape first gets turned upside down by the lens, which is then reflected by the mirror, to be reflected twice by the pentaprism, which is then directed to the viewfinder, to be imprinted on the retina, to be turned back upside down by the brain. And, like any good translation, this process is "seamless," running in the background, unnoticed.

At the time of writing, however, a new photography invention is poised to soon take over DSLR cameras in terms of popularity—the so-called "mirrorless" camera, which will adopt the functionality of the smartphone with the image quality of DSLRs. Because this new camera circumvents the mirrors and pentaprisms, it allows us to see the image to be taken on its display in exactly the same way as it would have been seen on the computer during post-editing. In fact, in mirrorless cameras the post-editing happens even before the picture is taken and the gap between the reality and its capture is blurred. In addition to including some editing tools in their software, these cameras also have Internet connectivity to make the images instantly shareable, a homage to Virilio's futurism of the instant. The sequestered darkroom will be brought outside, into the light, and the different facets of exposure discussed in this chapter will coalesce: camera settings, editing, meteorology, and distribution all rolled into one, impossible to separate one from another. The market prediction is that the capturing software will continue to steadily improve because lenses have physical limitations (anything from image distortion to those annoying specks of dust caught inside). When the software is augmented with AI tools that will help photographers drastically cut down on post-editing time, there will be no mass return to

DSLR (although there will always be late adopters of technology hesitant to make the switch, insistent on remaining fluent in both the mirrorless and the mirrored domains).

One effect of the breakneck technological advancement in capturing hardware and software is that the discussion of manipulation of nature is also becoming more abstract. If the editing decisions are made for us as part of the background processes of the camera, then photographers are inevitably trading off some of their creative agency. The more we do away with visible post-editing, the more we consign the images we take to the black box operation of computer code, the more inaccessible and automatic editing becomes. But what does it really mean that we stop tinkering with filters, developers, enlargers, paper, masks, layers, and sliders? Are we ever in control of the images of the world around us that we capture, modify, and interpret? We do, after all, live comfortably with our own blindspots, accept one eye as dominant, and allow the brain to intelligently do the legwork of filling in the missing pieces. When it comes to technology, it remains to be seen whether the decisions the cameras will make about nature will be just as "natural."

Notes

1 Since *Popular Photography* ceased publication, many of these articles are still available on magazine's eponymous website (popphoto.com), which is still being updated by Bonnier Corporation.

2 The U.S. Farm Security Administration was instrumental in organizing a large-scale federally subsidized documentary project between 1935 and 1943 to document the conditions of Americans during the Depression.

3 In an internal company-wide memo announcing the closure of *Popular Photography*, a Bonnier Corporation publication, CEO Eric Zinczenko explained that the decision to shut down the magazine had to do with "the rise of smartphone-camera technology and its increasing ability to capture quality images and share then socially" (cited in Mistry, 2017).

4 While RAW files contain more information than JPEGs and do not lose information when compressed, they may appear as more "bland" or less exciting than the latter. This seems counterintuitive, but only if one is not aware that a camera runs JPEGs through its image processor, automatically applying settings to improve the photos (contrast, white balance, color space, and sharpening).

5 The word "interesting" is often used (and even overused) in articles, blogs, and live streams dedicated to photography.

6 To adhere to the rule of thirds when framing photos, the photographer imagines breaking up the shot into thirds, horizontally and vertically. The most interesting subjects ("points of interest") are then positioned at one of the four intersections formed by the lines. If the rule is not used at the time of capture, rule of thirds can be easily applied during post-processing in Lightroom and Photoshop.

7 To an extent, some of the latest smartphones can make similar adjustments when shooting at night. Google Pixel smartphones are now equipped with a new feature that allows to take well defined, focused, and lit photos in "very dark situations." Night Sight mode captures up to fifteen low-light shots, "blending them to brighten up faces, provide sharp details, and saturate colors in a way that draws in the eye (Fowler, 2018).

8 When describing the stages of a hero's journey (separation–initiation–return) Campbell writes that "[a] hero comes back from this mysterious adventure with the power to bestow boons on his fellow man" (2004: 28). In other words, a gift or a bit of knowledge bestowed on those who remain at home.

References

Adams, Ansel. *Examples: The Making of 40 Photographs*. Boston, MA: Little, Brown and Company, 1983.

Campbell, Joseph. *The Hero with a Thousand Faces*. Princeton, NJ: Princeton University Press, 2004.

Craven, Scott. "How Horseshoe Bend Went Viral and What's Being Done to Manage the Crowds." *Arizona Republic* November 27, 2018. https://www.azcentral.com/story/travel/arizona/road-trips/2018/08/09/horseshoe-bend-scenic-hike-near-lake-powell/587733002/. Accessed May 2, 2019.

Defibaugh, Denis. "Landscape Photography." *Focal Encyclopedia of Photography*, Ed. Michael R. Peres. Waltham, MA: Focal Press, 2007. 333–334.

Feininger, Andreas. *Feininger on Photography*. New York: Crown Publishers, 1953.

"Dir. ElamStoltzfus. Live Oak Production Group, 2013. DVD.

Fowler, Geoffrey A. "Your Smartphone Photos Are Totally Fake—and You Love It." *The Washington Post* November 14,2018. https://www.washingtonpost.com/technology/2018/11/14/your-smartphone-photos-are-totally-fake-you-love-it/?tid=ss_mail&utm_term=.b2d1b71e5d3e

Frye, Michael. *Digital Landscape Photography: In the Footsteps of Ansel Adams and the Great Masters*. Lewes, UK: Ilex Press, 2009.

Gallagher, Peter B. "Florida Wildlife Corridor Expedition." *The Seminole Tribune* April 25,2012.

Gamerman, Ellen. "Do Digitally Altered Photos Represent Fact or Fiction? Social Media and New Editing Tools Are Recasting the Digital Landscape—and Its Rules—for Photojournalism." *The Wall Street Journal* August 11, 2016. ProQuest. Accessed May 2, 2019.

Gombrich, E. H. *Art and Illusion: A Study in the Psychology of Pictorial Representation*. London: Phaidon Press, 1984.

Grossman, Debbie. "Horizon Harmony." *Popular Photography & Imaging* 68. 6(2004): 52–53. ProQuest. Accessed May 2, 2019.

Grossman, Debbie. "Software Workshop: Creating a Fake Reflection." *Popular Photography* 75. 5(2011a): 42–44. ProQuest. May 2, 2019.

Grossman, Debbie. "How To: Optimize a Landscape in Photoshop." *Popphoto.com* February 23 (2011b). https://www.popphoto.com/gallery/how-optimize-landscape-photoshop. Accessed May 2, 2019.

Iribar, Ismael. Crescent Beach, Anastasia Island, Florida. August 2018.

Iribar, Ismael. Horseshoe Bend, Page, Arizona. October 2018.

Iribar, Ismael. Mather Point, Grand Canyon National Park, Arizona. October 2018.

Mistry, Phil. "*Popular Photography* is Dead after 80 Years as a Top Photo Magazine." *PetaPixel.com* March 7, 2017. https://petapixel.com/2017/03/07/popular-photography-dead-80-years-top-photo-magazine/. Accessed May 2, 2019.

Mora, Gilles. *Photospeak: A Guide to the Ideas, Movements, and Techniques of Photography, 1839 to the Present*. New York: Abbeville Press, 1998.

National Park Service. "Florida St. Augustine." https://www.nps.gov/nr/travel/geo-flor/24.htm. Accessed April 20, 2019.

Peres, Michael R., Ed. *Focal Encyclopedia of Photography*. 4th edn. Amsterdam: Focal Press, 2007.

Story, Louise. "What Adams Saw Through His Lens." *The New York Times*April 27, 2008. http://www.nytimes.com/2008/04/27/travel/27journeys.html

Virilio, Paul. *The Futurism of the Instant, Stop-Eject*. Trans. Julie Rose. Cambridge, UK: Polity, 2010.

Zuckerman, J. (2003). "Dramatizing boring skies." *Petersen's Photographic*, 32, 36–37.

10 (Re)coding environmental activism

An examination of *Hike Wild Montana*

Glen Southergill

When President Lyndon Johnson signed the Wilderness Protection Act into law in 1964, he codified a legal definition of wilderness as possessing a "primeval character and influence" that can be "recognized as an area where the earth and its community of life are untrammeled by man". In no small part, the Act and its noteworthy definition owes its inception to the lobbying efforts of citizen-activists, such as the founding members of the Montana Wilderness Association who began offering guided wilderness walks in 1958. These guided walks organized (and continue to organize) activists by facilitating experiences with the unique wilderness character eventually described by the Wilderness Protection Act. Consequently, these guided walks fulfill a significant communicative function as activities engineered to encourage wilderness advocacy and engagement in the process of writing public policy.[1]

In 2016, the Montana Wilderness Association's efforts to promote the "wilderness character" of federally protected spaces entered a new domain with the publication *Hike Wild Montana* (online at http://hike.wildmontana.org/). *Hike Wild Montana* is a web-based service that shares hiking trails, tips, reviews, and suggestions from other hikers. On one level, *Hike Wild Montana* represents a next-generation planning guide for hiking in the form of a participatory composition, such as explored by Sarah Arroyo (2013), but on another level it encourages the public to advocate for greater and more wilderness protections. It resulted from "a handful of guidebooks, a bunch of gigantic fold-out Forest Service maps, three topo maps, five websites, a half-dozen blogs, multiple calls to ranger stations … [and] the help of more than 70 Montana Wilderness Association volunteers" (Randzio, 2016). Despite the influence of analog texts in its development, it also affords a case study of how digital rhetoric in the form of code intervenes into environmental advocacy. While a lucrative analysis could certainly be done at the level of the interface by which visitors to *Hike Wild Montana* add or "see" content, this chapter focuses on the underlying programming which provides executable instructions that direct *Hike Wild Montana*'s behavior. By looking closely at the JavaScript programming of *Hike Wild Montana*, the chapter discusses how the work of environmental writing extends into domains of pixel and tracker, as well as deriving significant meaning from the discipline-specific languages and discourse communities of programmers.

Codes of environmental activism

"Of particular interest here is [Kenneth] Burke's argument that our understanding of the world comes through the symbols provided in our language. The way we use these symbols to represent the world is determined by the motives that emerge from the rhetorical scheme" (Herndl and Brown, 1996: 10).

With the coding of *Hike Wild Montana* and other virtual or digital sites of environmental communications, the symbolic actions of activism have encountered a new form of writing. Code can be approached in historical and cultural ways, as well as developed over time by programmers engaged in the craft of building both the code and conventions against which code conforms. Critically, code's functionality can be probed for questions of power relations, aesthetics, and a host of other concerns. However, we now speak in pluralities as codes interact, sometimes requiring human agents for direction and sometimes revealing selectively symbolic outputs to the human. The symbolic action of code exists beyond the discourse community of the programmer—it directs the display and conduct of devices and applications, which then interface with end users. We see in code studies, then, not merely a binary logic common to computing—a dramatism of discourse within programmer circles and between people mediated by programs—but a trinary that must also consider the execution language directed to nonhuman agents. I suggest that code as a subset of software studies displays symbolic actions even as it problematizes the identities of the fields to which it applies. Burke frames identification as a requisite component of symbolic action and a product of dialog for "reconciling opposites in a higher synthesis" (1962: 53). Code similarly operates with dialog across sets of human and nonhuman audiences. The first, the human programmers and the discursive communities they form, can be observed in the conventions often termed "best," "emerging," or "compliant" practices. The second, and second-order, would be the new programming done in response to existing programming.

Invariably looking at the communities of practice that develop software conventions or the various computational logics and languages that drive computing writ large begs important questions, including how (if at all) the "literacies" which have proven fertile soil for rhetorical theorization beget productive understandings of software. Code, Alexander Galloway asserts, "is the only language that is executable" (2004: 165). Galloway follows a logic whereby code acts by fiat—directing applications to display visual representations, permit participation through user input, or produce any form of output. As Galloway asserts "(hardware) cannot *do* anything, but must be transformed into code (software) to be effective"

(165). Wendy Hui Kyong Chun defines code "as source—as logos" (2013: 155), which maintains a generative logic to the coding enterprise. In a thread of scholarship he terms "critical code studies," Mark C. Marino (2006) asserts a need to study code for its "interpretation, the search for and production of meaning." To Marino, meaning stems not only from the computer as "one recipient of the code" (which in turn provides an interface that itself may contribute to the making of meaning by users), but also "there is the programmer, other programmers, and at times even users who have access to its text." Marino begins to nudge code specifically as a form of symbolic intervention.

Scholars of rhetoric and writing, such as Annette Vee, Estee Beck, Kevin Brock, James J. Brown, and Karl Stolley, have similarly begun exploring code as manifestations of writing, interrogating the underlying mechanics that both produce digital interfaces and serve as the subjects of study for programming communities. Vee, for instance, positions coding as not only a part of computer science, but a manifestation of the tradition of composition also aligned with rhetoric in order to place programming "in a longer historical and cultural context of information management and expression" (2017: 19). She further defines programming as "the act and practice of writing code that tells a computer what to do" (19). However, the relationships Vee constructs between code and action, programming and symbol are not so simple. She notes "programming—like writing—is a complex, social, expressive activity within a symbolic and technological system" (137). Such an awareness aligns with David J. Gunkel's post-structuralist resistance into the binary logics of computation, L.D. Introna's notion of encoding, and James J. Brown Jr.'s call for rhetors to "cross state lines" and engage in software studies (2015: 29). Sean Morey considers "writing as a system for representing nature, a technology used to signify an outside world" to situate images as a component of that system, which by a similar logic can begin including and critiquing coding (2009: 23). To the extent that writing in code contributes to understandings of digital rhetoric, such calls resonate with Douglas Eyman's assertion that digital rhetoric "is perhaps most simply defined as the application of rhetorical theory (as analytic method or heuristic for production) to digital texts and performances" (2015: 44).

In the specific case of *Hike Wild Montana*, code can become a species of environmental writing that can be historicized and contextualized alongside publications that announce or discuss wilderness hikes dated to the mid-20th century. M. Jimmie Killingsworth and Jacqueline S. Palmer interrogate relationships constructed "for the purpose of cooperative social action" (1992: 7). Code, then, especially in the participatory compositions that encourage encounters with and discussion of the environment, is a collaboratively written executable rhetoric derived from discourse communities that facilitates and forges social relations.

Javascripting *Hike Wild Montana*

In late 1995, JavaScript (JS) creator Brendan Eich joined Netscape, which was then seeking what Eich describes as a "glue language" that would "assemble components and automate their interactions [using higher order code]" (Hamilton, 2008). In this original intention, JS offered a needed scripting language embedded into HTML (Hypertext Markup Language) that would work in concert with the higher-order (and often proprietary) programming languages of internet applications like Firefox, Chrome, and Safari. Java-Script could then "touch elements of the [web]page, change their properties, and respond to events" that contributed to generating a "much livelier web consisting of pages that acted more like applications" (Hamilton). JavaScript enhanced the design of websites, but invited programmers who could quickly learn the language to begin experimenting with and generating novel solutions to website design on the client-side.

JavaScript functions in highly rhetorically noteworthy ways. First, it creates interactivity and behavior within web-based pages that can be subjected to investigation. While HTML or CSS (Cascading Style Sheets) controls the display of content, JS promotes behavioral characteristics by the web page. Next, JS development often relies on incorporating snippets of code provided by other programmers or organizations. Within the logic of JS, it becomes possible to anchor (in other words, redirect) the browser application rendering the content to draw code from and be maintained by another source. Thus developers work communally whenever they make snippets of code available for other developers to use or improve. When anchored, the source of the code is found not directly within the embedded script of the page, but rather in another source to which the browser application is directed. Finally, the logic of JS permits embedding comments that are clearly marked for the machine to ignore but a human reader to see. These comments are not rendered by browser applications for viewing by website users. To see them, a reader must examine the source code itself with enough knowledge of JS to see such comments for what they are: as a form of embedded note from programmer to programmer.

My reading of *Hike Wild Montana*'s JS focuses on several core questions: first, how does it function as a "glue" language? Second, how do *Hike Wild Montana*'s programmers engage within a discourse community by drawing from external sources of code? With JS, *Hike Wild Montana* employs several rather simple (but elegant) snippets of code. Each element of code reveals, through its operations and embedded notation, some signs of how the broader composition, *Hike Wild Montana*, becomes a cogent whole. The JS can be opened in a rather rudimentary text file, which with HTML and CSS tells browser applications how to display the website service on everything from type to placement of image, sound, or video files. However, each code segment bears a similar convention, the use of <> and </> to tag, or open and close, a given function. By beginning each "script" with tags, the code's transition to JS from HTML becomes clearer. Consequently, my analysis next moves to exploring in greater detail two specific and discrete code segments that are bounded by tags. In the course of any website, there may be several places where the programmer has embedded JS using tags as signposts. As discussed below, the location as well as the content of the tagged JS code is significant.

"Head" code example: Google Analytics

```
<!–Google Analytics–>
<script>
(function(i, s, o, g, r, a, m) {i['GoogleAnalyticsObject'] = r; i[r] = i[r] ||
function() {(i[r].q = i[r].q || []).push(arguments)}, i[r].l = 1 * new Date(); a =
s.createElement(o), m =s.getElementsByTagName(o)[0]; a.async = 1; a.src =
g; m.parentNode.insertBefore(a, m)})(window, document, 'script', '//www.
google-analytics.com/analytics.js', 'ga');
  ga('create', 'UA-37465504-1', 'auto');
  ga('send', 'pageview');
</script>
<!—End Google Analytics–>
```

Figure 10.1 Google Javascript tracking snippet.

In Fig. 10.1, the reader (machine or human) encounters the first instance of JS coding in *Hike Wild Montana*. In this section, I discuss and analyze the rhetorical features of Fig. 10.1 as well as pointing to its implications as an instance of environmental communication code-writing. At a macro level, webpages can be understood as divided into "Head" and "Body" categories. Head elements contain titles, styles, meta-information, and generalized information that relates to the whole of the site. Generally, head information exists more for the programmers to use to direct the user's selected browser application on general matters of display or behavior.

When read in the order by which a code would be run, the first line of JS appears after an embedded comment entitled "Google Analytics." Immediately prior to and after the script snippet, human readers will note lines with exclamation points, what looks like two mathematical symbols for greater or lesser than, and two hyphens before and after a "script" tag, which encapsulates the space of coding within HTML. These markers use HTML to relay a comment for human readership. Browser applications have themselves been programmed to ignore anything contained within them as unexecutable. Using Google Analytics, developers and their clients gain access to a broad range of user conduct, including information on page viewings and events (user interactions with content ranging from downloads to clicks). Enabling Analytics in code signals that the developer accepts Google's approach to collecting and measuring website visitation and usage, which

Google may modify and further refine at will. The simple remark "Google Analytics" also means, for instance, that *Hike Wild Montana*'s code defines visitation using Google's terminology, acting as a form of citation.

To learn more about how Google Analytics works and how to use the code, developers can visit Google's publication "Adding analytics.js to Your Site." There, Google describes that its JS tracking snippet accomplishes several symbolically rich actions. It in part redirects the browser application to pull code from a Google site, as indicated by the use of "a.src" which serves as an anchor point and directs the browser to draw code from www.google-a nalytics.com. In essence, the use of an anchor code represents a turn towards programmatic identification. The browser recognizes a direct instruction from the JS that could be translated to mean "go here and do what you find there directs you to do." Provided the point to which the browser has been directed and the browser application share an understandable language (or identification, to borrow rhetorical vernacular), the developer will be provided the analytics she requested. Should a browser application simply go directly to that site, it would simply display the code maintained by Google to manage its analytics function (in other words, a long string of code).

The Google Analytics snippet code in Fig. 10.1 also includes a code element termed "ga()" at the end of the sequence that uniquely marks *Hike Wild Montana* and tracks site-specific information. Google's developer kit defines this as a command queue, or "an interface for doing almost everything you need to do with the analytics JS Library." The proceeding lines which begin with "function" immediately after the opening script tag both "define" and "allow" the command queue. Essentially this use of code employs what Google calls a "create method," which first creates a tracker with an ID specific to *Hike Wild Montana* (a "UA" designator found within the "ga()" code lines). The second use of ga enables a transfer of data, when a "hit" corresponds to "page viewing" (an instance of a page being loaded in a browser). The executable side of the "ga()" language moves from "function" as definition to "ga" as instruction, resulting in a user's browser relaying information back to the web development team's analytics tracking apparatus.

From this one snippet, we see symbolic action in several noteworthy ways. A decision to communicate amongst coders with a primacy in HTML, prior to interjecting the code within the script hashtags, suggests the potential for developers to take critical or creative licenses with the grafting of code from one source into a new context. It signifies a cooperative relationship between the developers of the site and Google's analytics offerings. Such decisions may speak to the conventions the programmer chooses to follow or stress, and then speak to the ways in which the programmer is operating within a discourse community. Then the tracker code symbolizes not merely that page viewings are tracked, but that *Hike Wild Montana* employs Google as a third-party provider of how visitations are defined, monitored, and tracked.

"Body" code sample: "jQuery" Library

```
<script   src="https://cdnjs.cloudflare.com/ajax/libs/jquery/2.1.1/jquery.min.js">
</script>
<script>
$(function() {
  $(window).resize(function() {
    if ($(window).width() < 1025) {
      var windowHeight = $(window).height();
      var mastheadHeight = $('.relative').height();
      var iframeHeight = windowHeight - mastheadHeight;

      $('.map').css('height', iframeHeight + 'px');
    } else {
      // $('.map').css('height', '400px');
      // $('.content').css('height', '400px');
    }
  }).resize();
});

$('.mobile-nav-trigger').click(function(e) {
  e.preventDefault();
  $(this).toggleClass('open');
  $('.navigation-holder').toggleClass('closed');
});
</script>
```

Figure 10.2 jQuery snippet.

In Fig. 10.2, *Hike Wild Montana* uses code derived from jQuery library. Its use can be perhaps most readily identified by "script src" in the first line of code, which then references an external library housed on "cloudflare.com." When drawing from jQuery, developers incorporate lines of code from repositories that other developers contribute towards. In this case, the developers of *Hike Wild Montana* treat the size of a user's screen as an event. Feedback from the user's physical device then becomes a form of input, by which an alternative display designed for smaller screens is loaded by the browser application. To clarify, *Hike Wild Montana* would gather information from the user's browser application whether they are using a laptop or smartphone, for example. In the case of a smaller screen, the JS code from jQuery would instruct the browser application differently than a larger screen and more appropriately for the smaller screen. Users may visit the same website on a mobile device and see a different navigation window displayed, which in turn accomplishes similar and recognizable work. JavaScript provides the browser an ability to know what to do when confronted by a series of variables ("var") recognized by definition as a function of height and width. Each function contains a possible series of variables, presented as "if then" statements, that help guide the browser into rendering content as either developed with a larger or smaller display size. In this case, the core glue-like functions of JS respond to jQuery as a collaborative project by which assets can be grafted into new projects from existing libraries. Then there are functions with contained variables that require the browser application to recognize and adapt to the type of hardware in question. Consequently, the user's device becomes instructive to the JS solution used.

The use of a third-party solution from "jQuery" signifies a turn towards invoking emergent conventions amongst programming communities. Again, programmers function within discourse communities to recognize and resolve potential problems. As programmers heavily steeped in the language and best practices of a given language recognize commonly occurring problems, they may develop increasingly elegant solutions. In turn, these solutions become standardized not by fiat from either organizational pressure or convention by an organizing body, but by usage by peers. The solution employed by *Hike Wild Montana* represents one possible solution, one which has gained favor with the Montana Wilderness Association's development team. In time, however, as new hardware is introduced, the programming communities may find alternative approaches to producing snippets that find favor in the sight of the local developers. When read rhetorically, jQuery then provides a unique scene in which programmers share and use already-developed solutions to common problems. Consequently, as a scene of collaboration, contributors generally agree to certain generalized principles of practice—often termed open source. While jQuery provides documentation to help guide the flow of contributions, a type of rhetorical decorum to which contributors and users agree, ultimately the programmer-community serves as a form of dual agent. They both resolve the unique situational needs of a service, and also help other programmers who may face similar situations. In this case, the rhetorical dynamics of cooperation as a type of symbolic action moves beyond environmental writing, but speaks instead to the rhetorical nature of JS programming more generally.

Lessons learned, and towards the code of environmental activism to come

In *Hike Wild Montana*, the "glue" language envisioned by Eich becomes an alternative form of intervention within the history of a broader advocacy movement for wilderness. Relying upon analytics and responsive design, JS becomes a scene by which local and international programming communities remain in conversation. Whereas the participatory or representational nature of an application (such as a browser that displays a website) warrants careful study, beneath the surface of any given web-based services lies an alternative rhetorically rich language. Within these realms lies a domain of activism and collaboration. One such participatory composition, *Hike Wild Montana*, modifies the relationship of end-user computer with the Montana Wilderness Association. It also invokes decorums in the conventions of drawing from jQuery and Google to help meet the developer's aspirations. It suggests redefining places of open-source code libraries as rhetorical scenes that can be unpackaged for their conventions and contributions. It demonstrates uses of commenting for programmers to speak to one another within the space of the code itself using embedded commenting designed to be ignored by machine readerships. Ultimately, JS functions as a type of symbolic action of direct interest to environmental communications or writing that invokes discourse communities, symbolic gestures, and identifications.

Note

1 I would like to thank the Montana Wilderness Association for permission to reproduce significant components of their source code, and their unwavering advocacy for some of the most spectacular habitat on Earth.

References

Arroyo, Sarah. *Participatory Composition: Video Culture, Writing, and Electracy.* Carbondale, IL: Southern Illinois University Press, 2013.

Beck, Estee. "A Theory of Persuasive Computer Algorithms for Rhetorical Code Studies." *Enculturation: A Journal of Rhetoric, Writing, and Culture*November 22,2016. http://enculturation.net/a-theory-of-persuasive-computer-algorithms. Accessed January 1, 2017.

Brock, Kevin. *Engaging the Action-Oriented Nature of Computation: Towards a Rhetorical Code Studies.* NCSU Digital Repository. Raleigh, NC: North Carolina State University, 2013. http://repository.lib.ncsu.edu/ir/handle/1840.16/8460

Brown Jr., James J. "Crossing State Lines: Rhetoric and Software Studies." *Rhetoric and the Digital Humanities.* Eds. Jim Ridolfo and William Hart-Davidson. Chicago, IL: University of Chicago Press, 2015. 20–32.

Burke, Kenneth. *A Rhetoric of Motives.* Berkeley, CA: University of California Press, 1962.

Chun, Wendy Hui Kyong. *Programmed Visions: Software and Memory.* Cambridge, MA: MIT Press, 2013.

Cryer, Daniel A. "Withdrawal without Retreat: Responsible Conservation in a Doomed Age." *Rhetoric Society Quarterly* 48. 5(2018): 459–478.

Dobrin, Sidney I. and Sean Morey, Eds. *Ecosee: Image, Rhetoric, Nature.* New York: State University of New York Press, 2009.

Eyman, Douglas. *Digital Rhetoric: Theory, Method, Practice.* Ann Arbor, MI: University of Michigan Press, 2015.

Galloway, Alexander R. *Protocol: How Control Exists after Decentralization.* Cambridge, MA: MIT Press, 2004.

Google. "Google Analytics." https://developers.google.com/analytics/. Accessed April 15, 2018.

Google. "Adding analytics.js to Your Site." https://developers.google.com/analytics/devguides/collection/analyticsjs/. Accessed April 15, 2018.

Gunkel, David J. "Critique of Digital Reason." *Theorizing Digital Rhetoric*. Eds Aaron Hess and Amber Davidson. New York: Routledge, 2018. 19–31.

Hamilton, Naomi. "The A–Z of Programming Languages: JavaScript." *Computerworld*July 31, 2008. https://www.computerworld.com.au/article/255293/a-z_programming_languages_javascript/. Accessed December 18, 2018.

Herndl, Carl G. and Stuart C. Brown, Eds. *Green Culture: Environmental Rhetoric in Contemporary America*. Madison, WI: University of Wisconsin Press, 1996.

Introna, L. D. "The Enframing of Code: Agency, Originality and the Plagiarist." *Theory, Culture & Society* 28. 6(2011): 113–141.

Killingsworth, M. Jimmie and Jacqueline S. Palmer. *Ecospeak: Rhetoric and Environmental Politics in America*. Carbondale, IL: Southern Illinois University Press, 1992.

Kuglin, Tom. "Conservation champions honored by Montana Hall of Fame." *Ravalli Republic*December 2,2016. https://ravallirepublic.com/lifestyles/recreation/article_7d65d8bc-b8ff-11e6-8bfd-638fe183d9c3.html. Accessed May 3, 2018.

Marino, Mark. C. "Critical Code Studies." *electronic book review*December 4, 2006. http://www.electronicbookreview.com/thread/electropoetics/codology.   Accessed May 29, 2018.

Montana Wilderness Association. "About Us." https://wildmontana.org/about-us. Accessed May 15, 2018.

Montana Wilderness Association. "Hike Montana." Hike.wildmontana.org. Accessed May 3, 2018.

Morey, Sean. "A Rhetorical Look at Ecosee." *Ecosee: Image, Rhetoric, Nature*. Eds. Sidney I. Dobrin and Sean Morey. New York: State University of New York Press, 2009. 23–52.

Randzio, Kassia. "Welcome to HikeMontana.org." April 6, 2016. https://wildmontana.org/wild-life/welcome-to-hikewildmontanaorg. Accessed February 3, 2018.

Rivers, Nathaniel A. "Deep Ambivalence and Wild Objects: Towards a Strange Environmental Rhetoric." *Rhetoric Society Quarterly* 45. 4(2015): 420–440.

Simmons, W. Michele. *Participation and Power: Civic Discourse in Environmental Policy Decisions*. New York: State University of New York Press, 2007.

Stolley, Karl. "MVC, Materiality, and the Magus: The Rhetoric of Source -Level Production." *Rhetoric and the Digital Humanities*. Eds Jim Ridolfo and William Hart-Davidson. Chicago, IL: University of Chicago Press, 2015. 264–285.

Vee, Annette. *Coding Literacy: How Computer Programming is Changing Writing*. Cambridge, MA: MIT Press, 2017.

"Wilderness Act of 1964 (Public Law 88-577; 16 U.S.C. 1131–1136)." https://www.wilderness.net/nwps/legisact. Accessed April 15, 2018.

11 I See the Body Electrate

Jason Crider

I depend on digital media to stay alive. And while many people rely on digital technologies for various levels of day-to-day well being, recent events in my life have necessitated a moment-to-moment relationship with digital media and prosthetic technologies that irrevocably reshaped the way I interpret and use my body. As a type 1 diabetic, I now rely on cyborg technologies to help regulate my body's blood glucose levels, administer synthetic insulin, alert me to potentially life-threatening complications, and many other crucial tasks. Type 1 diabetes is a unique chronic illness in that its most effective contemporary treatment methods rely on digital technologies in order to manually simulate the functions of a "normal" human pancreas as accurately as possible. This new prosthetic situation challenges traditional conceptions of the body by shifting the boundaries between body and technology—while that relationship was always fluid, these medical technologies make that evident in new ways that have important implications for digital approaches to disability, cyborg bodies, and posthumanism. In particular, this chapter looks to the limitations of the "natural" body as a literate construct, and extends Gregory L. Ulmer's theory of electracy in order to demonstrate new affordances of the body via digital rhetoric. Just as the writing practices and technologies of literacy offered profound insights into the body via print-based logics and the natural sciences, so too might the emerging practices and technologies of networked, electronic media signal an ontological and epistemological shift in the ways we approach new rhetorical and affective potentials of the body. Ultimately, this chapter explores the ways in which my digital media prosthetics demonstrate one type of hybrid blending of body and technology and begins to theorize a "body electrate."

In the 2018 keywords special issue of *Rhetoric Society Quarterly*, Karma R. Chávez argues that the field of rhetoric mostly relies on either abstract or specific conceptions of the body, and that particular bodies only come to matter rhetorically when they are different from "the unspoken, yet specified, white, cisgender, able-bodied, heterosexual male standard" (2018: 242). While Chávez's primary example concerns a discussion of, and "textual stare" at, the body of black civil rights activist Fannie Lou Hamer (246–247), she notes the importance of this problem for disability rhetorics as well.

Ultimately, Chávez argues, "we cannot not nor should we try to reduce actual bodies to abstract conceptualizations of 'the body' because that at once reductive and totalizing move, like all such moves, enforces and animates systemic oppressions" (248). Poet Jillian Weise boldly identifies just such an oppression as it relates to cyborgism: "The [Cyborg M]anifesto coopts cyborg identity while eliminating reference to disabled people on which the notion of the cyborg is premised. Disabled people who use tech to live are cyborgs. Our lives are not metaphors" (2018). In theorizing a "body electrate," I hope to extend Chávez's important line of questioning to disabled and cyborg bodies, and ask how the functionings of these bodies might open up new rhetorical affordances and offer an escape from systemic, problematic logics in order to open new inventive possibilities via digital technologies. Or as Ulmer writes, "what literacy is to the analytical mind, electracy is to the affective body: a prosthesis that enhances and augments a natural or organic human potential" ("Electracy and Pedagogy"). By turning to my *actual* body's *literal* prosthetics and augmentations, I make literal Ulmer's approach to electracy in order to demonstrate new potentials for the posthuman body.

Type 1 diabetes (T1D), formerly known as juvenile diabetes, is often confused with the much more common type 2 diabetes, which is a metabolic disorder in which the body becomes more resistant to insulin. T1D on the other hand is an autoimmune disease in which the body's immune system attacks the pancreas' islet cells responsible for creating insulin. Insulin is a hormone necessary for regulating blood glucose levels in the body; without insulin, sugar builds up in the bloodstream instead of being used for energy, which can lead to the onset of many short- and long-term complications, and if left untreated is fatal. T1D accounts for only 5–10 percent of cases of diabetes, is not linked to lifestyle factors, and has no known cause or cure. It is not something I caused, but rather an unavoidable death of my "natural" body. Because a T1 diabetic's body no longer produces insulin, the only treatment consists of the administering of synthetic insulin[1] combined with close monitoring of blood glucose levels (American Diabetes Association, 2018).

Insulin is a *pharmakon* in the truest sense. As Derrida writes in "Plato's Pharmacy," "there is no such thing as a harmless remedy. The *pharmakon* can never be simply beneficial" (1983: 120–134). To put it in terms of Derrida's *pharmakon* of writing, synthetic insulin is both a remedy and a poison, a treatment and a toxin. If a T1 diabetic does not receive enough insulin, their body becomes unable to break down glucose in the bloodstream, causing blood glucose levels to rise and start destroying the body, which can in turn create complications that lead to blindness, loss of limbs, organ failure, or death. If a T1 diabetic administers too much insulin, the body's blood sugar will drop too low, essentially starving the body's cells and causing brain damage, seizures, coma, or death. Unlike many chronic illnesses, treatment for T1D demands constant intervention to keep a balance between hyperglycemia (high blood glucose) and hypoglycemia (low blood glucose), and almost anything can cause blood glucose to drop or spike—things like eating, exercise, lack of sleep, altitude changes, stress, and even thinking (the act of writing itself almost always causes my blood sugar to drop, and even as I write this my smartwatch alerts me to an impending hypoglycemic episode it reads via the glucose monitor implanted in my arm). Insulin therapy requires constant monitoring and tinkering, which rewrites the body as a location of perpetual revision.

Synthetic insulin is a body augmentation I depend on to stay alive, but also one I must monitor closely due to its volatility. Early methods of insulin therapy consisted of administering massive doses of insulin once or twice per day and then eating an amount of carbs roughly equal to the dosage. T1 diabetics at the time had to rely on affect to read their blood sugar levels— they waited to feel the physical symptoms of hypo- or hyperglycemia and then treated them to the best of their ability. Today, insulin treatment is much more accurate and personalized, and T1 diabetics can administer precise amounts of insulin to meet their needs, either via an insulin pump connected to their body or via multiple daily injections. And rather than waiting to feel the extreme symptoms of hypo- or hyperglycemia, T1 diabetics can now read their blood glucose levels with monitoring technologies and make extemporaneous adjustments as needed, allowing for greater control and minimizing the risk of eventual health complications. Traditional blood glucose monitoring consists of a small lancet tool to pierce the skin and extract a drop of blood. The blood is then applied to a chemically active test strip and read by a blood glucose monitor. T1 diabetics typically check their blood glucose levels this way at regular intervals throughout the day, before and after meals, and whenever they feel symptoms of hypo- or hyperglycemia. The much more recent, and more effective, alternative to this method is the continuous glucose monitor (CGM). Arguably the most useful tool in a T1 diabetic's arsenal (aside from, of course, insulin), a CGM consists of a small electrode placed under the skin that reads blood glucose levels via interstitial fluid and then transmits the data to a digital device. My CGM is a Dexcom G6, which gives me a blood glucose reading every five minutes, shows me how I am trending, and alerts me if my blood glucose levels will soon be dangerously high or low.[2] It sends all of this data to my smartphone and smartwatch, has mandatory alarms that alert me if I am in danger, and will even wake me up if I am dropping quickly in my sleep (see Fig. 11.1).[3] Despite it not being actually medicinal or in any way directly affecting blood glucose levels, the CGM is almost unanimously lauded by endocrinologists and T1 diabetic researchers as the most effective tool for lowering one's A1C, the three-month average blood test that is the primary method used for T1D management (Monaco, 2017).

The CGM is a writing technology. It translates chemical and biological data into typography; it does not write my identity, but rather writes relationships and changes in my body over time. To borrow again from Derrida, it shows me the *trace* of insulin as it mixes with my body. The CGM transforms insulin into data post-event, or rather, insulin was always data, and the CGM affords

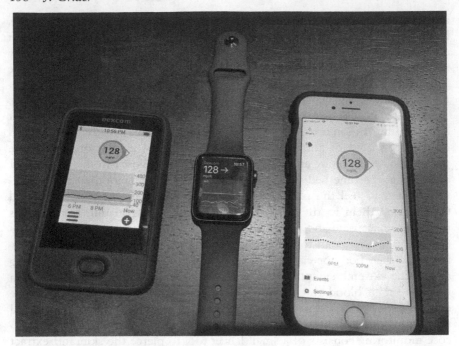

Figure 11.1 The Dexcom G6 CGM allows me to read my blood glucose values on multiple devices.

a means of translating that data and its effects on my body. Like many other health and bio-technologies, the CGM does not transform the body, but instead makes the body evident in new ways. In representing the trace of insulin's augmentation, it creates new potentials and demonstrates a fluidity of body and technology.

The overwhelming effectiveness of the CGM stems not only from its integration with the body, but from its uniquely digital operations. In terms of Wendy Chun's *Programmed Visions*, digital media "seek[s] to shape and predict—indeed embody—a future based on past data" (2011: xii). Every ten days I install a new Dexcom G6 sensor and transmitter into my arm or leg, according to the Food and Drug Administration (FDA)-mandated cutoff time (see Fig. 11.2). It takes time to calibrate, it collects data, it predicts, it learns. I supplement my Dexcom's informatics through third-party apps in order to generate actionable algorithms that help me identify trends and make smarter treatment decisions.[4] A functioning pancreas *thinks*—it reacts to changes in the body and makes decisions on how much insulin or glucagon to secrete in order to keep blood glucose levels within an optimal range. But for T1 cyborgs, that thinking is now performed via digital algorithms with treatment decisions made manually, all to try and simulate the noncyborg body as closely as possible. My body is in a constant state of becoming and overcoming its lack, forever working to attain a whole that it can never have. The CGM might represent a literal desiring machine—it structures my body's reality through its inclination towards upgrade. There is no longer a binary between body and nature, body and technology, body and other, but rather interconnected systems of production and desire.

As I move to theorize a post-literate, electrate body, I take up Ulmer's call in *Electronic Monuments* to "revisit our relationship to disaster," to locate myself as disaster. Questions of (dis)ability are questions of a group's value system, and cyborg technologies operate in direct relation to these value systems, most often in order to either simulate or augment the body in relation to said group's social construct of a "natural" body. For Ulmer, electracy is often introspective and personal, about locating oneself amongst the contingencies of a network. I examine my prosthetics in terms of electracy in order to find new connections in and amongst my body and the bodies of countless others who rely on digital technologies to live. As Ulmer writes, "to write the disaster is to find the group subject in me. What is to be done remains open to invention" (2015: 140).

On cyborgs and tryborgs

The CGM shares much in common with many emergent wearable technologies, particularly health-and-fitness devices and activity trackers. In the introduction to the 2016 *Rhetoric Society Quarterly* special issue "Wearables, Wearing, and the Rhetorics that Attend to Them," Catherine Gouge and John Jones "define wearables … as those technologies, electronic or otherwise, whose primary functionality requires that they be connected to bodies" (2016: 201). Most often these devices connect to bodies in order to measure or mediate health information, things like steps taken, heart rate, calories burned, and even offer medical coaching and other information. As Isabel Pedersen argues in *Ready to Wear*, "to *wear* a device is to integrate it with one's physical, political, social, and ontological makeup" (2013: 149, quoted in Gouge and Jones, 2016: 202). Our Fitbits and Apple Watches demonstrate a willingness to engage with our bodies in new ways by blurring the lines between our digital networks and our biological ones. These technologies measure physical activity and health statistics, and operate in many ways in the construction of the quantifiable self.

Gouge and Jones are quick to warn of the limits of discourses of the quantifiable self discourses, though, arguing that "positivist claims about the value of wearables and the data they generate participate in familiar anthropocentric calculations—particularly in health care—about the relationship between tools and our bodies, as users are promised mastery of the organized complexity of bodily systems" (2016: 200). While responsive health data obviously has many positive implications, and fitness wearables often help people learn about their bodies and lead healthier and more active lives, the rhetoric surrounding these devices frequently revolves around ableist conceptions of the body or implicit disability shaming. Gouge and Jones offer further warning against limiting critical approaches to wearables within these "logics of mastery and control," arguing that

> such approaches to wearables often reinforce what Rosemarie Garland Thomson and others have observed about ableist narratives of bodily mastery and control: That they privilege a "Cartesian image of [the] individual as a separate, isolated, efficient machine" and are, therefore, "focused on disciplining all bodies in the name of improvement".
>
> (2016: 202)

The quantifiable self is a limited self, and conceiving of wearables and other bodytech in these terms raises obvious questions of privacy and surveillance, and sets a precedent for body panopticism. Consider John Hancock, a life insurance company that has been around since the Civil War, and one of the largest life insurance providers in North America. In September 2018, the company announced that it will exclusively sell "interactive policies," requiring all policyholders to record and upload health-and-fitness data via wearable devices. This move comes after Hancock's partnership with Vitality Group, a platform that boldly claims wearable-equipped clients live thirteen to twenty-one years longer than those without them (Barlyn, 2018). I've experienced a similar corporate panopticism when a representative from Dexcom reprimanded me on the phone for hacking my G6 transmitter to extend a sensor past its ten-day FDA-mandated, forced cutoff date.[5] "We can see what you're doing," they say, before asking me to read a serial number off of my leg.

Limiting wearables to their ability to measure and quantify also limits the ways in which they offer us insights into a post-literate body. Wearable technologies more often than not operate in terms of literate identity formation, despite their digital media underpinnings. These devices collect and taxonomize data, they categorize bodily functions, and they allow for sophisticated record keeping and the outsourcing of memory. Gouge and Jones urge rhetorical studies of wearables to move beyond positivist notions of wearables. One of the ways they do so is by asking: in what ways might these devices allow us to perform our digital selves? (2016: 205). Pedersen argues that wearables "sit midway between media you carry ... and media you become" (2013: 4). Digital prosthetics and augmentations challenge our notions of media as things we use or wield, and as something we embody, and instead ask us to what degree media might embody us. The CGM is media I have become.

Weise (2016) offers a useful distinction between wearables and prosthetics in a *New York Times* opinion piece about her own cyborgism in relation to what she terms the "tryborg." Weise writes,

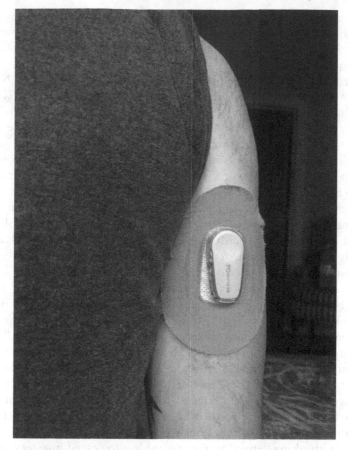

Figure 11.2 My Dexcom G6 sensor and transmitter.

Most cyborgs are disabled people who interface with technology. We depend on a computer for some major bodily function. The tryborg—a word I invented—is a nondisabled person who has no fundamental interface. The tryborg is a counterfeit cyborg. The tryborg tries to integrate with technology through the latest product or innovation. Tryborgs were the first to wear Google Glass. Today they wait in line for Snapchat Spectacles. The tryborg adopts the pose of a cyborg. But no matter how hard they try, the tryborg remains a pretender.

While I might not share Weise's humorous distaste for the tryborg, I do find the distinction she makes to be a crucial one. Tryborgs demonstrate a willingness to digitally engage with their body via wearables or the early adoption of bleeding-edge tech, but at the expense of sometimes coopting cyborg identities by falling into many of the problematic discourses of which Gouge and Jones warn. Cyborgs differ from tryborgs in that their body includes a fundamental interface, their body blends with technology in some inseparable or essential way. If a cyborg's prosthetic leg is removed, their mobility is altered. If a T1 cyborg's insulin pump is unplugged for a few days, they die.

Weise takes issue with self-proclaimed cyborg artists such as Neil Harbisson, who was touted by media outlets as the first cyborg in 2004 after he implanted an antenna in his skull that allegedly allows him to hear ultraviolet and infrared colors, and to connect his body to the internet via Bluetooth.[6] As Harbisson argues, "I've been a cyborg for 10 years now. I don't feel like I'm using technology, or wearing technology. I feel like I am technology. I don't think of my antenna as a device—it's a body part" (Jeffries, 2014). For Weise, statements like this represent the ultimate appropriation of cyborg identity. Cyborg identification comes down to a question of prosthetics, of using (often digital) technologies to confront a bodily lack. Harbisson's transhuman antenna might augment the body in a way that extends human potential, but it does not constitute a fundamental interface.

Weise also distinguishes cyborg from tryborg as constructs of language: "the tryborg is always distanced by metaphor, guesswork and desire ... To mistake them for cyborgs is to confuse the figurative with the literal." The term tryborg in many respects mirrors "disability drag," a term deployed by disability activists to identify able-bodied persons who "try on" disabilities, often in Hollywood. While this might seem like a mere semantic disagreement, these distinctions have profound impacts on the way we conceptualize and interface with the body. As an example, Weise explains that all of her prosthetic legs were designed for (athletic) men. By focusing primarily on functionality and ability, the designers fall prey to tryborg thinking, enacting the wearable "logics of mastery and control" that Gouge and Jones warn against, and as a result creates a new kind of lack, that of identity. "I have no complaint about androgyny," Weise writes, "but I'm just a regular femme who likes to show her legs" (2016). The cyborg body often represents a body created by an *other*, and raises questions of what it means to become technology, or how and when technology becomes us. Cyborg bodies help shed light on the way all bodies rhetorically perform, and resituate bodies as things we *do* and *are*, rather than things we simply *use*.

These digital interventions to the body raise questions of how we conceive of our bodies in terms of literacy. Building from Kelli Cargile Cook's notion of "layered literacies," Kristin Marie Bivens, Lora Arduser, Candice A. Welhausen, and Michael J. Faris approach this problem by "argu[ing] that health literacy is an embodied, multisensory experience that is invariably mediated by healthcare technologies." Bivens et al. demonstrate the ways in which "these technologies enable, constrain, and integrate multisensorial literacy practices in ways that complicate the concept of health literacy," and in doing so challenge traditional Cartesian mind/body dualisms by attending to the interconnectedness of sensory experience (2018). Their article works to complicate notions of health literacy, and to problematize traditional conceptions of literacy more generally.

In one branch of their article, Lora Arduser performs a case study on the use of medical technologies and prosthetics by T1 diabetics. She argues that T1 diabetics overcome limitations of health literacies by embodying them through their medical tech: "T1Ds act as lay scientists with regard to their own biology. As such, the complex relationships between T1Ds' bodies and medical technologies gives us fertile ground for re-embodying health literacy through the notion of tactility." She also notes the tendency of medical discourses to rely on a mind/body binary, stating that because of this, "the space of literacy is defined as being in the head as opposed to the body," citing the Patient Protection and Affordable Care Act of 2010 as one example (2018).

For Arduser, a key component of T1 diabetics' ability to embody multisensory literacies via tactility revolves around the various methods of bodyhacking and technological workarounds common in T1 communities. These include modifying the placement and application of CGMs, magnifying the volume of a CGM transmitter to better wake users during an overnight hypoglycemic episode, and a security researcher exploiting a software bug in his insulin pump that would have allowed a hacker to remotely kill him via overdose. I would add to these efforts by T1 bloggers to extend sensor and transmitter lifespans with custom smartphone apps and software hacks.[7] Arduser also includes two examples of biohacking via insulin pump—athletes who cut basal rates (the steady stream of insulin released by a pump) to balance out intense workouts, and users who dangerously cut insulin doses to quickly lose weight. She argues that conceiving of bodyhacking helps us think of literacies less hierarchically and more fluidly, as these actions move seamlessly across health, ethical, critical, and technological proficiencies (2018).

Literacy develops ways to study and change methods of thought, whereas the technologies I have discussed so far develop ways to study and change the body, and also make evident new roles the body plays in creating rhetorical capacities. As Arduser helps demonstrate through her theorizing of embodying health literacies, literate approaches to the body have their limitations. In the case of T1D, those limitations require a move beyond literacies of the "head" via tactile engagement with one's body via technology. T1 cyborgs engage with the limitations of literacy by engaging with what I will argue is an embodied electracy. As our bodies become increasingly digitally integrated and entwined, if we are to "become media," perhaps it is time to reform our relationship with literacy and the way we embody it, or rather maybe it is time to ask where an ontology not bound in literacy might lead us.

Cyborg electracy

Ulmer argues that the proliferation of digital media demands new methods of thinking and writing. He first proposed the term "electracy" in *Teletheory* in 1989 as a theoretical approach to developing the faculties needed to make full use of digital media's potential. Like orality and literacy before it, electracy is an apparatus. Electracy moves away from the instrumental logics and literal reasoning of literacy, and replaces literate paradigms such as true/false with new ones, such as attraction/repulsion. Just as literacy formed its ontology from the technology of alphabetic print, digital technologies now form the systems of thought and knowledge production in electracy, and Ulmer calls on us to invent new practices and possibilities within this emergent paradigm. Electracy differs from terms like digital literacy or technological literacy in the same way that literacy differs from orality; these terminological distinctions limit the scope of electracy's project. Or as Ulmer often says in conversation, referring to electracy as "digital literacy" is like referring to science as "nature magic." While literacies such as health literacies are effective ways of addressing medical problems, they are also somewhat limited in their reliance on science and historical dependency on the apparatus of print-based logics. This is not an either/or approach, but rather one that might work alongside literacy to address matters that literacy can not.

In *Orality and Literacy*, Walter Ong argues that our methods of conceptualizing the world rely heavily on the print-based technology of the map—we now imagine the world "laid out" in front of us, that the "writing and print reduced the oral-aural world to a world of visualized pages" (1982: 72). According to Ong, the shift from an oral culture to a literate culture created an epistemological rupture in our apparatus for accessing the world around us. Maps allow us to conceptualize the world as though it were laid out in front of us "ready to be 'explored.'" Ong argues that the "ancient oral world knew few 'explorers,' though it did know many itinerants, travelers, voyagers, adventurers, and pilgrims" (71). For Ong, to "explore" is to read the world as map, to triangulate our bodies in space according to the affordances of print-based logics. The map does not change the topography of the Earth, but does give us new ways of conceptualizing it and thus fundamentally changes our relationship to it. Just as the visualization of the map allows for new understandings of the world, so too do the visualizations of the CGM allow for new understandings of the body. The CGM does not alter my body, but it does allow me to access it in new ways. If we take Ong's ontological shift from orality to literacy and extend it to Ulmer's shift from literacy to electracy, what new potentials might emerge? Put another way, if we now "explore" the world after experiencing the print-based technology of the map, what new vocabulary is necessitated when I experience an electrate body?

There are few interventions on electracy and the body. Many digital rhetoric and writing scholars deploy electracy to explore how we embody place, but few have turned electracy to the body itself. Perhaps the first such attempt, Caleb Andrew Milligan's *Computers and Composition* article "Immanent Interbodies: Composing Disability through Embodied Choragraphy" argues for methods of composing disability by challenging the ableist underpinnings of digital pedagogies via Ulmer's notion of *choragraphy*. Milligan and Arduser both turn to the rhetorical notion of *mêtis* as alternatives to limited, ableist notions of the body, both drawing specifically from Jay Dolmage's work. *Mêtis* foregrounds practicality and cleverness, is "full of reversals and thus demanding resourcefulness" (2009: 6), an approach that Arduser argues is on full display in T1 bodyhacking efforts. Dolmage argues that his "*metis* historiography then wants to look like an extraordinary body: double, divergent, flawed, incomplete, surprising, in need of others" (quoted in Milligan, 2019) and Milligan extends this to videogames, where just such extraordinary bodies can occur. When it comes to Weise's computerized leg, or a T1 cyborg's digital insulin pump, *mêtis* becomes not only a crucial rhetorical strategy of embodiment, but a poetics for becoming media.

Mêtis reminds us that our bodies are sites of invention. In the hybrid video/print article "Haptic Heuretics: Electrate Tinkering as Rhetorical Making," Milligan and I argue that new digital technologies contain the potential for new discursive logics, and propose a simple method for moving away from hermeneutic remediation and towards (using Ulmer's term) heuretics, the logic of invention. In doing so, we take up Ian Bogost's call to not merely treat digital media as "black-boxed," abstracted machines, but to also engage with their materiality (2010: 28). Our experimental project introduces the WriteBox, which is not a material, singular "thing," but rather a practice that stresses customization and tinkering. "WriteBoxing" offers a methodology for digital rhetoricians to invent, and experiment with, their own writing interfaces as a material heuretic. In doing so we argue that perhaps we could learn from Friedrich Nietzsche, whom Friedrich Kittler calls "the first mechanized philosopher" (1999). Kittler explains that when Nietzsche was diagnosed with severe myopia he could no longer write for extended periods of time, so he turned to the recent invention of the typewriter, specifically Rasmus Malling-Hansen's "Writing Ball." As Nietzsche became blind to his own writing, he increasingly relied on the Writing Ball, later reflecting that not only did his style and delivery change, but his very thinking changed as well. Our WriteBox heuretic experiment thus attempts to simulate the rift Nietzsche faced when the mechanical substrate of his writing changed, and asks what might happen if we were to strategize the rift-making process as a part of our practices of rhetorical invention.

What happens when we extend a haptic heuretic to the body? When we seek to challenge ideal interfaces with Weise's notion of fundamental interfaces? The notion of touch is crucial to WriteBoxing, but as Arduser notes, T1 diabetics rely on tactility in a different way, as their medical prosthetics "sit on the surface of the skin but move beneath it as well" (Bivens et al., 2018). Now my biodata flows alongside digital data, forming new conceptions of networked being. Body technologies like the CGM make the unconscious processes of the body conscious, allowing for new opportunities to experience Nietzsche's discursive rift. If literacy facilitated a structuring of the mind, these technologies might allow electracy to facilitate a restructuring of the body. They create rhetorical opportunities to more fully realize the body's potential in the creation of meaning. As Debra Hawhee reminds us, the ancient sophists made no distinction between mind and body, and athleticism and rhetoric were linked by an "appreciation for the immediate relation between training practices and performance" (2014: 7). The electrate body extends these notions of training and performance to the contingencies of the network, allowing the body to become not a place of interpretation but of invention.

Ulmer makes rare mention of the body proper in his work, one such exception being in *Electronic Monuments*: "the face is produced only when the head ceases to be a part of the body, when it ceases to be coded by the body" (2015: 24). Might we now (de)code the fundamental interface in such a way? As Milligan argues, "to make an interface means to disavow the full spectrum of embodiment: *this* only works like *that*" (2019). When we confine the prosthetic to its use value, we instrumentalize the body and thus limit it within a literate paradigm. But what about when the interface becomes fundamental, or rather, when the interface becomes me? At what point does insulin become encoded by the body, or the computerized leg contribute to a new sense of self?

One of the ways I experience the electrate body consists of its involvement with networked writing and my life on social media. The body electrate has a fundamental interface, and that interface now contributes in my digital communication practices. When my phone buzzes with a notification, it might be a text message or calendar alert, or it might be my CGM alerting me to dangerous blood glucose levels and telling me to make a treatment decision, a digital daimon manifested as avatar. Or as a friend recently put it, "it's kind of like you're social media friends with your body." If orality inspired us via the muses, and literacy via the wills, perhaps the body's membra(i)n(e) can inform our electrate practices.

Let me put this another way. One of the most important conversations happening right now in the treatment of T1 diabetes is that of the "closed-loop" insulin delivery system. The bleeding-edge T1 cyborg currently deploys two prosthetics: the CGM and the insulin pump. The CGM reads blood glucose values in the body and transmits that data to the cyborg, who uses that data to make treatment decisions and input insulin distribution rates into their pump. The closed-loop system bypasses the cyborg's agency by putting the two prosthetics into conversation with one another. The CGM learns the body, and the pump subsequently learns how to best make adjustments to insulin basal rates, and administers insulin accordingly, closing the loop. The first FDA-approved closed-loop system, Medtronic's MiniMed 670G, just became commercially available in the spring of 2018, but looping has a history dating back to at least the early 2000s. Closed-loop systems were first developed in DIY and open-source circles,[8] often using the same single-chip Raspberry Pi computers with which Milligan and I built our first WriteBox. Just as Nietzsche once referred to his Writing Ball as a "thing like me" in a poem, does the material interface for our haptic heuretic become a thing like me? Or when I trust it to keep me alive at night, do I become a thing like it? The benefits of these closed-loop systems include requiring less human involvement, and in terms of DIY looping, bypass the strict guidelines put in place by device manufacturers and government regulation, common problems cited in the #wearenotwaiting movement. If we are to think in literate terms, these DIY looping systems raise questions of my confidence in my ability to code: do I trust my artificial pancreas not to inject me with a lethal overdose in my sleep? I have yet to tinker with a closed-loop system. I still use multiple daily injections instead of a pump. Maybe I'm not ready for a new body part just yet, a new fundamental interface. Maybe I'm not ready to let go of my heuretic rift. Maybe I'm not ready to be out of the loop.

This chapter's title is a nod to Walt Whitman's famous poem "I Sing the Body Electric" from *Leaves of Grass*. Whitman's strange, explicit poem celebrates the human body, focusing on both its individual parts and the way those parts work together holistically. His deployment of electricity reflects a desire to make connections and interpret bodies in new ways, in a certain sense to invent a new poetics for the body. As Whitman scholar Jerome Loving notes, the poem went untitled upon its inclusion in the original 1855 issue of *Leaves of Grass*. It was not until the 1867 edition that the title and opening line were added. Electricity was not yet a commonly used term at the time, just as electracy is not a commonly used term now. And as Steven Connor tells us of the poem's relationship to the word, at the time electricity "was used almost entirely for the production and display of shocking or exciting sensations," and its primary poetics at the time were "identified with the motive principle of life itself, and thought to be the means whereby sensation was transmitted through the living body," an invisible force that flowed between bodies and through boundaries (2015: 188). Just as electric was not a common term then, electrate is not a common one now, and maybe that is the operational shift needed in order to better see the full rhetorical and communicative potentials of the digital body, and to invent a healthier poetics for those of us stuck with fundamental interfaces.

Note

1 All uses of "insulin" from here on out refer to the medicinal version, not the version naturally produced by a properly functioning human pancreas.
2 And I often share this data with my wife, or friends I may be with, via Dexcom's "Share" feature.
3 A common fear for T1 diabetics is "dead in bed syndrome."
4 Primarily the smartphone application Sugarmate.

5 For any fellow T1 cyborgs looking to do the same, visit https://seemycgm.com/2018/06/11/restarting-g6-sensors-and-transmitter/.
6 There are several artists who attached robotics to their body before Harbisson, such as Stelarc.
7 For the sake of anonymity, I am not citing the efforts of these T1 hackers.
8 For a brief look into the history of DIY looping, see Melissa Lee's interview with BeyondType1 here: https://beyondtype1.org/melissa-lee-talks-diy-closed-loop-system/.

References

American Diabetes Association. "Type 1 Diabetes." American Diabetes Association. 2018. Available from: www.diabetes.org

Bivens, Kristin Marie, Lora Arduser, Candice A. Welhausen and Michael J. Faris. "A Multisensory Literacy Approach to Biomedical Healthcare Technologies: Aural, Tactile, and Visual Layered Health Literacies." *Kairos: A Journal of Rhetoric, Technology, and Pedagogy* 22. 2(2018). Available from: http://kairos.technorhetoric.net/22.2/topoi/bivens-et-al/index.html

Barlyn, Suzanne. "Strap on the Fitbit: John Hancock to Sell Only Interactive Life Insurance." *Reuters*, September 19, 2018. Available from: https://www.reuters.com/article/us-manulife-financi-john-hancock-lifeins/strap-on-the-fitbit-john-hancock-to-sell-only-interactive-life-insurance-idUSKCN1LZ1WL

Bogost, Ian. *Persuasive Games: The Expressive Power of Videogames*. Cambridge, MA: MIT Press, 2010.

Chávez, Karma R. "The Body: An Abstract and Actual Rhetorical Concept." *Rhetoric Society Quarterly* 48. 3(2018): 260–268.

Chun, Wendy Hui Kyong. *Programmed Visions: Software and Memory*. Cambridge, MA: MIT Press, 2011.

Connor, Steven. "Literature, Technology and the Senses." *The Cambridge Companion to the Body in Literature*. Eds David Hillman and Ulrika Maude. Cambridge, UK: Cambridge University Press, 2015. 177–196.

Crider, Jason and Caleb Andrew Milligan. "Haptic Heuretics: Electrate Tinkering as Rhetorical Making." *Textshop Experiments* 4(2018).

Derrida, Jacques. *Dissemination*. Trans. Barbara Johnson. Chicago, IL: University of Chicago Press, 1983. 120–134.

Derrida, Jacques. *Of Grammatology*. Ed. Gayatri Chakravorty Spivak. Baltimore, MD: Johns Hopkins University Press, 1998.

Dolmage, Jay Timothy. "Metis, Métis, Mestiza, Medusa: Rhetorical Bodies Across Rhetorical Traditions." *Rhetoric Review* 28. 1(2009).

Dolmage, Jay Timothy. *Disability Rhetoric*. Syracuse, NY: Syracuse University Press, 2014.

Gouge, Catherine and John Jones. "Wearables, Wearing, and the Rhetorics that Attend to Them." *Rhetoric Society Quarterly* 46. 3(2016).

Hawhee, Debra. *Bodily Arts: Rhetoric and Athletics in Ancient Greece*. Austin, TX: University of Texas Press, 2014.

Jeffries, Stuart. "Neil Harbisson: the world's first cyborg artist." *The Guardian* May 6, 2014. Available from: https://www.theguardian.com/artanddesign/2014/may/06/neil-harbisson-worlds-first-cyborg-artist

Kittler, Friedrich A. *Gramophone, Film, Typewriter*. Trans. Geoffrey Winthrop-Young and Michael Wutz. Palo Alto, CA: Stanford University Press, 1999.

Loving, Jerome. *Walt Whitman: Song of Himself*. Berkeley, CA: University of California Press, 2011.

Milligan, Caleb Andrew. "Immanent Interbodies: Composing Disability through Embodied Choragraphy." Computers and Composition in press. Available online May 31, 2019. https://doi.org/10.1016/j.compcom.2019.05.006

Monaco, Kristen. "CGM Benefits T1D Patients Who Use Daily Injections: Studies Reported Lower HbA1c Levels, Higher Rates of Satisfaction." *MedPage Today*January 24, 2017. Available from: https://www.medpagetoday.com/endocrinology/typeldiabetes/62693

Ong, Walter J. *Orality and Literacy: The Technologizing of the Word*. New York: Routledge, 1982.

Pedersen, Isabel. *Ready to Wear: A Rhetoric of Wearable Computers and Reality-shifting Media*. Anderson, SC: Parlor Press, 2013.

Ulmer, Gregory L. *Teletheory: Grammatology in the Age of Video*. London: Routledge, 1989.

Ulmer, Gregory L. *Electronic Monuments*. Minneapolis, MN: University of Minnesota Press, 2015.

Ulmer, Gregory L. "Electracy and Pedagogy." Available from: http://users.clas.ufl.edu/glue/longman/pedagogy/electracy.html

Weise, Jillian. "The Dawn of the 'Tryborg." *The New York Times*November 30, 2016. Available from: https://www.nytimes.com/2016/11/30/opinion/the-dawn-of-the-tryborg.html

Weise, Jillian. "Common Cyborg." *Granta* 144(2018). Available from: https://granta.com/common-cyborg/

Index

Printed in the United States
by Baker & Taylor Publisher Services